Urban Indicators

URBAN STUDIES INFORMATION GUIDE SERIES

Series Editor: Thomas P. Murphy, Special Assistant to the Secretary and Director of Executive Personnel and Career Development, U.S. Department of Health, Education, and Welfare, Washington, D.C.

The above series is part of the
GALE INFORMATION GUIDE LIBRARY

The Library consists of a number of separate series of guides covering major areas in the social sciences, humanities, and current affairs.

General Editor: Paul Wasserman, Professor and former Dean, School of Library and Information Services, University of Maryland

Managing Editor: Denise Allard Adzigian, Gale Research Company

Urban Indicators

A GUIDE TO INFORMATION SOURCES

Volume 10 in the Urban Studies Information Guide Series

Thomas P. Murphy

Special Assistant to the Secretary
and
Director of Executive Personnel and Career Development
U.S. Department of Health, Education, and Welfare
Washington, D.C.

Gale Research Company
Book Tower, Detroit, Michigan 48226

114584

Library of Congress Cataloging in Publication Data

Murphy, Thomas P   1931-
    Urban indicators.

    (Urban studies information guide series ; v. 10)
(Gale information guide library)
    Includes bibliographical references and indexes.
    1. Urban policy—United States. 2. Social
indicators—United States. I. Title. II. Series.
HT167.M87   307.7'6   80-13333
ISBN 0-8103-1451-7

VITA

Thomas P. Murphy received degrees in political science from Queen's College (1952), Georgetown University (1960), and St. John's University (1963). He currently is Special Assistant to the Secretary and the Director of Executive Personnel and Career Development of the U.S. Department of Health, Education, and Welfare.

Until 1978, he was the director of the Federal Executive Institute, Charlottesville, Virginia. From 1971 to 1976, he served as the founding director of the Institute for Urban Studies and as a professor of government and politics at the University of Maryland at College Park. He was also the founding director of the graduate program in Public Administration at the University of Missouri at Kansas City.

An administrator and practitioner, as well as an academician, he has been the county manager of Jackson County, Missouri, as well as a consultant to urban programs and departments in the cities of Fort Wayne, Indiana; Lancaster, Pennsylvania; Kansas City, Missouri; and Newark, New Jersey; the counties of St. Claire, Illinois; Jackson, Missouri; and Shelby, Tennessee; the metropolitan planning agencies in Kansas City, Memphis, and St. Louis; and the urban affairs and planning departments of the states of Alabama, Connecticut, Missouri, and New Jersey.

He has published articles in numerous journals including ADMINISTRATIVE LAW REVIEW, ADMINISTRATIVE SCIENCE QUARTERLY, AMERICAN JOURNAL OF ECONOMICS AND SOCIOLOGY, THE BUREAUCRAT, CONTEMPORARY REVIEW, THE ECONOMIST, ETHICS, NATURAL RESOURCES JOURNAL, NEW LEADER, PERFORMING ARTS REVIEW, POLITY, PUBLIC ADMINISTRATION REVIEW, REVIEW OF POLITICS, SOCIETY, SOUTHERN REVIEW OF PUBLIC ADMINISTRATION, URBANISM PAST AND PRESENT, and WESTERN POLITICAL QUARTERLY.

In addition to serving as series editor to this Urban Studies Information Guide, Murphy has compiled two others in the series: URBAN POLITICS and URBAN LAW. He has also published numerous works including INSIDE THE BUREAUCRACY (1978), coauthor; THE POLITICS OF CONGRESSIONAL COMMITTEES

(1978); URBAN POLITICS IN THE SUBURBAN ERA (1976), coauthor; NEW POLITICS CONGRESS (1975); UNIVERSITIES IN THE URBAN CRISIS (1975); ORGANIZING PUBLIC SERVICES IN METROPOLITAN AMERICA (1974), co-editor; GOVERNMENT MANAGEMENT INTERNSHIPS AND EXECUTIVE DE-VELOPMENT (1973); PRESSURES UPON CONGRESS (1972); SCIENCE, GEO-POLITICS, AND FEDERAL SPENDING (1971); EMERGING PATTERNS IN UR-BAN ADMINISTRATION (1970), coeditor; and METROPOLITICS AND THE UR-BAN COUNTY (1970).

Murphy is a member of the National Academy of Public Administration. He is also past president of the National Association of Schools of Public Affairs and Administration and of the National Center for Public Service Internships. He served for two years as cochairman of the International City Management Association--NASPAA Project on Improving Urban Management.

CONTENTS

PREFACE

This volume represents an attempt to provide an overview of the diverse and rapidly emerging field of urban indicators. Since citations of substantive material were deliberately used at the cost of eliminating peripheral items, much selectivity has been required. Because the field is totally interdisciplinary, it is very broad and it was necessary to attempt to balance the theory, the methodology, the technology of indicators and the applications. In organizing the volume, serious consideration was given to setting up separate chapters on different functional areas such as health, education, and social services. However, the final decision was to give the reader access to these areas by means of an extensive subject index. Since significant oversights may be corrected in a subsequent edition, comments are seriously solicited regarding items omitted or not effectively characterized.

In establishing selection priorities, preference has been given to publications since 1970, with some older classics also included. Likewise, preference has been given to the more widely used journals which are readily available in most libraries. For this reason, almost no theses, dissertations, or papers delivered at professional meetings have been included. However, the nature of this field is such that consultant reports had to be included, especially in the section on applications of indicators.

Research and editorial assistance was provided by Carol Boorman, Susan Hart, Doug Hastings, Lynn Kaplan Chasen, and Virginia Karas. The typing was handled by Joyce Carter, Susan Houchens, Jane Pender, and Jae Seward. George Ford, Wyatt Johnson, and Guy Brice handled the photocopying and index checking.

T.M.
Charlottesville

INTRODUCTION

The use of indicators to measure changes and to illustrate progress and slippage is not new. In the realm of economics, indexes such as the gross national product, the Dow Jones industrial average, or the consumer price index are as familiar to us now as the daily weather report. But how does one measure other components of life in American society? The quality of life, for instance, is not as easily quantifiable as is the growth of production in the American economy. Yet, it is as essential to the continued prosperity of our democratic system that we know how well we are doing in fulfilling the social aspirations of the citizenry as it is to know whether we are meeting their material needs.

President Lyndon Johnson fully realized that the success of his Great Society program rested on a clear understanding of social needs, priorities, and objectives, and on the ability to evaluate progress toward our goals. In March 1966 he directed the secretary of Health, Education, and Welfare to seek ways to improve the nation's ability to chart its social progress. Specifically, the department was told "to develop the necessary social statistics and indicators to supplement those prepared by the Bureau of Labor Statistics and the Council of Economic Advisors. With these yardsticks, we can better measure the distance we have come and plan for the way ahead."[1]

Implicitly, therefore, social indicator research is normative, in sharp contrast to the study of economic indicators. Mancur Olson, former deputy assistant secretary of the Department of Health, Education, and Welfare, who had the responsibility of responding to the Johnson challenge, defined social indicators as follows:

> A statistic of direct normative interest which facilitates concise, comprehensive and balanced judgments about the condition of major aspects of a society. It is in all cases a direct measure of welfare and is subject to the interpretation that, if it changes in the "right" direction, while other things remain equal, things have gotten better, or people are "better off."[2]

In little more than a decade the field of social indicator research has gained the substantial support of government, academic, and private research.

Introduction

Today it is recognized that indicators can be used to improve public policy-making by bringing our problems to light and by providing measures for better evaluating the success or failure of public programs. It is now assumed, not merely suggested, that government should involve itself in analysis of the quality of our environment, job satisfaction of the nation's work force, and the character of health service in this country among other social characteristics.

Urban indicator research, the subject of this volume, is an offshoot of the social indicator movement. Raymond Bauer, author-editor of a seminal 1966 volume on social indicators, defined them as "statistics, statistical series, and all other forms of evidence that enable us to assess where we stand and are going with respect to our values and goals, and to evaluate specific programs and determine their impact."[3]

Urban indicators seek to describe the social, economic, and political conditions of metropolitan areas--in short, every facet of urban living. Table 1 contains examples of national social indicators that can be adopted for analysis and evaluation of urban conditions. Some of these measures relate to basic capacities of the health delivery system and to the need for health services, while others are more concerned with value-oriented questions such as what percentage of the voting-age population vote or what percentage of women thirty-five to sixty-four work. In turn, these value questions (and there are value choices implicit in all the health indicators as well) raise philosophical questions about whether government should attempt to select societal goals, and if so, how. There even are value questions in determining how closely and with what techniques agreed upon societal goals should be monitored by government.[4] The field therefore is in the early stages of development.

The wealth of published books, articles, reports, and statistical information on the subject is clear testimony to the growing acceptance and practical importance now attached to urban indicator research. However, the rapid expansion of research has outpaced the ability of laymen and scholars alike to monitor and absorb existing information. This annotated bibliography is one of the first attempts to gather and review the major contributions to the field of urban indicator research that have taken place in recent years. It is by no means exhaustive. The volume is divided into six chapters, each presenting sources which deal with a different aspect of urban indicators. What follows in this introduction are summations of the material covered by the annotated sources in each of the six chapters of the bibliography.

CHAPTER 1: DEVELOPMENT OF URBAN INDICATORS

The pioneering efforts of the Russell Sage Foundation, which sought to study the social indicator movement, laid the base for using indicators in the field of urban analysis. The foundation began by analyzing family relationships, income and employment, methods of controlling labor input, and increased mechanization. Further, it examined existing data collection methods and began inventing new statistical approaches.

Table 1
SUGGESTED URBAN INDICATORS

Indicator	Present Experience	1976-79 Goal
1. Infant Mortality (per 1,000 live births)	22.1 (1967)	12
2. Maternal Mortality (per 100,000 live births)	28.9 (1967)	15
3. Family Planning Services (for Low-Income Women 15-44)	1 million (1968)	5 million
4. Deaths from Accidents (per 100,000 population)	55.1 (1967)	50
5. Number of Persons in State Mental Hospitals	426,000 (1967)	50,000
6. Expectancy of Healthy Life	68.2 years (1966)	70.2 years
7. Three- to five-year-olds in school or preschool	35.2% (1967)	95%
8. Persons 25 and older who graduate from high school	51.1% (1967)	65%
9. Persons 25 and older who graduate from college	10.1% (1967)	15%
10. Persons in Learning Force	100 million (1967)	150 million
11. Percent of Major Cities with public Community Colleges	66% (1968)	100%
12. Number of first-year students in Medical Schools	10,000 (1967)	18,000
13. Handicapped Persons Rehabilitated	208,000 (1968)	600,000
14. Average Weekly Hours of Work-- Manufacturing	40.6 (1967)	37.5
15. Labor Force Participation Rate for Women Aged 35-64	48% (1967)	60%
16. Average Annual Paid Vacation-- Manufacturing	2 weeks (1967)	4 weeks
17. Housing Units with Bathtub or Shower	85% (1960)	100%
18. Percent of Population Illiterate	2.4% (1960)	0
19. Voters as a Percentage of Voting Age Population	63% (1964)	80%
20. Private Philanthropy as a percent of GNP	1.9% (1967)	2.7%
21. Public and Private Expenditures for Health, Education and Welfare as a percent of GNP	19.8% (1968)	25%
22. Percent of Population in Poverty	12.8% (1968)	0
23. Income of Lowest Fifth of population	5.3% (1967)	10%
24. Persons who work during the year	88 million (1967)	110 million
25. Life Expectancy	70.2 years (1966)	72 years

Source: U.S. Department of Health, Education, and Welfare, TOWARD A SOCIAL REPORT (Ann Arbor: University of Michigan Press, 1970), pp. ix-x.

Social indicator systems continued to grow and in 1969 the Department of Health, Education, and Welfare added the capstone with the preparation and publication of TOWARD A SOCIAL REPORT--in response to President Johnson's 1966 request. Since that time SOCIAL INDICATORS, 1973 and SOCIAL INDICA-TORS, 1976 were produced by the Statistical Policy Division of the Office of Management and Budget (OMB). OMB also published the 1973 version, whereas SOCIAL INDICATORS, 1976 was published by the Bureau of the Census, U.S. Department of Commerce. Both volumes were printed by the Government Printing Office. The OMB group, led by Denis F. Johnston, was assisted and advised by an Interagency Committee on Social Indicators as well as by a body of outside researchers, the OMB Advisory Committee on Social Indicators. As of 1976, not only the United States but also Austria, Canada, France, Japan, the Netherlands, Norway, Spain, Sweden, the United Kingdom, and West Germany have issued "social indicator" reports.[5]

It is important to note that the biases of the analysts will necessarily be reflected in a system of urban indicators. There is no way to remove all the political questions involved in establishing social indexes. For example, the way in which urban indicators are developed is likely to have considerable influence in determining which level of government will end up dealing with the problem. Urban indicators should be subject to disaggregation and correlation and, while it would be dangerous if they were to become a purely political tool, they should take into account a wide variety of political interests if they are to be useful. Future data needs, as well as those of the present, require the use of urban indicators to provide comparisons between local data, average national data, and data corresponding to "best practice" in various fields. Finally, indicators must be revised as experience leads to more reliable ways of designing them

The process of developing meaningful and useful composite urban indicators can be outlined as a four-step procedure: (1) selecting a dimension of urban life to be measured, (2) establishing a statistical series to measure the aspects of this dimension, (3) constructing a methodology to combine these series, and (4) analyzing this composite measure in various neighborhoods of the metropolitan area. Although the statistical methods that create the index numbers and the geographic location codes are sophisticated, there are relatively simple ways to use these outputs to produce specific inferences on which to base actions.

CHAPTER 2: TYPES OF INDICATORS AND MEASURES

Urban indicators developed as a result of the need for accurate measurement of changes in the metropolitan environment. But indicators can also be of use in other important endeavors, such as the establishment of urban goals and priorities, program evaluations, and the development of social accounts to provide guidance in situations of choice.

There are at least three different types of urban indicators, each designed for a different use: (1) problem and policy oriented indicators, (2) indicators describing urban society and its changes, and (3) analytic indicators serving as components of causal models. Criteria for determining the significance of these indicators include the following: (1) Does it relate to a local, state, or national goal? (2) Does it help to describe an emerging goal (which may not be an issue for several years but on which longitudinal data will be essential)? (3) Does it facilitate the attainment of an intended change?

While the computation of urban indicators depends to a great extent on basic statistics, the most significant factor is the type of data used in the statistical computations. For example, urban administrators in Nashville and St. Petersburg wanted to evaluate service effectiveness in their respective cities. To do this they designed measures of solid waste collection and disposal, recreation, library services, crime control, fire protection, local transportation (including public transportation, traffic control, and street maintenance), water supply services, and the handling of citizen complaints and suggestions. In this particular circumstance, sample questionnaires were used to secure citizen perceptions.

But once these questionnaires are tabulated, what is done with the raw numbers? Several works annotated in this chapter suggest the use of statistical methodologies such as a Lorenz curve, the Gini index, the Schultze coefficent, and matrix equations. Some calculations look at input when developing indicators which are sometimes based on expenditure levels by urban area governments. Other calculations are more concerned with output; that is, they stress results and relevance to the objectives of individuals, families, and urban societies.

CHAPTER 3: PROBLEMS WITH URBAN INDICATORS

Anytime numbers are used to describe a social condition problems are bound to occur. Difficulties occur when mixed indicators are calculated, and there is always the question of how indicators will be interpreted. The statistics are most useful when used comparatively and to emphasize trends. Measuring the quality of services is best accomplished by output measures. Most authors annotated in this chapter warn that the significance of the statistics and statistical correlations must be carefully reviewed. Some authors look at particular indicators and suggest ways of making the indicators more accurate and more useful for analysis.

One frequently mentioned concern is that of "outdated norms." Tests of relevance must be applied, and many models are suggested for that purpose, including goal-oriented development. The models that are established must be dynamic and responsive to change. For example, evaluation and accountability are potential change agents within public welfare organizations. However, evaluations usually have political overtones when mandated by legislative bodies and these political influences may affect the objectivity of the evaluation. With a clarification of ultimate, intermediate, and proximate objectives, efficiency and effectiveness studies can begin to determine accountability. Evaluation programs, which are flexible and provide for redefinition and regrouping of data as problem definitions improve, appear to be the most viable.

Using indicators for future research raises several problems. It is important to note that the biases of the analysts will inevitably be reflected in any system of urban indicators. The character of assumptions that the future researcher makes about human behavior will reflect his personal style. Furthermore, future researchers formulate historical constructs. Since these input factors are the basis for prediction and forecasting and each depends upon contingencies, they can easily lead to distorted results. On the other hand, they can be very useful in suggesting new overviews or approaches that traditional analysis might miss or treat as unfeasible.

CHAPTER 4: APPLICATIONS OF URBAN INDICATORS

Although urban indicators are relatively new, urban policy analysts have wasted no time in applying them to the decision-making process. Urban indicators involve various factors such as types of mass transit, number of schools, available hospital beds, degree of racial integration, availability of housing, the quality of streets, and countless others. Measuring these factors greatly facilitates comparison of governmental units, evaluating governmental services, and more generally looking at the quality of life in urban areas.

Education is a frequent focus of urban indicator research. Analysts often concentrate on identifying basic data sets that bear on twentieth century trends in the output and distribution of schooling in America. Much of this data is collected by the U.S. Bureau of the Census. Significantly, the bureau has pioneered the use of the demographer's concept of cohort, which refers to information collected for a group of people who have in common the timing of an event defining their membership, such as birth in a common year.

Indicators of health services include an analysis of service delivery by public agencies and voluntary and private institutions. In presenting a model of the application of systems analysis to problems of health services in a metropolitan area, the factors involved include population characteristics; the potential capacity and services of municipal hospitals; available medical manpower; the impact of city, state, and federal funding; and the functions and roles of city executive agencies in relation to health care services. Existing resources should be reviewed and analyzed with references to sources of new funds and technological advances in the medical and support fields, such as information systems and chemical laboratories.

Recently, several community groups have sued their local governments claiming an inadequate or disproportionate provision of public services. In a Washington, D.C., lawsuit, urban indicators were used to demonstrate an alleged inequality in the distribution of police services in a black community. Evaluation measures included property crime rates and trends, violent crime rates, citizen satisfaction, services calls per officer, police per ten thousand residents, number of service requests per police car, and daily average police per square mile. Studies of this sort are very useful because they can be applied to other cities and can provide a basis for comparison.

"Quality of life" is an elusive concept, yet much of current social and urban indicator research focuses on just this topic. One author has divided quality of life into four areas: pollution, systems of misgovernment, social groups, and leisure. Popular magazines have picked up the cue and are advising their readers which cities are most and least desirable. HARPER'S ranked the top and bottom twenty-five cities by incorporating such indicators as number of places of amusement, percentage of household telephones, and number of doctors.[6]

CHAPTER 5: INDICATOR-RELATED PROGRAM EVALUATIONS

One of the specific purposes of urban indicators is to provide measures of particular urban conditions. The expectation is that programs can be designed to ameliorate negative conditions. The existence of the indicator data base should provide a means for determining whether a new urban program is achieving its purpose. In other words, urban indicators can contribute both to defining the nature of a problem and to evaluating the success of the solution.

Not surprisingly, program evaluation has become a specialty of its own. Many federal grant programs, for example, began a decade ago to require grantees to set aside a fixed proportion of their grant for the purpose of evaluating the program. Without evaluations there was no way to learn from the research effort the expected benefit of similar projects in the future. Further, it became clear that if the evaluation process and criteria were not designed at the outset, it would prove impossible to recapture the data or to agree upon appropriate evaluation criteria. The experience of operating the project would make it difficult for the participants to be objective about evaluation criteria.

Some organizations, such as the Urban Institute, a nonprofit think tank funded by a combination of federal and foundation grants as well as contracts, became specialists in urban program analysis and evaluation. The experience of designing evaluation criteria was highly relevant to designing indicators. Thus, many such organizations have also become specialists in urban indicators. Accordingly, a number of the program analyses included in this chapter were performed by nonprofit groups and related to federally financed programs conducted by state and local governments.

CHAPTER 6: FUTURE OF URBAN INDICATORS

There is a need for an effective calculus to measure social change and social values. Economic indicators are inadequate for this purpose and so a system of social and urban accounts is necessary. The major concern of society today is no longer the production of goods but the improvement of service, promotion of public education and understanding, and the expansion of opportunities to appreciate and enjoy the amenities of late twentieth-century living.

Government by experts, advisors, and technocrats is increasingly replacing or supplementing the market as the primary decision maker. Yet some of society's problems cannot be readily resolved with technical criteria because they involve values and political choices and because there is presently no effective social calculus which can provide a true measure of the total costs and total benefits of policy decisions. What is needed is a series of indicators which would help to measure the social as well as the private costs of enterprises, the costs of social ills, and the quality of life. These indicators would supplement the traditional measures like standard of living and income earning capacity.

The call is out for the federal government to issue regular social reports on the state of the nation's urban areas. Current federal statistics fall far short in measuring national welfare, especially in terms of "the things that make life worth living," such as the success of education and research, the culture of the cities, and the strength of the family. Indicators are needed to assess these conditions of society, to identify problem areas, and to evaluate the impact of urban programs.

As a U.S. senator, Walter Mondale sought passage of the Full Opportunity and National Goals and Priorities Act. The bill which was passed by the Senate but not acted upon by the House, called for a council of social advisors composed of social analysts. The council would have been responsible for monitoring conditions in the nation which affect the social opportunities of its citizens. The bill also called on the president to report annually on the nation's social status including education, health, housing, alienation, political participation, personnel security, and social mobility.

Monitoring of local government is also needed. Economy in government is one test of performance but other standards are needed to supplement it. While efficiency is a useful guide in managing the everyday delivery of municipal services, it cannot be the sole factor in determining what programs should be funded and at what level. Evaluating program effectiveness is a new challenge to the current way of doing things. It is directed at uncovering which programs succeed in obtaining their goals and which ones do not. An accurate rating of performance can help in setting city priorities and in allocating scarce resources to different departments and functions of governments.

CONCLUSION

The field of urban indicators has grown rapidly from its humble beginnings only slightly over a decade ago. Instigated by the academic community and by private research institutes such as the Urban Institute, the Rand Corporation, and the Midwest Research Institute, various levels of government have taken an active interest in the concept. Basic statistics have developed a new appearance, making them more useful to policy analysts and citizens alike.

Of course, as with any new, quickly developing concept, problems are bound to occur. Chapter 3 of this volume directs the student of urban indicators to sources that deal with these methodological problems. As an indication of the strength of the urban indicator movement, chapter 4, the largest chapter of this volume outlines various attempts at using urban indicators. The rapid acceptance of urban indicators in such a short time demonstrates the potential of this approach, however, there still remains tremendous potential for growth.

The last chapter contains annotations dealing with the call for further implementation of urban indicator systems. Government is being asked to take the lead in this effort.

NOTES

1. U.S. Department of Health, Education, and Welfare, TOWARD A SOCIAL REPORT (Washington, D.C.: Government Printing Office, 1969), p. iii.

2. Ibid., p. 97.

3. Raymond A. Bauer, ed., SOCIAL INDICATORS (Cambridge: MIT Press, 1966), p. 1.

4. Peter J. Henriot, "Political Questions about Social Indicators," WESTERN POLITICAL QUARTERLY 23 (June 1970): 235-55.

5. Denis F. Johnston, "The OMB Report, SOCIAL INDICATORS, 1976," paper presented at the 136th annual meeting of the American Statistical Association, Boston, Mass., 23-26 August 1976. (Washington, D.C.: Social Indicators Project, U.S. Office of Management and Budget, August 1976), p. 11.

6. Arthur Louis, "The Worst American City," HARPER'S, January 1975, pp. 67-71.

Chapter 1

DEVELOPMENT OF URBAN INDICATORS

1   Abt, Clark C. "An Approach to Methods of Combined Sociotechnological Forecasting." TECHNOLOGICAL FORECASTING AND SOCIAL CHANGE 2, no. 1 (1970): 17-22.

> Effective technological forecasting requires social forecasting also. More disaggregated approaches would help overcome the complexity of social forecasting. Possible approaches would be functional (health, education, etc.), industrial (chemical, electronic, etc.), disciplinary (economics, sociology, engineering, etc.), or utilization of consumption and production functions. Seven steps are proposed for social forecasting.

2   Alberts, David S. A PLAN FOR MEASURING THE PERFORMANCE OF SOCIAL PROGRAMS. New York: Praeger, 1970. 157 p.

> In light of the fact that we are in the midst of significant expansion of social programs, the author is disturbed that no overall evaluative methodology has been developed to tell us how effective these efforts are. The purpose of this book is to provide a framework in which the performance of a social action can be measured.
>
> Using two viewpoints--that of the individual in society and that of society at large--the author traces methods by which these alternative perspectives lead to operational criteria and programs or actions. Chapters deal with such topics as formulation of social viewpoints from these two perspectives and analysis of the effectiveness of actual programs. Tables, appendixes, and a bibliography are included.

3   Albuquerque Urban Observatory. SOCIAL REPORTING FOR ALBUQUERQUE: DEVELOPMENT OF A SOCIAL INDICES SYSTEM. Albuquerque, N. Mex.: 1971. 90 p.

> Albuquerque is one of eight cities participating in a two-year social indicator study funded by the U.S. Department of Housing and Urban Development (HUD). This report identifies the social

indicators which will be tested for reliability in phase two of
the study. The Albuquerque model utilizes education, health,
community participation, equality of opportunity, and level
of living as indicators of quality of life. The appendix
summarizes the rest of the project work in Atlanta, Cleveland,
Denver, Kansas City, Milwaukee, Nashville, and San Diego.

4   Bardach, Eugene. "Gathering Data for Policy Research." JOURNAL OF
       URBAN ANALYSIS 2, no. 1 (1974): 117-44.

       The author discusses the design and execution of a research
       strategy involving the search for relevant sources. Trade-offs
       must be made to balance the depth with which strategies
       appropriate to different kinds of sources are pursued.

5   Bauer, Raymond A. "Detection and Anticipation of Impact: The Nature
       of the Task." In his SOCIAL INDICATORS, pp. 1-67. Cambridge:
       MIT Press, 1966.

       In looking at the activities of the National Aeronautics and
       Space Administration (NASA) the author attempts to define a
       statistical method of analyzing the consequences or benefits
       of the nation's space program. An information system is
       designed to build a feedback mechanism providing a yardstick
       by which to measure policies. Attainment of the goal of the
       nation's space exploration program is a social indicator, but it
       is pointed out that many of the secondary effects of the program
       must also be analyzed.

6   _____. "Societal Feedback." ANNALS OF THE AMERICAN ACADEMY
       OF POLITICAL AND SOCIAL SCIENCE 373 (September 1967): 180-92.
       Reprinted in SOCIAL INTELLIGENCE FOR AMERICA'S FUTURE, edited by
       Bertram M. Gross, pp. 63-77. Boston: Allyn and Bacon, 1969.

       This essay examines the nature of a societal information system.
       Given the breadth, complexity, and uniqueness of social problems,
       the information needs which must be met, and the lack of con-
       sensus on any model of our society, any set of social indicators
       can only be put to a few potential uses. Bauer points out that
       in the selection of indicators, one must rely on consensus that
       certain aspects of the society are important regardless of the
       societal model to which one subscribes.

7   Bell, Daniel. "The Adequacy of Our Concept." In A GREAT SOCIETY?,
       edited by Bertram M. Gross, pp. 127-61. New York: Basic Books, 1968.

       See 612.

8   _____. "The Measurement of Knowledge and Technology." In INDICA-
       TORS OF SOCIAL CHANGE: CONCEPTS AND MEASUREMENTS, edited

by Eleanor B. Sheldon and Wilbert E. Moore, pp. 145-246. New York: Russell Sage Foundation, 1968.

> Bell reviews the basic structural trends of society as they affect knowledge and technology and relates this analysis to post-industrial society. He states that it is important to appreciate the aspect of the environment for which social indicators are being proposed.

9 _____. "Toward a Social Report: I." PUBLIC INTEREST 15 (Spring 1969): 72-84.

> The recent and rapidly growing use of social indicators is discussed with comparisons to other types of indicators, such as gross national product. Social indicators are analyzed from the standpoint of social costs and social trends. The author claims that research into social indicators lagged until the New and Great Societies of the Kennedy-Johnson years needed to develop a measurement of the programs' effectiveness. The article views continued social indicator research as threatened by the incoming Nixon administration. Disappointment is expressed over the failure of former Senator Walter Mondale's bill entitled the Full Opportunity and Social Accounting Act.

10 Betz, Michael. "The City as a System Generating Income Equality." SOCIAL FORCES 51 (December 1972): 192-98.

> This is an empirical test of a model of the relationship between urbanization and income equality. The model tests the manner in which city size, industrial diversification, percentage of non-whites within a population income level, and income inequality relate to one another. Betz found that city sizes influenced income level and percentage of nonwhites in a population, but had no direct effect on income inequality. Industrial diversification was related to income inequality.

11 Bixhorn, Herbert, and Mindlin, Albert. "The Construction and Use of Composite Social Indicators by Local Governments." TRENDS 3 (October-December 1973): 1-9.

> See 133.

12 Boyce, David E. "Toward a Framework for Defining and Applying Urban Indicators in Plan-Making." URBAN AFFAIRS QUARTERLY 6 (December 1970): 145-71.

> Urban indicators research tries to measure and quantify urban problems and trends so social science research can be applied to public policy goals. Urban indicators are applied to standards, criteria, and forecasts in the planning process to develop an interdependent definition of performance characteristics.

Standards and criteria are labeled normative while indicators and forecasts are viewed as nonnormative. Indicators concern past and present performance, forecasts are future oriented and standards and criteria can be past, present, or future in character. Six major metropolitan land use and transportation studies are examined.

13   Bryce, Herrington J.; Erber, Ernest; and Clay, Phillip. "Minorities and the Future of the Cities." In URBAN GOVERNANCE AND MINORITIES, edited by Herrington J. Bryce, pp. 3-13. New York: Praeger, 1976.

See 367.

14   Buckley, Walter, ed. MODERN SYSTEMS RESEARCH FOR THE BEHAVIORAL SCIENTIST: A SOURCEBOOK. Chicago: Aldine, 1968. 525 p.

Fifty-nine selections provide exposure to both recent literature on general systems research in behavioral science and to seminal classic statements of more general principles, including works by Ludwig von Bertalanffy, Norbert Wiener, David Easton, Anatol Rapoport, and Gordon Allport.

Selections cover the historical development of systems theory in various disciplines of the behavioral sciences, the way that the parts of a system are interrelated to result in characteristic properties, a contrast of open and closed systems, the homeostasis and purposefulness of open systems, the psychological aspect of open systems, and a general systems approach to sociocultural systems.

15   Burton, Richard M.; Damon, William W.; and Dellinger, David C. "Estimating the Impact of Health Services in a Community." BEHAVIORAL SCIENCE 21 (November 1976): 478-89.

Bayesian statistics can reinforce the clinical and mechanical combination of observations for purposes of prediction. This technique is of particular value where there are few observations to supplement a prior expert judgment. It also gives a basis for evaluating relative expertise and tracing the learning experience of experts. The technique is very general and is therefore applicable to any situation where the judgments of several experts must be coordinated to make a single prediction.

16   Caldwell, Catherine. "Social Science as Ammunition." PSYCHOLOGY TODAY, September 1970, pp. 38-41, 72-73.

Caldwell analyzes the aftermath of a Department of Health, Education, and Welfare, Office of Education-sponsored survey conducted and written by James S. Coleman on education and race, titled EQUALITY OF EDUCATIONAL OPPORTUNITY, 1966.

The concept of equal educational opportunity is defined in terms of (1) the extent of segregation in the schools, (2) resource differentials and (3) differential student achievement scores. The author notes the relative lack of implementation.

17   Canadian Council on Social Development. SOCIAL INDICATORS: PROCEEDINGS OF A SEMINAR, OTTAWA JANUARY 13-14, 1972. Ottawa: 1972. 180 p.

These are the proceedings of the first Canadian seminar held on the topic of social indicators. It was attended by scholars and representatives of both governmental and nongovernmental bodies working in this field. In general the proceedings reflect the beginning of the "state of the art" in Canada and illustrate some of the philosophical, conceptual, and methodological problems besetting researchers. The publication includes remarks, papers, and discussions put forth during the 2 1/2-day seminar.

18   Chiang, C.L. AN INDEX OF HEALTH MATHEMATICAL MODELS. Publication no. 1000, Series 2-no. 5. Washington, D.C.: National Center for Health Statistics, Public Health Service, 1965. 19 p.

Models based on frequency and duration of illness, severity of illness and number of deaths, are proposed as individual components for an overall health index.

19   Clark, Terry Nichols. "Community Social Indicators: From Analytical Models to Policy Applications." URBAN AFFAIRS QUARTERLY 9 (September 1973): 3-36.

This is a discussion of criteria for community indicators. Clark points out that any indicator should be measurable, socially significant, important for policy formulation, and integrated into a theoretical model. He offers several examples of such models, and makes some suggestions for measurability. He recommends that indicator collecting should be standardized in the near future.

20   Colorado Department of Social Services. SOCIAL SERVICES INFORMATION SYSTEM: MANAGEMENT OVERVIEW MANUAL. Denver: 1975. 54 p.

This manual summarizes the Social Services Information System (SSIS) of the Colorado Department of Social Services. It emphasizes the management and use of the system by local jurisdictions, and describes the system's approach to case tracking as well as what the system offers local jurisdictions. This is supplemented by four other manuals on different aspects of the SSIS.

21   Community Council of Greater New York. SOCIAL INDICATORS IN
      COMMUNITY RESEARCH. New York: Research and Program Planning
      Information Development, 1976. 187 p.

      This is a record of the presentations given at five meetings
      sponsored by the Committee of Community Social Researchers of
      the Community Council of Greater New York on the subject of
      social indicators. The specific topics included the classifica-
      tion of indicators as resource, event, and functional, with a
      description of current research; the problems and potential
      of health indicators and their use in New York City; the
      interrelationships among the indicators of child health and wel-
      fare, and the implications of a New York City case study for
      a nationwide study; the relative measurements of poverty; and
      the use of social indicators as an analytical and policy tool
      with which to monitor social change.

22   Coombs, Clyde H. "Theory and Methods of Social Measurement." In
      RESEARCH METHODS IN THE BEHAVIORAL SCIENCES, edited by Leon
      Festinger and Daniel Katz, pp. 471-535. New York: Dryden Press,
      1953.

      Coombs reviews the basic levels of social sciences measure-
      ment (nominal, ordinal, interval, and ratio) and discusses the
      pitfalls associated with selecting one over another. He then
      presents a theory of data which has its bases in both informa-
      tion collected on overt individual behavior and in the relation-
      ship between overt behavior and the individual's latent level
      of behavior. Finally, he details methods of collecting data
      on overt and underlying latent behavior and discusses methods
      of analyzing data including the parallelogram technique, the
      unfolding technique, Thurstone's law of comparative judgment,
      the method of similarities, Lazarfeld's latent distance model
      and latent structure analysis, Guttman scales, and group scales.

23   Dahlstrom, Basil. AN EXPLORATION OF THE CONCEPT OF REGION-
      AL DATA CENTERS. Boise, Idaho: Boise Center for Urban Research,
      1976. 118 p.

      Dahlstrom discusses the effort of local governments in metro-
      politan Boise to establish an information system, and details the
      technical and economic feasibility of a regional data system
      serving all of the local governments.

24   Danziger, James N. "Computers, Local Governments, and the Litany to
      EDP." PUBLIC ADMINISTRATION REVIEW 37 (January-February 1977):
      28-37.

      One proposed solution to problems facing urban and suburban
      local governments is the extensive use of computers and elec-
      tronic data processing (EDP). Although the contributions of

EDP are unquestionably substantial, the author argues that many local government officials overestimate the value of EDP. A case study analysis in twelve cities and counties identifies major components of this overestimation. These include the beliefs that EDP is staff reducing and cost reducing, that EDP provides better information for decision makers, and that EDP increases the supervisor's ability to monitor subordinates. The author suggests that such beliefs can be misleading or even incorrect.

25   Downs, Anthony. "A Realistic Look at the Final Payoffs from Urban Data Systems." PUBLIC ADMINISTRATION REVIEW 27 (September 1967): 204-10.

This article examines the final payoffs--improvements in government or private action--resulting from the decision to implement an urban data bank system. Several reasons are presented for the lack of detailed analyses on the final payoffs. Technical improvements in data caused by urban data systems are discussed and these are related to estimates of technical payoffs from these improvements. Power payoffs are the direct result of changes in organizational structure or decision-making processes, but these are usually clouded by discussions of technical improvements. Downs examines the power shifts caused by automated data systems and the way in which power payoffs influence the type of urban data systems used.

26   Downs, Roger M., and Stea, David, eds. IMAGE AND ENVIRON-MENT: COGNITIVE MAPPING AND SPATIAL BEHAVIOR. Chicago: Aldine, 1973. 439 p.

This collection of nineteen articles was the first attempt to explore the area of cognitive mapping in all of its dimensions. Each section in the book has an extensive introduction by the editors. The articles are divided into six sections: theory, cognitive representations, spatial preference, the development of spatial cognition, geographical and spatial orientation, and cognitive distance.

27   Dror, Yehezekal. PUBLIC POLICYMAKING REEXAMINED. San Francisco: Chandler Publishing Co., 1968. 370 p.

See 285.

28   Duecker, Kenneth J. "Urban Information Systems and Urban Indicators." URBAN AFFAIRS QUARTERLY 6 (December 1970): 173-78.

The relationship between urban indicators and urban information systems is examined. While the terms are similar, urban indicators are concerned with information requirements, whereas urban information systems focus on the means of providing information, or the data processing aspects. The similarity is pertinent in their efforts to use urban data to develop measures which describe specific subsystem relationships. Another model emphasizing cost effectiveness is introduced and the model depends upon both urban information systems and urban indicators to delineate costs. Both systems are necessary components in developing a planning-effectiveness model.

29 Duncan, Otis Dudley. INTRODUCTION TO STRUCTURAL EQUATION MODELS. New York: Academic Press, 1975. 180 p.

The author prepares the reader to understand the emerging sociological literature which uses structural equation models or discusses questions pertaining to them. Rather than presenting a computer-ready program model, he instructs students on how to think for themselves about the properties of the mathematical and structural models and how to decide what kind of model their research requires. Some of the matters he covers are recursive models, specifications errors, measurement errors, and path coefficients.

30 Duncan, Otis Dudley; Featherman, David L.; and Duncan, Beverly. SOCIOECONOMIC BACKGROUND AND ACHIEVEMENT. New York: Seminar Press, 1972. 284 p.

The authors describe this book as an "effort at systematic model construction for the process of social mobility." They present a multitude of models, both diagrammatic and algebraic as well as tables and formulas which attempt to measure the interrelationships between education, occupation, and income. The presentation is sophisticated and comprehensive, beginning with a simple explanation of models and methods and quickly introducing difficult, detailed examples. It attempts to "model" all possible variables, and contingencies, and influences which are measurable, for example, education of father, number of siblings, ethnic background, education, father's income, and motivation weakened by lower actual level of achievement.

31 Emery, F.E. "The Next Thirty Years: Concepts, Methods and Anticipations." HUMAN RELATIONS 20 (August 1967): 199-237.

This article is concerned with prediction and planning in social sciences as well as the way in which emergence of predicted capabilities will affect the environment for which they are planned. Extremely detailed, technical and comprehensive. Concerned with abstract theory of social sciences.

32 Evans, James W. "Public Finance and Urban Information Systems." GOVERNMENTAL FINANCE 1 (May 1972): 27-30.

The author discusses the use of computers to automate routine manual tasks in functional areas. Emphasis is placed on public finance. The author suggests that using integrated municipal information systems based on automation of routine operations and a constantly updated integrated data base common to all city functions would assist city administrators in planning as well as reducing costs and increasing service delivery.

33   Field, Arthur J. URBAN POWER STRUCTURES: PROBLEMS IN THEORY AND RESEARCH. Cambridge, Mass.: Schenkman, 1970. 60 p.

This small book contains a paper presented at the Ohio Valley Sociological Society, the comments of four respondents, and discussion from the floor. It reviews and criticizes power structure studies as being too narrowly defined and focusing only on political decisions. Three basic questions are raised: (1) How much are we trying to explain and why? (2) What kinds of institutions, organizations, and individuals have power and in what amount? (3) What is the total amount of power available in an area? The book has a selective bibliography.

34   Finsterbusch, Kurt. "The Potential Role of Social Impact Assessments in Instituting Public Policies." In METHODOLOGY OF SOCIAL IMPACT ASSESSMENT, edited by Kurt Finsterbusch and C.P. Wolf, pp. 2-20. Stroudsburg, Pa.: Dowden, Hutchinson and Ross, 1977.

Social impact assessment (SIA) aims to facilitate decision making by determining the full range of costs and benefits of alternative proposed courses of action. It includes three major aspects: policy selection, policy design, and policy administration. Political forces may cause SIAs to alter some basic features or may rule out using the information obtained. Nevertheless, SIAs can increase the social utility of policy decisions.

35   Fitzsimmons, Stephen J., and Lavey, Warren G. "Social Economic Accounts System (SEAS): Toward a Comprehensive, Community Level Assessment Procedure." SOCIAL INDICATORS RESEARCH 2 (1976): 384-452.

The Social Economic Accounts System (SEAS) was developed to help policy planners and officials understand "quality of life," "relative social position," and "social well-being" at the (lower) community level. SEAS consists of over four hundred variables within fifteen sectors of community life, each subdivided into "sector state," "sector system" and "relevant condition" variables. According to the authors, SEAS is sensitive to time-series analysis and indicative of special community needs.

36   Fox, Karl A. "Operations Research and Complex Social Systems." In ECONOMIC ANALYSIS AND OPERATIONS RESEARCH: OPTIMIZATION TECHNIQUES IN QUANTITATIVE ECONOMIC MODELS, edited by

Jati K. Sengupta and Karl A. Fox, pp. 452–67. Amsterdam: North-Holland Publishing Co., 1969.

Fox discusses theories and formulas for quantifying inputs and outputs for a gross social product (GSP) system.

37 _____. SOCIAL INDICATORS AND SOCIAL THEORY: ELEMENTS OF AN OPERATIONAL SYSTEM. New York: John Wiley and Sons, 1974. 328 p.

This book presents a sophisticated effort to take available data and use "social indicators" to build social theories. It is extremely comprehensive in scope--from the individual id, ego, and superego, to communities, cities, and regions, and finally to national and world models. It is what the author describes as the "vertical integration of theory, methods and data." He selects various theories and methods from sociology, psychology, economics, mathematics, and statistics, and combines them with such concepts as an "individual social income" and total income and various "behavior settings." He also uses Becker's theory of the allocation of time, nonmarket components of national income, total income models for individuals and families, demographic accounting and model building, and resource allocation problems. Admittedly "rough and preliminary" by the author, it is nonetheless quite an extensive effort. Contains approximately thirty tables, many graphs, various formulas, and so forth, supporting the author's many models.

38 Friedmann, John, and Alonso, William, eds. REGIONAL DEVELOP-MENT AND PLANNING, A READER. Cambridge: MIT Press, 1964. 722 p.

The editors gathered prominent pace-setting articles of the leaders in social economic, geographic, and regional services delivery planning. Included are William Alonso, Brian Berry, John Friedmann, Edgar Hoover, Eric Lampard, Richard Morse, Harvey Perloff, Lloyd Rodwin, Charles Tiebout, Edward Ullman, Lowdon Wingo, Jr., and Paul Ilvisaker. Articles cover the following topics: regional policy issues; organization of regions; theories of regional growth based on natural resource availability, external trade, or population migrations; the role of cities in development; problems of backward areas; national policy for regional development; definition of optimal planning regions and regional objectives; evaluation of regional economic progress; and national regional development strategies.

39 Fullerton, Herbert H., and Prescott, James R. AN ECONOMIC SIMU-LATION MODEL FOR REGIONAL DEVELOPMENT PLANNING. Ann Arbor, Mich.: Ann Arbor Science Publishers, 1975. 133 p.

The authors seek to develop a quantitative model capable of

providing economic and demographic projections which are
needed for regional planning. They describe the simulation
model and examine some of the data generated through its use.

40 Galnoor, Itzhak. "Social Information for What?" ANNALS OF THE
AMERICAN ACADEMY OF POLITICAL AND SOCIAL SCIENCE 393
(January 1971): 1-19.

This article examines uses of social information for developed
and developing countries. It begins with an explanation of the
terms "social," "social accounting," "social reporting," and
"social information." The need for more and better information,
and for development of a theoretical basis is stated. The author
examines the definitions of developing and developed countries
and calls for additional emphasis on social aspects and the role
that "social information" could play in that situation. He
suggests specific areas where he believes improvement to be most
likely and beneficial in uses of data for both developed and
developing countries.

41 Garn, Harvey A.; Flax, Michael J.; Springer, Michael; and Taylor,
Jeremy B. MODELS FOR INDICATOR DEVELOPMENT: A FRAME-
WORK FOR POLICY ANALYSIS. Washington, D.C.: Urban Institute,
1976. 61 p.

Urban indicators as well as policy analysis require the use of
performance measures to determine the efficiency and effectiveness of urban service delivery and the impact of different policies. The authors provide a model to monitor inputs and outputs as well as the contributions of various participants in the
process, including governments, industry, the nonprofit sector,
and the consumer. They deal with accountability and evaluation
models, and relate all the measures to policy analysis.

42 Goodman, Leonard H., ed. ECONOMIC PROGRESS AND SOCIAL
WELFARE. New York: Columbia University Press, 1966. 233 p.

The material in this book was prepared for presentation at the
1966 Annual Forum of the National Conference on Social Welfare.
Seven papers were presented dealing with various aspects of
Great Society problems and goals, including one on measurement of social change by Eleanor B. Sheldon and Wilbert Moore.

43 Gottehrer, Barry. "Urban Conditions: New York City." ANNALS OF
THE AMERICAN ACADEMY OF POLITICAL AND SOCIAL SCIENCE 371
(May 1967): 141-58. Reprinted in SOCIAL INTELLIGENCE FOR AMER-
ICA'S FUTURE: EXPLORATIONS IN SOCIETAL PROBLEMS, edited by
Bertram M. Gross. Boston: Allyn and Bacon, 1969.

Gottehrer was assistant to former Mayor Lindsay when he wrote
this article in 1967. He outlines problems inherited from the

previous administration of Mayor Wagner and what Lindsay did,
in the author's opinion, to correct Wagner's errors. He points
out how the Lindsay administration used social indicators, and
discusses program budgeting, additional aid, and regional approach to problems.

44   Gross, Bertram M. "The State of the Nation: Social Systems Accounting."
In SOCIAL INDICATORS, edited by Raymond A. Bauer, pp. 154–271.
Cambridge: MIT Press, 1966.

Gross argues for social systems accounting through integration
of concepts from economics, sociology, political science, anthropology, psychology, and social psychology. He proposes a two-
dimensional social systems model involving the system structure
(the internal relations among the system's parts), and the system
performance (the acquiring of inputs and their transformations
into outputs). This model can be adapted to different stages of
development. He warns that attention must be paid to keeping
the intangible values from being swallowed up by the quantitative factors, and cautions against a "new philistinism"--the use
of monetary units as the common denominator of the important
things in human life.

45   _____ . "Social Goals and Indicators for American Society." ANNALS
OF THE AMERICAN ACADEMY OF POLITICAL AND SOCIAL SCIENCE
371 (May 1967): entire issue; 373 (September 1967): entire issue.

Two entire editions of this journal are devoted to social goals
and indicators for American society. Twenty-one articles explore
the issues surrounding the collection and validity of social measurement.

46   _____ , ed. SOCIAL INTELLIGENCE FOR AMERICA'S FUTURE: EX-
PLORATIONS IN SOCIETAL PROBLEMS. Boston: Allyn and Bacon,
1969. 541 p.

The book was originally to be a locally run social report analo-
gous to the economic report of the president. What resulted
was a series of articles by individual authors who have written
what they believe a social report ought to be, including ideas
about the way it could be used to set social goals, plan programs,
and implement public policy. The articles include suggestions
for social statistics and indicators that would be included in the
social report and which could be collated to develop an appraisal
of social problems and progress. The articles address the broad
spectrum of societal concerns including politics, culture, health,
poverty, racial discrimination, the natural environment, and the
cities.

47   Gross, Bertram M., and Springer, Michael. "A New Orientation in
American Government." ANNALS OF THE AMERICAN ACADEMY OF

POLITICAL AND SOCIAL SCIENCE 371 (May 1967): 1-19.

This brief but comprehensive article was written at the beginning
of the current social indicator movement and attempts to explain
the other articles contained in the volume as they all relate
to social indicators. The authors explain that this volume of the
ANNALS and a future volume will be devoted to the new
movement of social indicators. They give brief explanations of
each and the overall perspective behind the publication of the
articles. They include a table of "Indicator Suggestions,"
that is, new data and better use of existing data from various
sources. The development of the need for social indicators
is reviewed, as well as their potential uses and abuses.

48 _____, eds. "Political Intelligence for America's Future." ANNALS
OF THE AMERICAN ACADEMY OF POLITICAL AND SOCIAL SCIENCE
388 (March 1970): entire issue.

See 643.

49 Gross, Bertram M., et al., eds. A GREAT SOCIETY? New York:
Basic Books, 1968. 362 p.

This is a compilation of articles by persons from the university
community regarding the Great Society. It provides a brief
history of the social indicator movement and President Johnson's
efforts to get the academic community involved in his pursuit of
the Great Society. The dialogue which was initiated covered
a wide range of topics--political science, sociology, economics,
history, and public and business administration.

50 Harrison, David, Jr., and Kain, John F. "Cumulative Urban Growth
and Urban Density Functions." JOURNAL OF URBAN ECONOMICS 1
(January 1974): 61-98.

This is a conceptual discussion of a model of urban density
functions. In this model, urban growth is a layering process
and urban spatial structure is the result of a cumulative process
of growth. Current levels of population, commuting costs, and
transportation costs are determined by the density of development
during this period, but past and future densities are determined
by the level of those variables at that time. The authors
demonstrate that this model can generate reasonable density
functions.

51 Hatry, Harry P. "Measuring the Quality of Public Services." In
IMPROVING URBAN MANAGEMENT, edited by Willis D. Hawley and
David Rogers, pp. 3-27. Beverly Hills, Calif.: Sage Publications, 1974.

Efforts to measure the quality of public services have increased
in recent years as new management tools have been developed
and have become available to local governments. Benefits

derived from public service quality measurement are problem identification, program information feedback, evaluation of employee and management performance, and increased community involvement. Quality of public service has different meanings. The major components of such a program include intended purposes, negative effects, adequate quantity, equitable distribution, response time, citizen input, perceived satisfaction, and efficiency. The author discusses different ways quality measurement can be undertaken, including how to set quality targets or standards. The people and institutions who should be responsible for measuring public service quality are the local government, citizen groups, universities, and legislatures.

52   Hatry, Harry P.; Winnie, Richard E.; and Fisk, Donald M. PRACTICAL PROGRAM EVALUATION FOR STATE AND LOCAL GOVERNMENTS. Washington, D.C.: Urban Institute, 1973. 134 p.

This study is a guide for public officials who wish to assess and evaluate the impact of spend programs. A step-by-step plan for implementing the evaluation system is presented as well as a method for defining objectives, establishing criteria, and identifying client groups for the study. Several evaluation designs are discussed, including a variety of techniques to be used. The authors also make suggestions on data collection, cost, and staffing estimates which officials should undertake in the evaluation, and how evaluation results can be translated into public policies.

53   Hauser, Philip M. SOCIAL STATISTICS IN USE. New York: Russell Sage Foundation, 1975. 385 p.

The author provides an honest overview of social statistics in use today and offers a readable introduction to the subject--what the social statistics are and where they may be found. The work was commissioned by the Russell Sage Foundation in pursuit of its aim to better inform the general public of the value of such social science research. The focus is on social (rather than economic) statistics, essentially those compiled by various government agencies. A number of experts were consulted and have contributed to the description of the nature and uses of data in their fields of specialization. Useful selected bibliographies accompany each chapter.

54   Hearle, Edward F.R. "The Scope of Management Information Systems in Governmental Administration." In GOVERNING URBAN SOCIETY: NEW SCIENTIFIC APPROACHES, edited by Stephen B. Sweeney and James C. Charlesworth, pp. 197-208. Philadelphia: American Academy of Political and Social Science, 1967.

Management information systems are rapidly becoming a vital tool in the public sector administrator's arsenal. In the near future we will be using optical readers; computers that produce output in printed, vocal, or graphic form; unlimited storage; increased processing speed; remote input and output devices linked to central computers; and smaller, cheaper computers. As a result, public sector managers will be able to obtain more data on their environment, monitor their agency's internal operations, expand interagency information systems, bypass middle management, utilize national and regional data centers, and share equipment with other agencies. Not all information a manager receives should be systematized. Much of the information he receives through informal and ad hoc channels is important in the decision-making process.

55   Heise, David R. "Group Dynamic and Attitude-Behavior Relations." SOCIOLOGICAL METHODS AND RESEARCH 5 (February 1977): 259-88.

Heise presents a dynamic model of social deviance. Attitudes have effects on behaviors, behaviors are compared against norms to define deviance, and deviance has a return, corrective effect on attitudes through mechanisms of social control. Through social interactions, these individual processes are linked to form a single interpersonal system within a group. The results of a preliminary empirical study show that the proposed system is viable with some modifications.

56   Henshel, Richard L. ON THE FUTURE OF SOCIAL PREDICTION. Indianapolis: Bobbs-Merrill, 1976. 77 p.

Sociologists have become increasingly interested in social prediction. Whereas the earlier emphasis was on probablistic studies of specific social problems, in recent years there has been a movement toward viewing sociology as a policy science aimed at designing sophisticated alternative social structures. The author points out two factors which determine the predictive potential of any discipline: the sophistication of its theory, and the validity of its determinants of predictability. For sociology, since most social phenomena do not lend themselves to prediction in their natural state, predictive models and systems must be scientifically grounded, and this grounding, the author concludes, has not been emphasized.

57   Holleb, Doris. "Social Statistics for Social Policy." In PLANNING, edited by American Society of Planning Officials, pp. 80-85. Chicago: American Society of Planning Officials, 1968.

See 301.

58   Hughes, James W. URBAN INDICATORS, METROPOLITAN EVALUATION, AND PUBLIC POLICY. Rutgers, N.J.: Rutgers-The State University, 1972. 233 p.

See 305.

59   James, Franklin J., and Hughes, James W. ECONOMIC GROWTH
      AND RESIDENTIAL PATTERNS: A METHODOLOGICAL INVESTIGATION.
      New Brunswick, N.J.: Rutgers-The State University, Center for Urban
      Policy Research, 1972. 211 p.

      This is a report on the development and testing of a model of
      employment and household growth. Its purpose is to examine
      the effects of decentralization of economic activities with its
      associated redistribution of housing demand to suburban areas.
      The model permits a test of possible "locking out" of middle-
      and low-income workers from suburban housing markets. Employ-
      ment allocation, household generation, and residential demand
      are the key variables of the shift-share model which is developed
      and tested.

60   Janson, Carl-Gunnar. "Some Problems of Ecological Factor Analysis."
      In QUANTITATIVE ECOLOGICAL ANALYSIS IN SOCIAL SCIENCES,
      edited by Mattei Dogan and Stein Rokkan, pp. 301-41. Cambridge:
      MIT Press, 1969.

      Factor analysis, that is, "component analysis," of the human
      ecology is both a controversial and a popular contemporary topic.
      The author attempts a review of studies on this subject and
      acknowledges a heavy Scandinavian-American, sociological,
      and egocentric bias in the thirty-seven-page summary. His
      review concerns aspects of urban spatial structure (within communi-
      ties), and analyses concerned with variations among communities
      or social units. He further discusses, in some detail, basic
      assumptions underlying factor analyses, including many technical
      ones. Throughout the review, factor analysis is discussed as a
      descriptive tool, not as a causal model, although noncausal
      inferential implications are included in the author's descriptive
      definition of the factor analytic approach. A useful bibliogra-
      phy is included.

61   Kemeny, John G. "The City and the Computer Revolution." In GOV-
      ERNING URBAN SOCIETY: NEW SCIENTIFIC APPROACHES, edited by
      Stephen B. Sweeney and James C. Charlesworth, pp. 49-62. Philadel-
      phia: American Academy of Political and Social Science, 1967.

      The basic premise of this article is that the computer will help
      us to deal with many of the complexities of modern society and
      will relieve some of the problems of our cities. The evolution
      of computers can be viewed in three stages: the dawn of
      computing, the coming of time sharing, and the era of a com-
      puter in every home. Cities have been slow to use computers
      and have generally done so only for the most elementary tasks,
      ignoring, for instance, the value of simulation in traffic, pollu-
      tion, and planning. Time sharing has permitted all users to
      take advantage of high speed computers. This is being done in
      medical care quality control, crime records, and traffic control.
      Eventually computers will become available to every citizen,

thus reducing many of the functions cities perform and at the same time resolving many of our urban problems.

62 Kraemer, Kenneth L. "Local Government, Information Systems, and Technology Transfer: Evaluating Some Common Assertions About Computer Application Transfer." PUBLIC ADMINISTRATION REVIEW, July–August 1977, pp. 368–82.

This article is part of a research project entitled "Evaluation of Information Technology in Local Government" which is supported by a grant from the U.S. National Science Foundation. It examines the transfer of computer technology into city and county governments in the United States, comparing the alleged benefits of these transfers. It is a quantitative analysis which does not make qualitative judgments about the real transfer experiences, but attempts to provide a rational framework in which to evaluate such technological transfers.

63 _____. POLICY ANALYSIS IN LOCAL GOVERNMENT: A SYSTEMS APPROACH TO DECISION-MAKING. Washington, D.C.: International City Management Association, 1973. 65 p.

Kraemer advises that he has written this text for the policymaker rather than the expert analyst. He states that policy analysis is an important part of the decision-making process, and describes a changing environment that makes analysis possible and necessary. He presents various methods that may be employed with limitations, the use and misuse of analysis, and the necessary preconditions for analysis. Kraemer describes the process of analysis and the operational, programming, and developmental problems. He also explains modeling and other quantitative and nonquantitative techniques. There is a brief bibliography as well as several graphs and charts.

64 Land, Kenneth C. "The Role of Quality of Employment Indicators in General Social Reporting Systems." AMERICAN BEHAVIORAL SCIENTIST 18 (January–February 1975): 304–32.

The author discusses the development of the social indicator movement, outlines definitional problems, and describes two different, but complementary, types of social indicators. In addition, he places quality-of-employment indicators in this broader context and introduces the notion of social indicator models as aids in interpreting social indicators. His purpose as he describes it is to "locate the place of quality of employment indicators within the larger social indicator perspective and to indicate some ways in which procedures for the analysis of general social indicators can be related to changes in employment indicators."

65 _____. "Theories, Models and Indicators of Social Change." INTER-
NATIONAL SOCIAL SCIENCE JOURNAL 27, no. 1 (1975): 7-37.

See 192.

66 Land, Kenneth C., and Spilerman, Seymour, eds. SOCIAL INDICATOR
MODELS. New York: Russell Sage Foundation, 1975. 411 p.

This book represents a very comprehensive effort, rather advanced
in its perception of the status of the social indicator movement.
It contains a selection of fifteen different articles, most of
them dealing with either replication models or longitudinal and
dynamic models. Some are general in scope and others specific.
Models presented here are less comprehensive than models which
attempt to use all indicators together. They are limited to only
those few indicators which involve one area of study. The
editors indicate in the introduction that they believe world
models and the like to be premature and unrealistic, considering
the present state of science. Land presents a well-written overview of the social indicator movement to date, and social indicator models in particular. The book does have many tables
and involved formulas, but it is not difficult reading.

67 Lasswell, Harold D. A PRE-VIEW OF POLICY SCIENCES. Policy
Science Book Series 1. New York: American Elsevier, 1971. 173 p.

This is a short sketch of one of many possible approaches to the
policy sciences by one of the pioneers of the field. Over
twenty years ago the author, together with Daniel Lerner, introduced the concept of "policy science," and laid its earliest
foundations. For years the field has been obscured or overtaken
by other types and methods of social science research, but re-
newed interest in policy science is now clearly evident.

68 Lazarsfeld, Paul F. "Social Accounting." In THE USES OF SOCIOLOGY,
edited by Paul F. Lazarsfeld, William S. Sewell, and Harold Wilensky,
pp. 839-75. New York: Basic Books, 1967.

This is a broad background overview of the history of census
taking in the United States and the part played therein by
statistics. The article also reviews the role of social statistics
in terms of its interrelationships, in the broadest sense, with
public policy and the decision-making process. Lazarsfeld gives
a historical perspective of the social indicator movement. The
latter idea, however, is not very extensively pursued. He calls
for centralization of data collection, and broader dissemination
of accumulated data, and a social "accounting" system.

69 Lear, John. "Where is Society Going? The Search for Landmarks."
SATURDAY REVIEW, 15 April 1972, pp. 34-39.

This is a brief readable history of the people and the milestones associated with social science research, both public and private, with particular emphasis on the work of the Russell Sage Foundation. The author also gives special mention to the pioneering work of Eleanor Sheldon. In addition, he reports in some detail the results of a 1971 national survey of the quality of American life, financed by the Russell Sage Foundation.

70   Lebergott, Stanley. "Labor Force and Employment Trends." In INDICA-TORS OF SOCIAL CHANGE: CONCEPTS AND MEASUREMENTS, edited by Eleanor B. Sheldon and Wilbert E. Moore, pp. 97-114. New York: Russell Sage Foundation, 1968.

This early effort was supported by the Russell Sage Foundation to study the social indicator movement. Sixteen authors have contributed to this study of the current status and possible application of developing indicators. This chapter reviews major changes in labor supply and employment since 1900. It begins with the relationship between family income and employment, discusses methods of controlling labor input in relation to changes in demands for goods and services, analyzes how such changes led to advanced mechanization, and finally proposes changes in existing data collection methods. Many aspects of possible sociological impact are explored in some depth.

71   Lehman, Edward W. "Social Indicators and Social Problems." In HAND-BOOK ON THE STUDY OF SOCIAL PROBLEMS, edited by Erwin O. Smigel, pp. 149-76. Chicago: Rand McNally, 1971.

This article is a general description of what social and urban indicators are, and a report on the status of the movement. Easy to read, it is a good stepping-off point for anyone interested in urban indicators. It is also a well-balanced report containing the pros and cons--in a very general sense--as well as the restrictions on utilization of indicators and an analysis of the likely degree of success in the future.

72   Lepawsky, Albert. "The Planning Apparatus: A Vignette of the New Deal." JOURNAL OF THE AMERICAN INSTITUTE OF PLANNERS 42 (January 1976): 16-32.

An analysis of Franklin Roosevelt's major New Deal program, the National Resources Planning Board (NRPB). The NRPB concerned itself with a great number of subjects, including the following: social security and public welfare, consumption and production, income and investment, natural resources and public works, conservation and development, urbanism and ruralism, metropolitanism and regionalism, housing and community facilities, health and demography, education and scientific research, and transportation and technology. The author contends that the NRPB reports were relatively unsophisticated when compared with the thoroughly analytic work of the Council of Economic

Advisers, which followed in 1946 as America's first full-fledged agency for fiscal policy and economic planning. Nevertheless, the NRPB helped identify various economic problem areas, estimated the effects of alternative allocations of resources, improved data collection and methods, and proposed various methods of government fiscal management.

73   Lineberry, Robert L. "Equality, Public Policy and Public Services: The Under Class Hypothesis and the Limits to Equality." POLICY AND POLITICS 4 (December 1975): 67-84.

This article provides an assessment of the problems of applying equality to the allocation of urban public services. It describes three types of underclass, that is, those which result from race preference, class preference, or power elite. Using San Antonio, Texas, as a model, he analyzes the hypothesis using various indicators such as proximity to and quality of fire protection, or parks.

74   Liu, Ben-Chieh. "Local Government Finance and Metropolitan Employment Growth: A Simultaneous-Equation Model." SOUTHERN ECONOMIC JOURNAL 43 (January 1977): 1379-85.

Economists have generally ignored the effects of local government finance and fiscal policies on regional growth. The author presents a simultaneous equation model, employing four variables: differential growth in per capita local government expenditures, and differential growth in average tax rates. The estimates of the model are based on observations of the seventy-five largest S.M.S.A.s from 1960 to 1967. The results showed clearly that the changes in the levels of public services are important determinants of the locational and expansional decisions of industries. Moreover, the model indicates that per capita local government public expenditures have a positive influence on net migration, which also contributes to regional employment growth.

75   Logan, John R. "Industrialization and the Stratification of Cities in Suburban Regions." AMERICAN JOURNAL OF SOCIOLOGY 82 (September 1976): 333-48.

A significant analysis of the factors affecting the pattern of suburban growth in American metropolitan areas. The author suggests that a model for this process must include regional growth, suburban interdependence, local governmental decisions, social characteristics of residents, and the group politics within each community. Census data from 1950 to 1970 is used to generate a tentative model.

76   Long, Norton E. "Indicators of Change in Political Institutions." ANNALS OF THE AMERICAN ACADEMY OF POLITICAL AND SOCIAL SCIENCE 388 (March 1970): 35-45.

This article contains a narrative critique of social indicators with particular reference to those used in the Kerner Commission report and the Skolnick report. The author claims that indicators are of little value in studies like the Kerner and Skolnick reports because they do necessarily support the conclusions. The author believes that studying the "patterns of history" is more valuable and that indicators must be supported with a theory that explains the phenomena, trends, and institutions of society.

77   Lundberg, Fred J. "Development of Large Urban Information Systems." MUNICIPAL FINANCE 40 (November 1967): 73-79.

The author cites three reasons why urban governments have not developed and used large scale information systems--lack of resources, lack of skilled manpower, and data banks being used only for special projects. Eight characteristics are listed as being basic to the design and implementation of a large-scale system. The urban data center in Cincinnati is located at the university to free it from any local governmental restrictions. Different models being used are described and techniques of combining different systems already in use around the country are presented. Urban data banks are difficult and time-consuming projects, but they can be successfully implemented.

78   McCall, Storrs. "Quality of Life." SOCIAL INDICATORS RESEARCH 2 (September 1975): 229-48.

This is another attempt to define the term "quality of life." This author defines the concept in terms of obtaining the necessary conditions for happiness throughout society, rather than, as other authors do, by treating it as a summation of the individual happiness of all members of society. The author finds that the conditions of happiness are necessary but not sufficient factors for quality of life and consequently high "quality of life" may actually be compatible with unhappiness.

79   McGranahan, Donald. "Development Indicators and Development Models." THE JOURNAL OF DEVELOPMENT STUDIES 8 (April 1972): 91-102.

This discussion focuses on twin topics: the semantics of indicators and the concepts of development. In addition, the author examines procedures for the selection and validation of indicators and contrasts the systems model with other approaches to the measurement of development. The article is a revision of a working paper prepared while the author was director of the United Nations Research Institute for Social Development at Geneva, Switzerland.

80   Merton, R.K. SOCIAL THEORY AND SOCIAL STRUCTURE. Enl. ed. New York: Free Press, 1968. 702 p.

Merton addresses two interests in this reworked collection of his earlier papers plus additional new articles. The two interests center around the connection between social research and theory and the codification of both theory and procedures of qualitative analysis. He commences with a review of social theory, then examines three groupings of related problems in sociological theories: problems with functional analysis, with the related sociologies of knowledge and mass communications as well as public opinions, and with the sociology of science. This brings under consideration a wide range of subjects: social dynamics and change, bureaucratic structure and personality, bureaucratic dysfunctions, sociological analysis of occupations, reference group behavior, relative deprivation, influence structures in communities, self-fulfilling prophecy, existentialism, relativism, propaganda analysis, the relation of science to the political order and to social values, universalism, communism, and skepticism.

81   Michelson, William. "Urbanism as Ways of Living: The Changing Views of Planning Researchers." EKISTICS 40 (July 1975): 20–26.

This is a discussion of the role of planning in terms of the conception of the quality of life. Quality of life is coming to be seen as relative to one's life-style, and the evaluation of quality is adjusted upward with improving quality. This leads to a concern for providing people with the opportunity to maximize their own desires. The ethical implication of this is that who does the planning for whom is significant.

82   Mitchell, Joyce M., and Mitchell, William C. "The Changing Politics of American Life." In INDICATORS OF SOCIAL CHANGE: CONCEPTS AND MEASUREMENTS, edited by Eleanor B. Sheldon and Wilbert E. Moore, pp. 247–94. New York: Russell Sage Foundation, 1968.

This paper seeks to distinguish what changes have occurred in American political life within a loose formulation of systems analysis. It implements a review of historical data and broad estimates are used to provide a summary view of what has happened in American political history. It highlights the changing political system including the formal political structures and processes, policy and policymaking, changing political activities of citizens, changing governmental activities, and changing impacts of policy and society. Indicators used include historical data from the U.S. Bureau of Census and other sources on taxation, governmental indebtedness, governmental units, and public employment.

83   Monts, J. Kenneth. "Responsibility: Relevance or Realism? The Case of Urban Dynamics." SOCIAL SCIENCE QUARTERLY 57 (December 1976): 520–34.

This article analyzes Forrester's influential URBAN DYNAMICS (Cambridge, Mass.: MIT Press, 1969). The author agrees that Forrester's systems approach is a brilliant formulation and the most promising mode of understanding urban dynamics. However, the author posits that there must be the additional criterion of realism. The problem chosen to be studied must accord with the realities of the urban crisis. The final goal should be to restructure Forrester's model so that it incorporates valid assumptions and still generates the same phenomenon.

84   Moser, C.A. "Some General Developments in Social Statistics." In SOCIAL TRENDS, edited by Muriel Missel, pp. 7-11. London: Her Majesty's Central Statistical Office, 1970.

Social statistics are becoming more significant in the United Kingdom. This article reports on the use of statistics by the Office of Population Censuses and Surveys and the General Household Survey, and discusses a system of social statistics which integrates many statistics on social conditions, resources, and the flow of people.

85   Moynihan, Daniel P. "Urban Conditions: General." ANNALS OF THE AMERICAN ACADEMY OF POLITICAL AND SOCIAL SCIENCE 371 (May 1967): 159-77.

It is essential that all concerned with the development of a system of urban social indicators be prepared in advance for being accused of betraying supposedly allied causes. Social scientists do not always take the side of these causes. The way in which urban indicators are developed is likely to have considerable influence on the level of government which deals with the problems. The indicators are going to be developed by people with certain values. Urban social indicators should be in the realm of disaggregation and correlation. Urban social indicators cannot be apolitical, but they should cater to a wide selection of political interests. The future must be dealt with as well as the present. Urban indicators should seek to provide comparisons between local data, average national data, and data corresponding to "best practice" in various fields. The author suggests changes and additions to indicators concerning individuals, families, and institutions.

86   Murphy, Thomas P. "Management Information Systems." In DEVELOPING THE MUNICIPAL ORGANIZATION, edited by Stanley Powers, F. Gerald Brown, and David S. Arnold, pp. 211-26. Washington, D.C.: International City Management Association, 1974.

Management information systems (MIS) are a vital part of local governmental organizations. They provide the necessary information for managers to coordinate the daily operations of local government, and they assist in policy analysis and long-range planning. Management information systems are not used solely by chief administrators. They are of value to councilmen, department heads, and citizens. MIS makes major contributions in records storage and retrieval, budget information and control, decision making, data processing, program information, internal communications, and interdepartmental coordination. The author discusses the types of data needed for the system and the problems of centralization versus decentralization. Human problems encountered in implementing new systems are examined as is the impact of MIS on the organization. The author concludes with a discussion of urban information systems.

87   Ontell, Robert. WHAT IS A SOCIAL INDICATOR? San Diego, Calif.: Urban Observatory, 1971. 47 p.

The author reviews a variety of social indicator definitions. Some definitions stress the relationship of a social statistic to social systems models and others require that indicators be output measures. The conclusion is that while there is general agreement that a social indicator is a kind of social statistic, there is less agreement about what social indicators actually measure--other than the quality of life in a very general way.

88   Parker, John K. "Information Requirements for Urban Research Programs." In GOVERNING URBAN SOCIETY: NEW SCIENTIFIC APPROACHES, edited by Stephen B. Sweeney and James C. Charlesworth, pp. 241-50. Philadelphia: American Academy of Political and Social Science, 1967.

See 673.

89   Perle, Eugene D. "Editor's Introduction." URBAN AFFAIRS QUARTERLY 6 (December 1970): 135-44.

An introduction to a special issue with six articles on urban indicators; three report on the state of the art and the other three present original research.

90   Popenoe, David. "On the Meaning of Urban in Urban Studies." URBAN AFFAIRS QUARTERLY 1 (September 1965): 17-34.

The article attempts to define "urban affairs." The author outlines the growth of academic research in this interdisciplinary field, giving the topic some conceptual framework to assist new students of the field. Popenoe explains that the study is concerned with both a structural-functional and a process approach. The article treats such topics as: the nature of communities, the urban process, and how they interact.

91   Rice, Stuart A. "Social Accounting and Statistics for the Great Society." PUBLIC ADMINISTRATION REVIEW 27 (June 1967): 169-74.

The author reviews SOCIAL INDICATORS, edited by Raymond A. Bauer (Cambridge, Mass.: MIT Press, 1966). He agrees with

the book's editor and contributors that social indicators are needed
which will reflect the interrelations between technological and
social changes. No longer can technological change be deemed
a variable independent of social change. Just as technology
affects social conditions, so too must social considerations affect
technology. Because society has now seen some ill-effects of
technology, it is necessary to redirect properly its advancements
by taking into consideration their possible social consequences.
Social indicators are quantitative information which reflect
qualitative concepts of social conditions, for example, health,
happiness, and prosperity. They must be developed to serve as
feedback from society and the environment to help identify social
conditions related to technology. They are needed to help determine the present state of the nation's social health as well as
the changes which would result from anticipated technological
activity, such as the space program. They are needed to find
pathways through the maze of social interconnections with technology. The author believes that SOCIAL INDICATORS is one
of a growing number of related studies which are part of a trend
in "social investigation" whose purpose is to help mankind ulti-
mately control its destiny.

92   Richard, Robert. SUBJECTIVE SOCIAL INDICATORS. Chicago: National
      Opinion Research Center, University of Chicago, 1969. 210 p.

      Richard presents methodological study of the design validation
      and measurement of variables necessary to construct a social pro-
      file for inclusion as a chapter of the HOUSEHOLD SURVEY
      MANUAL (Washington, D.C.: U.S. Bureau of the Budget,
      1969). Such profiles serve as analytical tools for policymaking
      and social-action agencies.

93   Riecken, Henry W. "Social Sciences and Social Problems." SOCIAL
      SCIENCE INFORMATION 8 (February-June 1969): 101-29.

      The author points to a renewed sense of determination to solve
      social problems. There is the assumption that the social sciences
      have much to contribute. There is a history of the application
      of the social sciences. An "orientation and stance" of the
      social sciences is presented. There are three significant obstacles
      to applying social science to social problems: (1) manipulability--
      manipulable elements are not identified, (2) the Hawthorne effect--
      changes in behavior that result from the fact that the individuals
      are the subjects in an experimental study, rather than from the
      actual effects of the factors or variables that are being manipulated,
      and (3) the defects of indirect data--the human memory distorts,
      omits, and fabricates events as well as underreporting data. All
      social problems require the efforts of more than one discipline.
      Members of these disciplines must be able to work together pro-
      ductively and effectively. The products of social science are
      almost always intangible. Practices and routines having to do

with human behavior are harder to teach than are those of the physical sciences. There is a need for change in human relationships. What should be the relationship between the social scientist or social engineer-developer and the people he is trying to help or influence?

94   Rivlin, Alice M. SYSTEMATIC THINKING FOR SOCIAL ACTION. Washington, D.C.: Brookings Institution, 1971.

Rivlin evaluates the progress of the analysts in improving the basis for public decisions on social action programs by measuring social needs, evaluating the effectiveness of government programs to meet them, and estimating the cost versus the benefits of alternative programs. She asserts that considerable progress has been made in identifying social problems, estimating who would gain if social programs were successful. Yet little progress has been made in comparing the benefits of different social programs, or in distinguishing more effective from less effective approaches. She concludes that high priority should be given to developing refining measures of performance whether decisions are made at the federal, state, or local levels, or alternatively if social services are turned over to the private market.

95   Rosenberg, Barry. EVALUATION OF THE STATUS AND EFFECTIVENESS OF STATE AND LOCAL HUMAN SERVICES INFORMATION SYSTEMS. SYSTEM PROFILE: SOCIAL INDICATORS PROJECT. Silver Spring, Md.: Applied Management Sciences, 1976.

The Social Indicators Project of the Center for Social Research and Development (CSRD), a division of the Denver Research Institute of the University of Denver, is described. The project was conducted by CSRD for Department of Health, Education and Welfare and was designed to identify indicators of social problems and progress in social development at the county level to create a single data bank for gathering, storing, and analyzing data to identify relationships between socioeconomic conditions and social problems, and to produce information useful for regional and state human service planning and evaluation. Exhibits summarizing the Social Indicators Project data base and listing the publications of the Social Indicators Project are provided.

96   Rossi, Peter H., and Wright, Sonia R. "Evaluation Research: An Assessment of Theory, Practice, and Politics." EVALUATION QUARTERLY 1 (February 1977): 5-52.

Social policy evaluation involves special methodological problems since it attempts to answer questions posed by policymakers rather than academicians. Thus, precise definition of the program itself, its goals, and the criteria for its success can only be supplied by the policymakers, not by the researcher. Moreover, evaluation research takes place in an "acting setting," so that the evaluation researcher may have to forego considerable control over the problem specification, the variables to be included, and the sample to be used. And finally, findings must be reported in a form and style such that policymakers and their staffs can understand them. The authors present a survey of existing research designs and accompanying techniques and briefly assess their usefulness for different social programs.

97 Sheldon, Eleanor Bernert, and Freeman, Howard E. "Notes on Social Indicators: Promises and Potential." POLICY SCIENCES 1 (Spring 1970): 97-111.

See 327.

98 Sheldon, Eleanor Bernert, and Land, Kenneth C. "Social Reporting for the 1970's: A Review and Programmatic Statement." POLICY SCIENCES 3 (July 1972): 137-51.

The authors review the root of the demand for social indicators-- the obvious social change occurring in America in the 1960's could be assessed only with measures of change. The authors believe that social indicators could be used for more than the assessment of change, such as in the establishment of social goals and priorities, the evaluation of programs, and the development of a system of social accounts to provide guidance in situations of choice. There are three different types of indicators designed for different uses: problem-oriented or policy-oriented indicators, indicators descriptive of society and its changes, and analytic indicators to serve as components of causal models. Criteria for adding or dropping social indicators include the following: (1) Does it represent a national goal, for example, better health or more social mobility? (2) Does it describe an emerging social goal which may not be an issue for several years, for example, better mental health? (3) Does it facilitate the attainment of intended change, for example, totaling homicides does not reduce the number of murders whereas measurement of interpersonal tensions might? The authors illustrate their comments by looking at the social indicators of two content areas: public safety and youth. The authors organize social indicators into twenty social indicator content areas grouped under five major headings. A selected bibliography is included.

99 Sheldon, Eleanor Bernert; Land, Kenneth C.; and Bauer, Raymond A. "Social Reporting for the 1970's." In THE PRESIDENT'S COMMISSION ON FEDERAL STATISTICS II, pp. 403-35. Washington, D.C.: Government Printing Office, 1971.

The authors propose a long-term program for the development of social indicators with their recommendations made in general terms and illustrated by examples. The social change occurring in American society creates a demand for development of social indicators. Common objectives for these demands include the establishment of social goals and priorities, the evaluation of public programs, the development of a system of social accounts, the furtherance of knowledge about the functioning of society, and the enhancement of our capacity in social prediction. Emerging from these demands is a recognition of three types of indicators: problem-oriented or policy-oriented indicators, indicators descriptive of society and its changes, and analytic indicators to serve as components of causal models. The authors illustrate their comments by looking at four social indicator content areas: public safety, health, social mobility, and youth. They make recommendations to the federal government regarding the development of social indicators in these four areas. They recommend some organizational arrangements to federal and private agencies for a continuing effort to develop social indicators.

100   Sheldon, Eleanor Bernert, and Moore, Wilbert E., eds. INDICATORS OF SOCIAL CHANGE: CONCEPTS AND MEASUREMENTS. New York: Russell Sage Foundation, 1968. 822 p.

The theoretical rather than the practical side of social indicators development is explored in this volume containing chapters by fourteen specialists. It presents trends in American life based on an implicit or explicit theory or model of society. It does not usually design social indicators which stand for a set of correlated changes which program administrators can utilize in their program planning. Changes covered include those in the population's composition and geographic distribution, economic growth, employment, labor force, technology, politics, family, religious beliefs, consumerism, leisure, health status, schooling, social stratification related to mobility, and welfare.

101   Siedman, Eileen. "Why Not Qualitative Analysis?" PUBLIC ADMINIS-TRATION REVIEW 37 (July-August 1977): 415-17.

In an attempt to create a science of management, program analysts have over emphasized quantitative criteria. Comprehensive analysis should include the assessment of qualitative factors such as the specific impact of the program on its intended beneficiaries.

102   Smith, Tom W. "Social Change and the General Social Survey: An Annotated Bibliography." SOCIAL INDICATORS RESEARCH 2 (June 1975): 9-38.

This bibliography was compiled for the Social Change Project, directed by James A. Davis and supported by the U.S. National Science Foundation. It includes a subject index.

103   Southern California Association of Governments. GUIDE TO SOCIAL INDICATORS FOR LOCAL GOVERNMENT OR HOW TO IMPROVE YOUR POLICY DECISIONS WITH INFORMATION YOU DIDN'T KNOW YOU HAD. Los Angeles: 1975. 31 p.

This publication defines social indicators as statistics on the conditions of society that facilitate social policy choices. These statistics provide a quantitative measure of each condition. The guide illustrates the use of social indicators for estimation of community needs and the allocation of resources in programs such as: child care centers, mental health, and senior citizen nutrition. It emphasizes that social indicators are not substitutes for the political process, should not be used to accumulate data about individuals, and can facilitate, but are not sufficient to provide, program evaluation.

104   Springer, Michael. "Social Indicators, Reports and Accounts: Toward the Management of Society." ANNALS OF THE AMERICAN ACADEMY OF POLITICAL AND SOCIAL SCIENCE 388 (March 1970): 1-13.

Springer notes that the two most prominent social indicators systems (those of Mancur Olson and Bertram Gross) make different assumptions about the ideal social order. He argues for a system based on values of democracy as well as on rational management.

105   United Nations. Secretariat. "System of Social and Demographic Statistics: Draft Outlines on Social Indicators." 26 April 1974. 56 p. Mimeo.

This document examines the international activity concerning social indicators and looks at the purposes and scope of social indicators. It includes guidelines for social indicators for use by the United Nations Statistics Commission. Criteria for developing social indicators and techniques for their construction are discussed. A list of proposed indicators is also presented.

106   U.S. Department of Health, Education, and Welfare. TOWARD A SOCIAL REPORT. Washington, D.C.: Government Printing Office, 11 January 1969. 101 p.

This report resulted from a presidentially mandated directive of March 1966 in which the secretary of the Department of Health, Education, and Welfare (HEW) was asked to search for ways to improve the nation's ability to chart its social progress. These recommendations and findings were intended to supplement the social statistics and indicators already prepared by the U.S. Bureau of Labor Statistics and the Council of Economic Advisers.

The HEW report, a landmark in the field of social indicator research, deals with such aspects of the quality of American life as health and illness; social mobility; the physical environment; income and poverty; public order and safety; learning, science, and art; and participation and alienation.

107 U.S. National Goals Research Staff. TOWARD BALANCED GROWTH: QUANTITY WITH QUALITY. Washington, D.C.: Government Printing Office, 1970. 228 p.

See 563.

108 U.S. National Science Foundation. National Science Board. SCIENCE INDICATORS--1974. Washington, D.C.: Government Printing Office, 1975. 242 p.

The National Science Board is continuing its attempt to develop a series of indicators to measure the state of science in the United States. The indicators used deal with human and financial resources for scientific research and development. The value of science indicators is discussed.

This report presents indicators of science and technology in an international context of resources for research and development, of the state of basic research, of industrial research, development, and innovation, of the magnitude and character of the nation's population of scientists and engineers, and of the public's attitudes toward science and technology.

109 U.S. Office of Management and Budget. Statistical Policy Division. SOCIAL INDICATORS 1973: SELECTED STATISTICS ON SOCIAL TRENDS AND CONDITIONS IN THE UNITED STATES. Washington, D.C.: Government Printing Office, 1973. 258 p.

A book of statistics organized to describe social trends and conditions in the United States. It is the first book of its kind to be published by the federal government. Eight major social areas are examined: health, public safety, education, employment, income, housing, leisure and recreation, and population. In each category, areas of social interest, based on widely held social objectives, are identified. For each concern one or more indicators are given and explained. The indicators measure individual and family well being. The indicators are primarily time series showing national totals. This is a serious effort by the federal government, through the U.S. Office of Management and Budget, to make sound use of available data on social indicators. The data used are mainly from federal sources. The publication makes a realistic appraisal of society based on present indicators. It contains a multitude of graphs and charts.

110   von Bertalanffy, Ludwig. GENERAL SYSTEM THEORY: FOUNDATIONS, DEVELOPMENT, APPLICATIONS. New York: George Braziller, 1968. 289 p.

Von Bertalanffy presents a broad overview of the current state and future progress of "systems theory" as well as a history of its development over the last thirty years, up to 1968. All of the chapters involve at least some previously published material which the author has adapted to his purposes. He reviews "open systems" aspects of systems theory in biology, psychology, and psychiatry as well as various other sciences and disciplines. The book includes several graphs, a table, and formulas.

111   Wilcox, Leslie D., and Brooks, Ralph M. "Social Indicators: An Alternative Approach for Future Research." Paper presented at the annual meeting of the Rural Sociological Society, Denver, Colo., August 1971. Mimeo.

The paper suggests a possible empirical approach to the development of a system of social indicators. The authors present an alternative to the macromodel approach, in terms of a more inductive approach. They describe a three-step model: (1) conceptualizing social indicators that reflect the human meaning of societal change and development by examination of the life experience of people at the nonmetropolitan community level, (2) working inductively toward the macrolevel by combining these empirical indicators into more abstract indicators that provide relational models of community systems, and (3) drawing causal inferences by the use of controlled indicators designed to measure the social effects of major demographic changes as one strategic force in societal change.

112   Wilcox, Leslie D.; Brooks, Ralph M.; Beal, George M.; and Klonglan, Gerald E. SOCIAL INDICATORS AND SOCIETAL MONITORING: AN ANNOTATED BIBLIOGRAPHY. Washington, D.C.: Jossey-Bass, 1972. 464 p.

This annotated bibliography is intended both as a tool for those interested in acquiring initial knowledge about social indicators and as a reference work for those with more specialized interests in social indicator research. It is the result of an extensive literature search and correspondence with individuals working in many disciplines.

Chapter 2

TYPES OF INDICATORS AND MEASURES

113 Aiken, Michael, and Alford, Robert R. "Community Structure and Innovation: The Case of Public Housing." AMERICAN POLITICAL SCIENCE REVIEW 64 (September 1970): 843-64.

This article reviews 646 communities regarding variables affecting participation in public housing programs. The authors conclude that it is important to consider the community as the basic unit of analysis, organizations as the key actors, and their coordination as crucial to understanding the outcomes. Availability of federal urban renewal funds, ethnicity, income, voting behavior, political structure, industrial character, educational level, city age and size, unemployment, migration, housing, and nonwhite composition were the primary variables considered.

114 Albrecht, Stan L., and Green, Miles. "Attitudes Toward the Police and the Larger Attitude Complex: Implications for Police-Community Relations." CRIMINOLOGY 15 (May 1977): 67-86.

Concern over negative public attitudes toward the police has led to numerous efforts to improve the image of the police and to facilitate more positive relationships with the community. However, such programs must take into consideration the fact that public attitudes toward the police do not exist in isolation, but are part of a broader complex of attitudes toward the system of legal justice. Four different samples in a western state were taken to test this hypothesis. The results show that negative attitudes toward the police are closely related to negative attitudes toward the court system and the lack of legal justice in this country. A potentially important strategy for changing the public image of the police would be to emphasize their community service function in an effort to offset the high visibility of their coercive function.

115 Alford, Robert R. "A Critical Evaluation of the Principles of City Classification." In CITY CLASSIFICATION HANDBOOK: NEW METHODS AND EVOLVING USES, edited by Brian Berry, pp. 331-60. New York: John Wiley and Sons, 1972.

Alford uses various factors in analyzing cities and developing classifications, including socioeconomic and political characteristics of cities. Various correlations are developed based on these characteristic statistics. Alford concludes that a broader range of data is needed when developing classifications and that knowledge of variations within major types of cities may be more useful than a restatement of parameters already discovered.

116 _____. "Data Resources for Comparative Studies of Urban Administration." SOCIAL SCIENCE INFORMATION 9 (June 1970): 193-203.

See 608.

117 Alker, H.R., Jr., and Russett, B.M. "On Measuring Inequality." BEHAVIORAL SCIENCE 9 (July 1964): 207-18.

Alker and Russett examine measures of inequality, including measures of extremeness, minimal majority, the Lorenz curve, the Gini index of concentration, the equal share point, and the Schultz coefficient. These measures are applied to representation in state upper houses, and to data on land distribution. The results are compared. The authors evaluate the usefulness of the different measures of inequality.

118 American Institute of Planners. STATE LAND USE ACTIVITY. Washington, D.C.: 1976. 524 p.

This publication summarized each state's approach to meeting the land use planning requirements of the Comprehensive Planning Assistance Program. The report does not provide a quantitative or qualitative assessment of each state's land use planning activities, but rather a description of the state-of-the-art report on land use planning.

119 Anderson, James G. "Causal Models and Social Indicators: Toward the Development of Social Systems Models." AMERICAN SOCIOLOGICAL REVIEW 38 (June 1973): 285-301.

Anderson discusses the need for theoretical models of social systems specifying the nature of relationships among the various indicators in the model. The author claims efforts without sound definitions and models are meaningless. He then constructs such a model for health care based on a system serving New Mexico, explaining each step.

120 Andrews, Frank M., and Withey, Stephen B. SOCIAL INDICATORS OF WELL-BEING: AMERICA'S PERCEPTIONS OF LIFE QUALITY. New York: Plenum Press, 1976. 455 p.

This study about perceptions is based on findings from data
collected from more than five thousand Americans, including
results from four separate samplings of the American population.
It examines how perceptions of well-being are organized in
the minds of various groups of American adults and it attempts
to find valid ways of measuring these perceptions.

121 Arrow, Kenneth Joseph. SOCIAL CHOICE AND INDIVIDUAL VALUES.
New York: John Wiley and Sons, 1963. 124 p.

Arrow is concerned with the formal aspects of collective
decision making. He explores the possibility of developing a
procedure for moving from a set of known individual tastes
to a method of social choice. He discusses the rationality
and consistency of some value judgments concerning collective
decision making. Arrow defines and elaborates a social welfare
function and illustrates contradictions in the majority rule system.

122 Barabba, Vincent P. "The National Setting: Regional Shifts, Metropolitan
Decline, and Urban Decay." In POST INDUSTRIAL AMERICA: METRO-
POLITAN DECLINE AND INTER-REGIONAL JOB SHIFTS, edited by
George Sternlieb and James W. Hughes, pp. 39-76. New Brunswick, N.J.:
Rutgers-The State University, Center for Urban Policy Research, 1975.

See 351.

123 Barrows, Richard L., and Shaffer, Ron E. "Indicators of Development
in Wisconsin Counties: 1970." SOCIAL INDICATORS RESEARCH 2
(December 1975): 333-60.

This research effort focuses on the measurement of several components of society which are generally considered important by
its citizens. Each concept is measured by a multivariable
index. Using these indexes is advantageous because they
collapse several interrelated measures into a single more easily
interpreted number. The author discusses the theoretical justification for selecting the indicators he uses and treats some of
the data problems which confront him.

124 Bauer, Raymond A. "Detection and Anticipation of Impact: The Nature
of the Task." In his SOCIAL INDICATORS, pp. 1-67. Cambridge:
MIT Press, 1966.

See 5.

125 _____. "Societal Feedback." ANNALS OF THE AMERICAN ACADEMY
OF POLITICAL AND SOCIAL SCIENCE 373 (September 1967): 180-92.
Reprinted in SOCIAL INTELLIGENCE FOR AMERICA'S FUTURE, edited
by Bertram M. Gross, pp. 63-77. Boston: Allyn and Bacon, 1969.

See 6.

126 _____, ed. SOCIAL INDICATORS. Cambridge: MIT Press, 1966.
357 p.

This book is comprised of five essays which explore the possibilities and the problems of developing various statistical data
which would help to evaluate the social state of a nation.
The health of a nation's social state is described in terms of
such things as equality for all, improved living conditions,
increased efficacy of the democratic process, safety from crime,
and the development of the arts and sciences. Social indicators
are used to measure America's success in achieving these social
goals. The indicators include such statistics as income distribution, employment rates, population growth, educational
level, and crime rates.

127 Beardsley, Philip L.; Kovenock, David M.; and Reynolds, William C.
MEASURING PUBLIC OPINION ON NATIONAL PRIORITIES: A REPORT
ON A PILOT STUDY. Beverly Hills, Calif.: Sage Publications, 1974.
49 p.

An effort is made to develop and test devices to gauge public
opinion with emphasis on national priorities. A detailed report
on how the study was conducted, its purpose, and conclusions,
is presented. The authors deal entirely with the matter of
preferences of individuals regarding national goals and how
resources should be spent.

128 Bell, Roger A. NEEDS ASSESSMENT IN HEALTH AND HUMAN SER-
VICES. PROCEEDINGS OF THE LOUISVILLE NATIONAL CONFERENCE,
1976. Louisville, Ky.: University of Louisville, 1976. 372 p.

This publication is the proceedings of a national conference
on needs assessment in health and human services. The presentations covered the following: identifying and assessing needs,
social mandates and federal legislation (implications for health
and planning), the definition and identification of human service
needs in a community context, socioecological determinants
of health status, application of systems theory in assessment of
community needs, measurement of health status, process steps
for converting need assessment data into program operations,
and a case study of a need assessment. Other topics include
the following: use of social indicators in estimating health
needs, use of client utilization data to determine social planning
needs, use of the field survey to estimate health needs in the
general population, the value of epidemiological study of mental
illness for need assessment, the nominal group method in the
assessment of community needs, a convergent assessment model
for determining health status and assessing need, translating
need assessment and resource identification data into human
service goals, and integrating need assessment with evaluation.

129 Berry, Brian J.L., ed. CITY CLASSIFICATION HANDBOOK: NEW METHODS AND EVOLVING USES. New York: John Wiley and Sons, 1972. 394 p.

> This handbook is a collection of papers from different fields that explore the urban process. The twelve essays develop different methodologies and report their results and limitations. The essays illustrate how the classification of variation can be used for a more systematic political and social study. Part 1 talks about the methodology of classification. Part 2 discusses whether the classifications are related to the characteristics of American cities that are of primary importance for political and social analysis. In Part 3 a variety of classification methods are developed. Part 4 explains the weaknesses and strengths of the variety of methods of classification discussed. The overview discusses the applications and growth of city classification.

130 Bestuzhev-Lada, Igor. "Forecasting—An Approach to the Problems of the Future." INTERNATIONAL SOCIAL SCIENCE JOURNAL 21, no. 4 (1969): 526-34.

> This article makes distinctions between the terms forecasting, planning, programming, and design and control with special emphasis on forecasting and planning and the various inter-relationships and perceptions of the two.

131 Bettman, James R. "Measuring Individuals' Priorities for National Goals: A Methodology and Empirical Example." POLICY SCIENCES 2 (December 1971): 373-90.

> Bettman presents a methodology for measuring individuals' priorities for national goals on an interval scale. He utilizes multivariate, discriminant, and cluster analytic procedures to gain policy insights from the interval scale data. The methodology is applied to national priorities for eight possible national goals.

132 Biderman, Albert D. KINOSTATISTICS FOR SOCIAL INDICATORS. Washington, D.C.: Bureau of Social Research, 1971. 7 p.

> Biderman argues that the print medium is not adequate to display indicator information and urges experimentation with other display approaches. "Kinostatistics" means the substantive integration of content, techniques of analysis, and methods of display.

133 Bixhorn, Herbert, and Mindlin, Albert. "The Construction and Use of Composite Social Indicators by Local Government." TRENDS 3 (October-December 1973): 1-9.

> The Mayor's Office of Planning and Management in the District of Columbia through its statistical systems groups, has been

working to develop meaningful and useful composite indicators.
The procedure involves selecting a dimension of community life,
determining statistical series to measure aspects of this dimension,
constructing a methodology to combine these series, and analyzing
this composite measure over neighborhoods of the city.
According to the authors, the District of Columbia social
indicator project has successfully established an objective and
scientific methodology for distinguishing neighborhoods of the
city with respect to meaningful dimensions of community life.
The principal task now is to familiarize city agencies with the
methodology, and thereby move forward toward setting up a
social indicator system as a regular, ongoing tool for planning,
programming, and evaluation in operating agencies.

134   Blair, Louis H., and Schwartz, Alfred I.   HOW CLEAN IS OUR CITY?
A GUIDE FOR MEASURING THE EFFECTIVENESS OF SOLID WASTE
COLLECTION ACTIVITIES. Washington, D.C.: Urban Institute, 1972.
67 p.

The Urban Institute and the city of Washington, D.C. developed
and tested a system for measuring the effectiveness of solid
waste collection and street and alley cleaning operations.
The essence of the system is periodic inspections, citizen surveys,
and a cleanliness rating system that is constructed by using
photographs depicting varying degrees of litter. The authors
also discuss establishment of the measurement system, training
of inspectors, analyzing citizen complaints, survey techniques,
and interpretation of findings and estimated costs.

135   Blair, Louis H., and Sessler, John. DRUG PROGRAM ASSESSMENT: A
COMMUNITY GUIDE. Washington, D.C.: Drug Abuse Council, 1974.
50 p.

This publication provides communities with guidelines to evaluate
their drug abuse programs and estimate the potential effectiveness of other treatment strategies.

136   Blalock, Hubert, M., ed. CAUSAL MODELS IN THE SOCIAL SCIENCES.
Chicago: Aldine-Atherton, 1971. 512 p.

The volume is an attempt to collect the main developments
in the study of causal models and structural systems of equations
which cut across several different disciplines. The author
builds this study in methodology on works of a number of
econometricians but recognizes that their contributions may be
too technical for most sociologists and political scientists. On
the other hand, he is convinced that the sociologists and political
scientists must master some of the technical literature if they
are ever to overcome the important methodological problems
facing social scientists. The book is technical and mathematical in its discussion of methodology.

137 Bloedorn, Jack C. DESIGNING SOCIAL SERVICE SYSTEMS. Chicago:
American Public Welfare Association, 1970. 101 p.

Bloedorn reviews policy and planning aspects of the Pennsylvania
and Maine social service system models. He stresses four steps
to planning a public social service system: (1) formulation of
overall objectives, (2) development of subobjectives, (3) selection of a subset of alternative concepts and ideas which meet
the criteria, and (4) selection of functional and organizational
structures. Bloedorn discusses concepts and issues involving
the separation of aid and service functions, risk and target
populations, community development, scope and content of
services, and client programming. He relates an input and
output social service system model to an integrated public social
services system.

138 Boots, Andrew J. III; Dawson, Grace; Silverman, William; and Hatry,
Harry P. INEQUALITY IN LOCAL GOVERNMENT SERVICES: A CASE
OF NEIGHBORHOOD ROADS. Washington, D.C.: Urban Institute, 1972.
55 p.

The author prescribes a technique for measuring the level of
public services. This method was developed to answer the
question of whether Fairfax County, Virginia was providing
a fair percentage of roads in black neighborhoods.

139 Booz-Allen and Hamilton, Inc. ASSESSING SOCIAL SERVICE NEEDS
AND RESOURCES. AN IMPLEMENTATION MANUAL. Washington, D.C.:
1973. 683 p.

This manual provides tools to assess social service needs and
resources. It proposes several methods for assessing social
service needs: collection and analysis of data such as census
and public department statistics; working with data on social
service cases through a case record or client contact analysis;
and the use of surveys of the service eligible population. The
methodology for determining the effect of the resources available through public and private social service agencies is
reviewed.

140 Brail, Richard K., and Chapin, F. Stuart, Jr. "Activity Patterns of
Urban Residents." ENVIRONMENT AND BEHAVIOR 5 (June 1973):
163-90.

This paper presents both a conceptual framework for social
activity analysis and the empirical results of such a study.
Brail and Chapin found that life-style differences in activity
patterns could be explained by four variables: sex, family
responsibility, income, and employment status. They found no
differences in the amount of discretionary time available to
low-income and high-income householders, although high-income
householders were more likely to spend their discretionary

time outside the home in participatory and socially-interactive activities.

141 Buchanan, James M. THE DEMAND AND SUPPLY OF PUBLIC GOODS. Chicago: Rand McNally, 1968. 214 p.

Buchanan uses the economic model of the marketplace to explain political behavior. His theory of "public economy" describes the outcomes of the process of voluntary exchange by individuals of goods generated through political institutions. He devises many models to illustrate this theory of the demand and supply of public goods. He supplements it with another theory of fiscal institutions to explain the built-in rigidities in the institutions of fiscal choice.

Problems he raises include the free rider who will not contribute voluntarily to the cost of public provision of the goods at a level sufficient to generate optimal provision of the goods, and the decision as to which goods should be public.

142 Christenson, James A. "Quality of Community Services: A Macro-Unidimensional Approach with Experimental Data." RURAL SOCIOLOGY 41 (Winter 1976): 509-25.

This study assesses whether the degree of unidimensional differentiations of the quality and availability of community services (as perceived by the individual in a macroframework) is related to degree of population concentration. Based on experiential data from one hundred North Carolina counties, the study shows encouraging possibilities for the macrostructural approach to community services with experiential data. The findings also indicate that in the public's view, the availability of community services is more often related to population concentration than is the quality of community services.

143 Clewett, Robert L., and Olson, Kerry C. SOCIAL INDICATORS AND MARKETING. Washington, D.C.: American Marketing Association, 1974. 193 p.

There are fifteen papers included in this book which is divided into two sections. The first draws from the 1972 American Marketing Association conference and reflects its theme; it examines social indicators and their usefulness to marketing and business in general.

Part 2 draws primarily from the 1973 conferences and has a broader orientation. It focuses on how businesses are responding to changing social values and the tools that can be developed to guide them.

144 Conner, Louise, and Oborn, Parket T. EMPIRICAL DEVELOPMENT OF
COMPOSITE SOCIAL INDICATORS. Denver: Denver University, Colorado
Center for Social Research and Development, 1975. 106 p.

> Factor analysis techniques are applied to county-level data
> from 1970 for four states (Montana, North Dakota, South Dakota,
> and Colorado). The results indicate that if conceptually
> organized groups of data are analyzed, subgroups of variables
> may still be found to exist, and that if relationships among
> variables which are prominent in the subgroups are studied,
> the boundaries of the conceptual groups dissolve in a multi-
> tude of cross-group relationships.

145 Converse, Philip E. "Change in the American Electorate." In THE
HUMAN MEANING OF SOCIAL CHANGE, edited by Angus Campbell
and Philip E. Converse, pp. 263-337. New York: Russell Sage
Foundation, 1972.

> Converse focuses on long-term, "permanent" longitudinal change
> in the American public's electoral response. Reformulations
> in electoral law in the nineteenth century, including the
> Australian ballot and voter registration, resulted in changes
> in the pattern of electoral vote. In the twentieth century, the
> reenfranchisement of blacks in the South, changing patterns
> of partisanship, and the erosion of party fidelity in the late
> 1960's represent changes that could become long-term realign-
> ments rather than the short term oscillations. One sure long-
> term permanent change of the twentieth century is not itself
> political, but has political effects: the rapid increase in levels
> of formal education of the adult electorate. Education as a
> predictor of voter behavior is most useful in explorations of
> popular involvement and participation in politics.

146 Culyer, A.J.; Lavers, R.J.; and Williams, Alan. "Social Indicators--
Health." SOCIAL TRENDS 2 (1971): 31-42.

> Culyer asserts that three kinds of social indicators are needed
> to set health policy: measures of the state of health, measures
> of the need for health, and measures of the effectiveness of
> health-affecting activities.

147 Davies, Ross. "Using the Census for Planning." PLANNER 62 (January
1976): 15-19.

> See 284.

148 Dear, M.; Fincher, Ruth; and Currie, Lise. "Measuring the External
Effects of Public Programs." ENVIRONMENT AND PLANNING 9
(February 1977): 137-47.

> Decision makers are increasingly concerned about undesirable
> externalities associated with public programs. Specifically,

intangible externalities (such as invasion of privacy or fear for
personal safety), which can have a great impact on environmental quality, should, according to the authors, be analyzed and
incorporated into planning strategies. Two approaches are
suggested for use in systematic analyses of external effects.
The first technique, multidimensional scaling (MSD), considers
individuals' judgments or perceptions of objects and can be
used to determine how people judge public programs. The
second technique, the differential semantic method, measures
connotative aspects of meaning and can be used to determine
that judgment in a given population. The authors recommend
using MDS and the semantic differential in sequence--the
former to establish dimensions, the latter to measure them.

149 de Neufville, Judith Innes. SOCIAL INDICATORS AND PUBLIC POLICY:
INTERACTIVE PROCESSES OF DESIGN AND APPLICATION. New York:
Elsevier Scientific Publishing Co., 1975. 311 p.

The author discusses how to design indicators that can be useful
to policy and how to design processes to make better use of
such information. Case material is used to identify problems
relating to using indicators for public decision. This work deals
with the role of quantitative measures in problem definition,
the setting and context for projected systems of indicator use
in U.S. statistical policy, the criteria for choosing among data
collection processes, and the danger of letting data be used
for short-term political considerations.

150 Dewees, D. N. "The Effect of a Subway on Residential Property Values
in Toronto." JOURNAL OF URBAN ECONOMICS 3 (October 1976):
357-69.

This study attempts to isolate the relationship between land values
and transportation facilities in Toronto, Canada. To do this
the author examined sale prices of residential properties and
their characteristics in conjunction with access to subway
stations. Quantitative methods and the results of the empirical
study are explained.

151 Dogan, Mattei, and Rokkan, Stein, eds. QUANTITATIVE ECOLOGICAL
ANALYSIS IN THE SOCIAL SCIENCES. Cambridge: MIT Press, 1969.
607 p.

This volume grew out of a core of European-American scientists
responding to the needs of comparative politics for such a work.
It illuminates the debate between the American political scientists who favor use of sample surveys to discover trends and
Europeans who favor geographic-historical in-depth analysis
of official statistical sources. It also suggests an optimal mix
of the two approaches be employed in research in the future,
concentrating on various analyses options such as regression,

covariance, linear analysis, factor analysis, and time series analysis. It also reveals how computers have greatly expanded the European approach of trend analysis by simplifying ecological data archiving.

152 Duncan, Otis Dudley. "Methodological Issues in the Analysis of Social Mobility." In SOCIAL STRUCTURE AND MOBILITY IN ECONOMIC DEVELOPMENT, edited by N.J. Smelser and S.M. Lipset, pp. 51-97. Chicago: Aldine, 1966.

Duncan covers some of the technological and methodological issues raised in the literature on intergenerational occupational mobility. His discussion centers on the relationship of social mobility to economic development and problems which result from the unavoidable series of contingent postulates which must be strung together before a relationship can be deduced.

Those problems he foresees include the following: (1) the complexity which makes dangerous the translating of occupational change into occupational mobility, (2) the inadequate measurement techniques, classification procedures, and analytic models in intergenerational mobility studies which hinder its effectiveness, (3) the noncomparability of study procedures in studies on interspatial comparisons of mobility patterns or rates which hampers these studies, (4) the intrinsic structural differences which render any equating of occupational categories dubious, and (5) the effort to infer a "mobility effect" as one of the consequences of mobility for individual behavior which has unnecessarily complicated the subject.

153 Easton, David. A SYSTEMS ANALYSIS OF POLITICAL LIFE. New York: John Wiley and Sons, 1965. 507 p.

Easton, first to adapt political science to the functional approach of general systems theory, refined and expanded his theory here. The focus is on the process, not the structural arrangement, of a political situation. The political process depicted involves input from the environment to the political system, conversion within the system, and a consequent output from the system back to the environment. He chose demands and supports as the key input indicators for the system. These impose stress on the system. The system responds to the stress by outputs to abort, coerce, or satisfy the individual or group demands causing stress. Once satisfied, the individual groups put in sufficient support to the system to maintain the system. His basic level of analysis is political interactions through which values and valued things are authoritatively allocated by government for a society.

154 Ennis, Phillip. "The Definition and Measurement of Leisure." In INDICATORS OF SOCIAL CHANGE: CONCEPTS AND MEASUREMENTS, edited

by Eleanor B. Sheldon and Wilbert E. Moore, pp. 525-27. New York: Russell Sage Foundation, 1968.

Ennis discusses the definition and measurement of leisure with attention to its distribution and quality.

155 Entry deleted.

156 Etzioni, Amitai. "Indicators of the Capacities for Societal Guidance." ANNALS OF THE AMERICAN ACADEMY OF POLITICAL AND SOCIAL SCIENCE 388 (March 1970): 25-34.

Etzioni discusses development indicators for macrosociological concepts. Measurements of the areas of societal knowledge and societal mobilization are illustrated. The relative value of various indicators is explored.

157 Fava, Sylvia, comp. URBANISM IN WORLD PERSPECTIVE, A READER. New York: Thomas Y. Crowell Co., 1968. 620 p.

Both informational and analytic aspects of urbanism are covered in this urban sociology reader. The articles approach urbanism from many directions--ecologically, historically, demographically, organizationally, and analytically through functions or problems in an effort to determine what is urban. Familiar scholars appear: Louis Wirth, Herbert Gans, Philip Hauser, Homer Hoyt, Edgar Hoover, Raymond Vernon, Charles Abrams, and Bernard Weissbourd. A wealth of urban indicators are introduced, not all hinging on sociology. These include city population density, spatial patterns, heterogeneity, personality characteristics, social interaction characteristics, level of industrialism, class structure, and ethnicity.

158 Ferriss, Abbott L. "National Approaches to Developing Social Indicators." SOCIAL INDICATORS RESEARCH 2 (June 1975): 81-92.

Ferriss discusses the process of selecting social indicators in the United States and compares this to the experience in other selected countries. He then analyzes the selection of time series (as a criteria) in studying social processes and organizations within the United States. A bibliography is included indentifying national U.S. reports available.

159 Fisher, Joseph L. "The Natural Environment." In ANNALS OF THE AMERICAN ACADEMY OF POLITICAL AND SOCIAL SCIENCE 371 (May 1967): 127-40. Reprinted in SOCIAL INTELLIGENCE FOR AMERICAN'S FUTURE, edited by Bertram M. Gross, pp. 455-71. Boston: Allyn and Bacon, 1969.

While the quantitative side of pollution control is under careful scrutiny, the qualitative side is much less clearly defined. Qualitative goals and indicators are more difficult to work with because the more subjective problems of individual and social welfare must be taken into account. Using interquality studies of the Delaware Estuary, this article outlines different methods of measuring this social welfare function of pollution control.

160 Fisk, Donald M., and Lancer, Cynthia A. EQUALITY OF DISTRIBUTION OF RECREATION SERVICES: A CASE STUDY OF WASHINGTON, D.C. Washington, D.C.: Urban Institute, 1974. 46 p.

See 584.

161 Friedmann, John. "Two Concepts for Urbanization: A Comment." URBAN AFFAIRS QUARTERLY 1 (June 1966): 78-84.

The author distinguishes between urbanization and urban processes, the former being a spatial manifestation of the latter. Urbanization refers to processes that (1) incorporate growing populations into urban settlement patterns with the city becoming the basic ecological matrix for social life and production, and (2) incorporate growing populations into urban structures and styles of life, leading to modification and transformation of these structures. This distinction is essential because there are cities that are not wholly urban in the sociocultural sense and there are urban populations that do not live in cities.

The traditional U.S. city is dissolving into an urban field where geographic mobility and community are substituted for place. Ring theories and sector theories of ecological patterns need to be replaced by more dynamic models to describe this transformation. The author terms this transformation the post industrial urbanism and he predicts its spread over the entire globe. Its characteristics include the technologies of computers, lasers, communications satellites, a multinational social integration, and the civil servant as the social prototype.

162 Galtung, Johan. THEORY AND METHODS OF SOCIAL RESEARCH. New York: Columbia University Press, 1967. 534 p.

This book contains two main sections: data collections and data processing and the many approaches and applications in current use. Galtung attempts to place all collections in a common framework. He believes that exhibiting all together will be helpful to the theory and development of social research. This work is extremely comprehensive and complex with multiple charts, graphs, and formulas.

163 Gans, Herbert J. "The Positive Functions of Poverty." AMERICAN JOURNAL OF SOCIOLOGY 78 (September 1972): 275-89.

Although the conventional view looks at poverty as dysfunctional, Gans uses a Mertonian functional analysis to enumerate fifteen economic, social, and political functions of poverty that benefit the nonpoor. Alternatives are offered, but each is rejected since the higher costs of replacement would be dysfunctional for the nonpoor.

164   Gastil, Raymond D. "Social Indicators and Quality of Life." PUBLIC ADMINISTRATION REVIEW 30 (November–December 1970): 596–601.

See 294.

165   Giles, Peter B. "Systems Analysis and Urban Information." In DEVELOPING THE MUNICIPAL ORGANIZATION, edited by Stanley Powers, F. Gerald Brown, and David S. Arnold, pp. 193–210. Washington, D.C.: International City Management Association, 1974.

The author examines how data are collected and processed and describes systems project management and operating techniques. It assists urban administrators in understanding the essentials of information systems analysis, design, implementation, and project evaluation. The six topics discussed are as follows: the systems approach; systems project organization; project planning, scheduling and control; description and analysis; and design and evaluation. Diagrams and charts are presented throughout the article illustrating the different techniques discussed. Once the system has been installed actual costs should be measured against estimated costs and actual benefits against anticipated benefits. Users of the system should be involved in a qualitative identification of problems and reactions.

166   Goldman, Nathan. "Social Breakdown." ANNALS OF THE AMERICAN ACADEMY OF POLITICAL AND SOCIAL SCIENCE 373 (September 1967): 156–79. Reprinted in SOCIAL INTELLIGENCE FOR AMERICA'S FUTURE, edited by Bertram M. Gross, pp. 375–404. Boston: Allyn and Bacon, 1969.

The author reviews briefly those areas such as crime, divorce, alcoholism, and prostitution that are customarily referred to as indicators of social disorganization and social breakdown. He then examines their sources for reliability and validity. Goldman determines that much additional information is needed and readily available; that without it the varying definitions and differential reporting make it impossible to gauge status of society. He finally asserts that current indicators of disorganization may actually be indicators of reaction to strains within society. Goldman then explains many ills as "role" problems, that is, those unable or unwilling to fulfill the role society expects. He also notes the ambivalence of society regarding the enforcement of standards or roles and so forth and the effect of alienation and strain this has. The author sees the problem as twofold (1) identification and location of social problems (which is currently being done) and (2) identification and analysis of those processes within society which impede solution of social problems.

167　Goodman, Leo A. "A General Model for the Analysis of Surveys."
AMERICAN JOURNAL OF SOCIOLOGY 77 (May 1972): 1035-86.

> From their actual survey of 608 persons, researchers Wilner,
> Walkley, and Cook diagramed a causal system for the variables
> observed in their "contact study" of racial attitudes. This
> article takes their data and develops a more quantitatively
> explicit model than their causal diagram. The quantitative
> model can be used to study the relationships among many
> variables. The model estimates relationships among variables
> in a more direct and unified way and allows the survey data
> to be tested as to whether is supports or negates the causal
> diagram. The quantitative model involves usage of contingency
> tables, chi-square values, multiple correlation coefficients, and
> partial correlation coefficients. The author also develops
> a measure of association termed the partial expected odds ratio.

168　＿＿＿＿. "The Multivariate Analysis of Qualitative Data: Interactions
among Multiple Classifications." JOURNAL OF THE AMERICAN
STATISTICAL ASSOCIATION 65 (March 1970): 226-56.

> The author explains how different methods for the multivariate
> analysis of M qualitative variables complement each other,
> and together lead to a more complete analysis of the data
> through M-way contingency tables than previously assumed in
> earlier literature. The author introduces new methods for
> estimating variable relationships and for testing hypotheses
> based on these relationships. He extends and simplifies the
> classic chi-square approach in order to minimize its faults.
> Concepts covered include independence, equiprobability, con-
> ditional independence, and conditional equiprobability through
> use of techniques such as confidence intervals, fitted marginals,
> and maximum-likelihood estimates.

169　Greene, Kenneth V.; Neenan, William B.; and Scott, Claudia D.
FISCAL INTERACTIONS IN A METROPOLITAN AREA. Lexington, Mass.:
Lexington Books, 1974. 263 p.

> The authors provide a methodology for analyzing the net effects
> of costs and benefits of urban services provided to neighboring
> jurisdictions and citizens. This methodology is directly related
> to disputes over central city subsidizing of suburbanites as well
> as to the equity of commuter taxes.

170　Gross, Bertram M. "The Coming General Systems Models of Social
Systems." HUMAN RELATIONS 20 (November 1967): 357-74.

> See 640.

171　Gruber, Alan R. "The High Cost of Delivering Services." SOCIAL
WORK 18 (July 1973): 33-40.

One way to improve the delivery of social services is to encourage agency administrators and board members to recognize the importance of knowing how time is being spent by staff members and what the costs are of delivering services. The unit of service rendered by an organization can be equated with a product and service and cost accounting techniques can be implemented and applied to the system. Service agencies have to become cognizant of accountability to the public and service and cost accounting techniques are shown to facilitate this accountability. A detailed system of services and cost accounting is presented for the purchasing of services.

172 Gurr, T. "A Causal Model of Civil Strife: A Comparative Analysis Using New Indices." AMERICAN POLITICAL SCIENCE REVIEW 62 (December 1968): 1104-24.

This article describes a successful attempt to assess and refine a causal model of the general conditions of several forms of civil strife. The technique employed uses cross sectional analysis of data collected for 114 polities. The author stipulates a set of variables to determine the likelihood and magnitude of civil strife.

173 Harland, Douglas G. SOCIAL INDICATORS: A FRAMEWORK FOR MEASURING REGIONAL SOCIAL DISPARITIES. Ottawa: Department of Regional Economic Expansion, 1971. 132 p.

The Canadian Department of Regional Economic Expansion was established to overcome regional social economic disparities in Canada. This report presents a typology for planning and evaluation social adjustment strategies in collaboration with other Canadian government departments. Quality of life is analyzed in terms of level, standard, and norm of living. Social indicators are discussed in terms of goal specification, measurement of goal attainment and the construction of social indicator indexes within a social development framework.

174 Hatry, Harry P. "Issues in Productivity Measurement for Local Government." PUBLIC ADMINISTRATION REVIEW 32 (November-December 1972): 776-84.

See 645.

175 _____ . "Measuring the Quality of Public Services." In IMPROVING URBAN MANAGEMENT, edited by Willis D. Hawley and David Rodgers, pp. 3-27. Beverly Hills, Calif.: Sage Publications, 1974.

See 51.

176 Hatry, Harry P.; Blair, Louis H.; Fisk, Donald M.; and Kimmel, Wayne A. PROGRAM ANALYSIS FOR STATE AND LOCAL GOVERNMENTS. Washington, D.C.: Urban Institute, 1976. 155 p.

48

Program analysis is concerned with predicting the potential of proposals not yet implemented. The method involves problem definition identification of alternatives, specifying objectives, determining evaluation criteria, and making cost estimates.

177 Hatry, Harry P., and Dunn, Diana R. MEASURING THE EFFECTIVENESS OF LOCAL GOVERNMENT SERVICES: RECREATION. Washington, D.C.: Urban Institute, 1971. 47 p.

This guide is designed for local public officials to supplement to routine data they collect about local recreational facilities and activities. Some of the measures used are: accessibility, crowding, participation rates, safety, and perceptions of citizen satisfaction with recreational services. The authors provide estimated costs and techniques for collecting the necessary data.

178 Hatry, Harry P.; Winnie, Richard E.; and Fisk, Donald M. PRACTICAL PROGRAM EVALUATION FOR STATE AND LOCAL GOVERNMENTS. Washington, D.C.: Urban Institute, 1973. 134 p.

See 52.

179 Hatry, Harry P., et al. HOW EFFECTIVE ARE YOUR COMMUNITY SERVICES: PROCEDURES FOR MONITORING THE EFFECTIVENESS OF MUNICIPAL SERVICES. Washington, D.C.: Urban Institute, 1977. 318 p.

The authors propose measures and detailed procedures for data collection on the effectiveness of many basic local government services. Objectives for which measures are designed include (1) solid waste collection and disposal, (2) recreation, (3) library services, (4) crime control, (5) fire protection, (6) local transportation services, including public transit, traffic control, and street maintenance, (7) water supply services, and (8) the handling of citizen complaints and requests. The book includes sample questionnaires to secure citizen perception of the delivery of many of these services and reports on the detailed application of these procedures in Nashville and St. Petersburg.

180 Hatry, Harry P., et al. MEASURING THE EFFECTIVENESS OF BASIC MUNICIPAL SERVICES: INITIAL REPORT. Washington, D.C.: Urban Institute, 1974. 118 p.

See 587.

181 Hirsch, Gary B., and Riccio, Lucius J. "Measuring and Improving the Productivity of Police Patrol." JOURNAL OF POLICE SCIENCE AND ADMINISTRATION 2 (June 1974): 169-84.

Past studies of police productivity have focused on broad measures such as crime rate per capita or the number of police officers per capita. This study develops a framework of goals, objectives, and activities within which the performance of a police department's patrol function can be assessed. A process is presented for measuring the productivity of patrol activities, diagnosing the causes of poor productivity and taking the most effective action to improve patrol productivity. Suggestions based on programs being used by several agencies are offered for productivity improvement in each area in which poor performance is discovered.

182 Hobson, Richard, and Mann, Stuart H. "A Social Indicator Based on Time Allocation." SOCIAL INDICATORS RESEARCH 1 (March 1975): 439-57.

This article discusses an operations research approach to the development of a unitary social indicator called Lambda (2). Lambda is based on an objective measurement of the variance of time spent on activities within specified populations. The problems of inclusive variable listing and factor weighting are solved by use of a time-lease measure. A report of a pilot study using Lambda is included in the article.

183 Isserman, Andrew M. "The Location Quotient Approach to Estimating Regional Economic Impacts." JOURNAL OF THE AMERICAN INSTITUTE OF PLANNERS 43 (January 1977): 33-40.

The use of the location quotient for estimating regional economic impact multipliers has received a great deal of criticism recently. The article attempts to respond to this criticism by delineating four major theoretical assumptions behind the location quotient. Moreover, the author mentions certain modifications which could improve the location quotient approach. Further, he argues that although this approach requires more data than other approaches, it generates considerably more information regarding the types and levels of exogenous activity in the economy of the region studies. Also, the calculations involved in estimating the location quotient multiplier can be done easily. Because of increasing demand for quick impact analysis and moderate expenditure, the location-quotient approach can be a useful planning tool.

184 Jantsch, Erich. "Planning and Designing for the Future." FUTURES 1 (September 1969): 440-44.

Erich reviews three books, Rene Dubos's SO HUMAN AN ANIMAL (New York: Scribner's, 1968), Jay Forrester's URBAN DYNAMICS and Aurelio Peccei's THE CHASM AHEAD (New York: Macmillan, 1969). The author points to three themes in all of them: (1) future of man and society has to be dealt with within the context of systems which link them to the environment; (2) these systems form complex dynamic systems, high-order, multiple-loop, nonlinear, feedback structures emphasizing feedback; and (3) actively shaping and planning for the future implies hanging the structure of the systems, not just the variables. Forrester's model is based on 153 equations useful in exploring how various policy changes would affect urban conditions.

185   Johnston, Denis F. "Forecasting Methods in the Social Sciences." TECH-NOLOGICAL FORECASTING AND SOCIAL CHANGE 2 (July 1970): 173-87.

There are extremes of forecasting methods. The reasoned out-look statement is a thinly disguised argument in support of some particular panacea. At the other extreme might be highly technical demographic projections of population. The author distinguishes between predictions, projections, and forecasts, and describes methods of forecasting. He sees a need for social indicators (1) to give advance warnings of potential crises, and (2) to provide descriptions of the probable conse-quences of programs or policies. There may be a convergence in "qualitative and quantitative" approaches to social projection. Social indicators should be developed with the aim of pro-viding a more adequate monitoring of the changes in society. Complexity must be taken into account. A very intricate analysis of indicators follows.

186   Jones, Bryan D. "Distributional Considerations in Models of Government Service Provision." URBAN AFFAIRS QUARTERLY 12 (March 1977): 291-312.

Jones examines three models of the government service process: policy output analysis, policy impact analysis, and service dis-tribution. The first two models are based on systems analysis, which conceives of service output as a variable responding to input factors. In contrast, the service distribution model con-siders empirical factors such as decisions and attitudes of service providers, organizational constraints and arrangements, and leg-islative mandates. In making routine service decisions, local service delivery agencies adopt task performance rules. These rules, generally related to goal accomplishment and to the adjustment of interests within the organization, have an impact on distribution. Groups of citizens who are not members of the service agency are differentially affected by the rules, and citizens have a hard time getting service deliverers to deviate from their rules.

187   Kirby, Ronald F.; de Leeuw, Frank; and Silverman, William; assisted by Dawson, Grace. RESIDENTIAL ZONING AND EQUAL HOUSING OPPORTUNITIES: A CASE STUDY IN BLACK JACK, MISSOURI, Washington, D.C.: Urban Institute, 1972. 34 p.

See 459.

188   Koelle, H.H. "An Experimental Study on the Determination of a Definition for the 'Quality of Life.'" REGIONAL STUDIES 8 (Fall 1974): 1–10.

> This is a concise presentation of the format and data for a goal-structures determination of the quality of life. The survey is to go through eight rounds of a process of goal finding, goal analysis, and goal setting.

189   Kopkind, Andrew. "The Future-Planners." AMERICAN PSYCHOLOGIST 22 (November 1967): 1036–41.

> See 656.

190   Kraemer, Kenneth L. "The Evolution of an Information System for Urban Administration." PUBLIC ADMINISTRATION REVIEW 29 (July–August 1969): 389–402.

> Urban information systems have begun to receive increased attention by urban administrators seeking new ways to cope with complex issues. Four approaches are discussed: the housekeeping approach, the data-bank approach, the model-building approach, and the process control approach. Examples of how each approach is used are presented. The evolutionary steps are examined: the processing, analysis, and control capabilities of computers viewed as technical subsystems, creating urban information systems as part of integrated systems, and integration of technical subsystems and administrative processes. The four approaches are viewed as stages in the development of urban information systems and are discussed in terms of linkages and redefinition of the system. Improvements are needed in integrating information technology and decision processes, realigning organization structure, developing personnel, expanding our knowledge about information systems and changing the social climate in which they are built.

191   Krendel, Ezra S. "Social Indicators and Urban Systems Dynamics." SOCIO-ECONOMIC PLANNING SCIENCES 5 (August 1971): 387–93.

> The author presents the view that citizen's complaints may form the basis for determining the quality of life, but limits his effort here to indicate that such complaints may (and probably should) be used to establish indicators of how well the system functions or adapts to necessary change. Krendel claims that while citizen complaints are not a perfect indicator, they are useful.

192   Land, Kenneth C. "Theories, Models and Indicators of Social Change." INTERNATIONAL SOCIAL SCIENCE JOURNAL 27, no. 1 (1975): 7–37.

> Land discusses the difference between theory and measurement with regard to social change, and argues that most authors

have been concerned with the theory but not with measuring change. He mentions Obgum's efforts early in the century to measure change and project it for the future. He describes this as background or lead-in to his article on the development of the "social indicator movement." Land further reviews the present state of the conceptual and theoretical aspects to the indicator movement and illustrates the relationship between social indicators and social policy. There are some graphs, charts, and a few formulas but this is largely a nontechnical work.

193 Laszlo, C.A.; Levine, M.D.; and Milsum, J.H. "A General Systems Framework for Social Systems." BEHAVIORAL SCIENCE 19 (March 1974): 79-92.

See 309.

194 Levy, Shlomit, and Guttman, Louis. "On the Multivariate Structure of Wellbeing." SOCIAL INDICATORS RESEARCH 2 (December 1975): 361-88.

This paper sets forth a formal definition for the whole body of well-being items, and treats the empirical multivariate research which is guided by the definition. It presents a partial theory for the structure of intercorrelations among the varieties of well-being. The focus is on one aspect of empirical observation--the correlation matrix for well-being items for a population at a single point of time. Tables, charts, illustrations, and references are included.

195 Lovrich, Nicholas P., Jr., and Taylor, G. Thomas, Jr. "Neighborhood Evaluation of Local Government Services: A Citizen Survey Approach." URBAN AFFAIRS QUARTERLY 12 (December 1976): 197-222.

The authors attempt to synthesize the contributions of the "technocrats" and the "community control" advocates in local government service delivery. They focus on the opinions of identifiable Anglo, black, and Mexican-American neighborhoods in Denver using a sample survey of eight hundred local voters. The study shows that the negative attitudes toward local government were more pronounced among black and Mexican-American voters than among Anglos, and the perceptions of each ethnic group were strongly related to the condition of their neighborhoods. In particular, community attitudes toward the police were shown to be sensitive to the influences of ethnicity and the condition of the neighborhood. This sort of focused citizen survey is recommended as a feasible and politically acceptable method for collecting and utilizing neighborhood policy inputs.

196   Massey, D.; Minns, R.; Morrison, W.I.; and Whitbrend, M. "A Strategy for Urban and Regional Research." REGIONAL STUDIES 10, no. 4 (1976): 381-87.

197   Matras, J. "Development of Indicators and Development Models." JOURNAL OF DEVELOPMENTAL STUDIES 8 (April 1972): 91-102.

198   _____. "Social Mobility and Social Structure: Some Insights from the Linear Model." AMERICAN SOCIOLOGICAL REVIEW 32 (August 1967): 608-14.

> Matras reviews a mathematical model representing the relationship between social structure and social mobility. The form of the model is a matrix equation. Relationships between social mobility and social structure that are suggested by the model are noted and some of the problems concerning the relationship are listed. Matras makes some suggestions for additional analysis based on the matrix equation. A linear model of social mobility, changing social structure and population growth is also discussed. A knowledge of matrices and linear equations is needed to understand this article.

199   Moles, Abraham. "The Future Oriented Society: Axioms and Methodology." FUTURES 2 (December 1970): 312-26.

> Moles approaches future goals, developing a table showing the characteristics of time-ordered systems, with four time ranges. He relates the time periods to categories of people. He distinguishes various aspects of planning and forecasting.

200   Moriyama, Iwao M. "Problems in the Measurement of Health Status." In INDICATORS OF SOCIAL CHANGE: CONCEPTS AND MEASUREMENTS, edited by Eleanor B. Sheldon and Wilbert E. Moore, pp. 573-99. New York: Russell Sage Foundation, 1968.

> Moriyama examines the course of the infant mortality rate, as a statistical measure and sensitive index of the level of living and of sanitary conditions together with other indexes. Although there are measurement problems such as life expectancy at birth, the crude death rate, and the proportionate mortality rate for ages fifty and over, there are recommended indicators of level of living for international comparisons.
>
> The author asserts the inadequacy of health and morbidity statistics by surveys and recommends certain desirable properties for an index of health. He urges studies of conceptual problems especially those relating to the definition of health, since mortality rates have not been a particularly good index of health. A good review of data and indicators of health and disease.

201 Moynihan, Daniel P. "Urban Conditions: General." ANNALS OF THE AMERICAN ACADEMY OF POLITICAL AND SOCIAL SCIENCE 371 (May 1967): 159-77.

See 85.

202 Muller, Thomas, and Dawson, Grace. THE ECONOMIC EFFECTS OF ANNEXATION: A SECOND CASE STUDY IN RICHMOND, VIRGINIA. Washington, D.C.: Urban Institute, 1976. 91 p.

Blacks in Richmond contested a 1970 annexation on the basis that it was intended to dilute black political power. The courts agreed that the annexation was racially motivated but refused to order deannexation. The annexation was allowed to stand because the courts accepted Richmond's argument that it offered economic benefits to the city. The authors provide a methodology for cities to measure the costs and benefits of annexation.

203 Murphy, Raymond E. THE CENTRAL BUSINESS DISTRICT. Chicago: Aldine-Atherton, 1972. 193 p.

This work is a summary of the research on the central business district (CBD). The author reviews the theories of CBD size and structure, especially central-place theory, and the problem of defining its boundaries. He then turns to several studies of the CBD, including the U.S. Bureau of the Census's use of the term. The last part of the book is devoted to an evaluation of the function of the CBD, for manufacturing and transportation, as a competitor with the suburbs, and as it has changed and will continue to change through time.

204 Mushkin, Selma J., ed. PUBLIC PRICES FOR PUBLIC PRODUCTS. Washington, D.C.: Urban Institute, 1972. 400 p.

Fees to finance public services are reviewed in terms of revenue, potential equity between users and nonusers, economic efficiency, conservation of scarce resources, conservation of social property such as air and water, and involvement of the private sector in delivering public services. Public services include waste collection and disposal, air pollution control, public transportation, water supply, fire protection, recreation, hospitals, education, welfare, and subsidized housing.

205 National Planning Association. IMPROVEMENTS IN THE QUALITY OF LIFE: ESTIMATES OF POSSIBILITIES IN THE UNITED STATES, 1974-83. Washington, D.C.: 1975. 285 p.

This study both develops an analytical framework for measuring the quality of life and attempts some empirical estimates within the framework. The stress is on results rather than resource input, and this brings the analysis closer to the objectives

of families and individuals. The volume represents the findings
of two research projects undertaken by the author at the
National Planning Association over a seven-year period beginning in the late 1960's. Part 1 consists of the multioutput
productive relationships formulated in the activity matrices,
while part 2 provides a detailed discussion of particular fields
of social concern.

206 Neiman, Max. "Policy Analysis: An Alternative Strategy." AMERICAN
POLITICS QUARTERLY 5 (January 1977): 3-26.

This analysis of Deutsch's analogue model of political communication uses data from fifty-one American cities to select tentative indicators of several concepts in the theory, testing for
the model's bivariate relationships, and assessing the model's
multivariate linkages that account for observed correlations
among concept indicators. Neiman views urban political systems as communication networks linked to their environments
by communication flows. When inputs create tension, the
system must either adjust outputs in pursuit of long-standing
goals or change goals. Public policy outputs are the results
of political systems responding to information about the wants
and demands of newly mobilized groups. Response innovation
may include allocation of goods and services, symbols, and
regulation of behavior.

207 Newman, Sandra. "Objective and Subjective Determinants of Prospective
Residential Mobility." SOCIAL INDICATORS RESEARCH 2 (June 1975):
53-64.

This is the report of survey research into the relative importance
of objective and subjective indicators as explanatory variables
for the decision to move. Not only does Newman find that
subjective indicators are more powerful, she also finds that
they explain a considerable portion of the variance over and
above that explained by objective indicators. This superiority
holds only for short-term residents. For long-term residents,
the indicators are virtually identical.

208 Obudho, Robert A. "Social Indicators for Housing and Urban Development
in Africa: Towards a New Development Model." SOCIAL INDICATORS
RESEARCH 3 (December 1976): 431-49.

Social indicators should be based on their utility in policy
development. One set of important indicators concerns the
housing industry. Housing indicators must be interpreted with
regard to the type of climate and culture, the degree of urbanization, and the demographic, social, and economic structure
of the country in question. Although social indicators are still
far from being perfect tools, they can contribute more measuring the extent of development in Africa than the gross
national product.

209 Olson, Mancur, Jr. "An Analytic Framework for Social Reporting and Policy Analysis." ANNALS OF THE AMERICAN ACADEMY FOR POLITICAL AND SOCIAL SCIENCE 388 (March 1970): 112-26.

> Olson discusses the types of tools of thought that would be most helpful to organize the collection and classification of the statistical information that is geared to the strategic options facing society, in relation to the need for a presidential staff to deal with planning, research, and evaluation and to issue an annual social report. Two different general tools for organizing analyses in social science are considered: (1) the problem-solving approach, and (2) the structural-functional approach. The first approach is for use on problems that are narrower than the strategic ones, but this style has a sound logical structure and is able to illuminate practical policy choices. Structural-functional analysis can deal with strategic, society-wide questions but suffers from logical confusion and a lack of relevance to most practical policy choices. Olson outlines an approach which attempts to combine the best of both approaches and is called complex systems analysis.

210 _____ . THE LOGIC OF COLLECTIVE ACTION: PUBLIC GOODS AND THE THEORY OF GROUPS. Cambridge, Mass.: Harvard University Press, 1965. 176 p.

> The author employs economic analyses to examine when a common interest shared by individuals justifies the cost of organization. Sometimes the individual interest is served by an organizational effort but the mere existence of a common interest among a large group does not automatically justify collective action. There must be either compulsion or incentives to join together. The author demonstrates his theory by examining trade unionism, the concept of economic freedom, Marx's clan theory, orthodox theories of pressure groups, special interest groups, and unorganized groups.

211 Orcutt, Guy H.; Caldwell, Steven B.; and Wertheimer, Richard F. II. POLICY EXPLORATION THROUGH MICRO-ANALYTIC SIMULATION. Washington, D.C.: Urban Institute, 1976. 370 p.

> A reliable model of the economy is useful in establishing government policies on unemployment, social services, income distribution, education, and health. This volume describes the Urban Institute's Dynamic Simulation of Income Model (DYNASIM). The model is based on knowledge about how social and political processes actually function and respond to human actions. The focus of the model is on individual and family decisions, rather than with averages of the gross national product or of personal income.

212 Ostrom, Elinor. "Institutional Arrangements and the Measurement of Policy Consequences in Urban Areas." URBAN AFFAIRS QUARTERLY 6 (June 1971): 447-75.

> Ostrom proposes a model that provides negative feedback mechanisms which can help correct errors in the policy process resulting from poor data. The FBI Index of Crime is eliminated and new interpretations of the meaning of crime statistics, new indicators for the evaluation of police services, and new institutional arrangements for the provision of police services are called for.

213 _____. "On the Meaning and Measurement of Output and Efficiency in the Provision of Urban Police Services." JOURNAL OF CRIMINAL JUSTICE 1 (Summer 1973): 93-111.

> Proposals for changing the organization of police departments in metropolitan areas are usually presented with little supporting evidence for the change. It is assumed by many that large-scale police departments are more effective and more efficient. The author defines the concepts of output and efficiency for police agencies. Ostrom develops some potential measures of output and efficiency of differently organized police departments serving metropolitan areas. Four types of police activities are discussed as are the problems of measurement for each type.

214 Perkins, Dennis N.T. "Evaluating Social Interventions: A Conceptual Scheme." EVALUATION QUARTERLY 1 (November 1977): 639-56.

> This paper attempts to provide a set of conceptual reference points which may be used to distinguish among the various types of projects which are commonly called 'evaluation research.' It proposes a broad classification system and identifies a number of methodological alternatives. Tables, graphic illustrations, and a list of references are included.

215 Peterson, George E., ed. PROPERTY TAX REFORM. Washington, D.C.: Urban Institute, 1973. 188 p.

> Peterson provides measures for analyzing this effect of various property tax systems on homeowners in different categories. He also provides data on tax costs for nonresidential usages.

216 Quinn, James Brian. "Technological Forecasting." HARVARD BUSINESS REVIEW 45 (March-April 1967): 89-106.

> The author urges that organizations develop means for forecasting probable technological change and the impact of each change. Management needs to take such information into account when making decisions. Just as managers rely on

economic indicators and financial analyses, so too ought managers to consider technological forecasts to anticipate the opportunities and problems the organization will encounter in the future.

Technological forecasting may be based upon various kinds of study techniques. For example, using "demand assessment," future societal and individual needs are anticipated. Using "parameter analysis," the future capabilities and uses of technical systems are projected by taking into account current trends and substitution curves. Using "systems analysis," present weaknesses and probable future problems in the system are identified, and the characteristics of technology best suited to correct them are defined. In each of these methods of technological forecasting, the probabilities and the implication of these prospective technological advances are then analyzed, and this information becomes part of the data used to make better decisions.

Technological forecasting is of course limited to the extent that some developments in technology are unpredictable and some data, such as scientific research of private industry, is unavailable. Moreover, technological forecasting can be effective only to the extent that forecasts become part of the organization's regular executive decision-making apparatus. But it is unthinkable that executives will not use technological forecasting, but rather act on simple hunches concerning future technology.

217   Rapp, Brian, and Patitucci, Frank.   "Improving the Performance of City Government: A Third Alternative." PUBLIUS 6 (Fall 1976): 63-91.

Soaring costs and increased demand for more and better city services generally result in either raising taxes or cutting back services or both. This article poses a third alternative: increasing the efficiency and effectiveness of current services by strengthening local government management processes. It analyzes twelve internal and external factors that affect the management process of city government. Internal factors are those which exist within the formal legal, political, and administrative structure of local government; and external factors are those which exist outside that structure. The authors attempt to simplify the problem of understanding the interrelated conditions that affect the management process.

218   Rees, P.H.   "Concepts of Social Space: Toward an Urban Social Geography." In GEOGRAPHIC PERSPECTIVES ON URBAN SYSTEMS, edited by Brian J.L. Berry and Frank E. Horton, pp. 306-94. Englewood Cliffs, N.J.: Prentice-Hall, 1970.

A review and analysis of the principle findings in studies of the classical models of changing spatial structure (Burgess's Concentric Zone theory, and Hoyt's Sector Model), in relation to where people live, what they are like, and what determines their choice of residential location. The results of the study are based on the premise of urban location theory, which defines social area analysis and factor analysis. Three primary indicators are used: social rank, urbanization, and segregation.

219   Ridley, Clarence E., and Simon, Herbert A. MEASURING MUNICIPAL ACTIVITIES: A SURVEY OF SUGGESTED CRITERIA AND REPORTING FORMS FOR APPRAISING ADMINISTRATION. Chicago: International City Management Association, 1938. 75 p.

This study deals with the problem of measuring local government service output. It devotes a chapter each to fire, police, public works, public health, recreation, public welfare, public education, public libraries, personnel, municipal finance, and city planning. An appendix is provided with data gathering forms.

220   Rosenthal, Robert A., and Weiss, Robert S. "Problems of Organizational Feedback Process." In SOCIAL INDICATORS, edited by Raymond A. Bauer, pp. 302-40. Cambridge: MIT Press, 1966.

The authors examine the need for feedback systems in large organizations and the difficulties encountered in developing and using feedback information. Organizations require feedback to compare desired performance with actual performance. Organizations cannot usually predict all the consequences of their actions. Moreover, they themselves are affected by those consequences. They need feedback to determine the impact of their policies and how those policies can be redirected to effect the most desirable consequences.

To deal responsibly with the consequences of their actions, organizations need feedback from groups external as well as internal groups, indirectly as well as directly affected, and targets unintended as well as intended. Unfortunately, the structured relations of organizations sometimes obstruct the flow of vital feedback to decision makers. The development of research programs is one of the best ways to maintain appropriate feedback. What is needed are: continuing research within the organization which maintains close contact with the outside world, and ad hoc research studies undertaken by external groups whose objectivity is desired. For any feedback program to be effective, it must well established within the organization, and have a high status of acceptance. Only then will it be integrated into the decision-making processes.

221   Russett, Bruce M. "Indicators for America's Linkages with the Changing World." ANNALS OF THE AMERICAN ACADEMY OF POLITICAL AND SOCIAL SCIENCE 388 (March 1970): 82-96.

A world social indicators approach could utilize so many different indicators that it is difficult to determine which variables on which data are available. The author proposes that indicators might be classified into three categories: national attribute data, value achievement and aspiration differentials, and indicators of international linkage.

222 Sanders, Barkev S. "Measuring Community Health Levels." AMERICAN JOURNAL OF PUBLIC HEALTH 54 (July 1964): 1063-70.

Sanders suggests that the increased prevalence of various chronic diseases is an indication of better medical care, since fewer people are dying from these diseases. Thus the present morbidity rate is incorrect. Measurement of the efficiency of health care should be made in terms of its contribution to increasing productive man years.

223 Schaenman, Philip S., and Muller, Thomas. MEASURING IMPACTS OF LAND DEVELOPMENT: AN INITIAL APPROACH. Washington, D.C.: Urban Institute, 1974. 93 p.

This report suggests ways to estimate the impact of land development on local jurisdictions. The techniques are applicable to both proposed and past land developments. The authors recommend specific data collection procedures for evaluating land development impacts on economic, environmental, housing, and public service issues. Use of these techniques will enable local public officials to assess land use decisions in a systematic and a comprehensive way. The study outlines the issues to be confronted before the evaluation system can be implemented and illustrates how the measurement system can be used in short-term situations.

224 Schneider, Mark. "The Quality of Life in Large American Cities: Objective and Subjective Social Indicators." SOCIAL INDICATORS RESEARCH 1 (March 1975): 495-509.

See 326.

225 Scott, Douglas. MEASURES OF CITIZEN EVALUATION OF LOCAL GOVERNMENT SERVICES. Santa Monica, Calif.: RAND, 1976. 30 p.

Given the need for multiple sources of data in policy research, there is a problem of finding a methodology which incorporates both multiple measures and high probability. A classificatory scheme can be established relating data-collection methods to measurement techniques: questionnaire, interview, experiment, and other methods are related to several strategies, including single-indicators and single-method as well as single-indicator and multiple-method strategies plus multiple indicators differentiated into homogeneous and heterogeneous types. Two ordinal measurement techniques previously unused in policy research were implemented in the Los Angeles Metropolitan Area Survey (LAMAS VII): cluster analysis and a multitrait and multimethod matrix. The results were very favorable for quality aspects of the study.

226 Sheldon, Eleanor Bernert, and Land, Kenneth C. "Social Reporting for the 1970's: A Review and Programmatic Statement." POLICY SCIENCES 3 (July 1972): 137-51.

See 98.

227 Sheldon, Eleanor Bernert; Land, Kenneth C.; and Bauer, Raymond A. "Social Reporting for the 1970's." In THE PRESIDENT'S COMMISSION ON FEDERAL STATISTICS II, pp. 403-35. Washington, D.C.: Government Printing Office, 1971.

See 99.

228 Sheldon, Eleanor Bernert, and Moore, Wilbert E., eds. INDICATORS OF SOCIAL CHANGE: CONCEPTS AND MEASUREMENTS. New York: Russell Sage Foundation, 1968. 822 p.

See 100.

229 Shevky, Eshref, and Bell, Wendell. SOCIAL AREA ANALYSIS: THEORY, ILLUSTRATIVE APPLICATION, AND COMPUTATIONAL PROCEDURES. Stanford, Calif.: Stanford University Press, 1955. 70 p.

The authors develop three different indexes of urban behavior based on selected variables in social rank and economic status, urbanization and family status, and segregation and ethnic status. The combined indexes form a typology for urban stratification and differentiation. The authors then demonstrate the use of this typology as an analytic framework for the comparative study of American cities.

Two hypotheses were tested and found to be supportable: (1) the three indexes are necessary to account for observed social differentiation in census tract populations, and (2) the indexes are unidimensional measuring instruments. Description of census tract populations based on social rank, urbanization, and segregation captures most of the significant variation between tract populations.

230 Shinn, Allen, Jr. "Measuring the Utility of Housing: Demonstrating a Methodological Approach." SOCIAL SCIENCE QUARTERLY 52 (June 1971): 88-102.

Shinn reviews the utility of the "magnitude estimation" technique for measuring "utility functions." To know how well society is "doing" is not possible without measures of societal and group utility functions which "magnitude estimation" can measure.

231 Siegel, Paul M., and Hodge, Robert W. "A Causal Approach to the Study of Measurement Error." In METHODOLOGY IN SOCIAL RESEARCH, edited by Hubert M. Blalock and Ann B. Blalock, pp. 28-59. New York: McGraw-Hill, 1968.

See 328.

232 Smith, David M. THE GEOGRAPHY OF SOCIAL WELL BEING IN THE UNITED STATES: AN INTRODUCTION TO TERRITORIAL SOCIAL INDI-CATORS. New York: McGraw-Hill, 1973. 144 p.

This volume includes the development of new ways of viewing the geography of national territories with emphasis on the spatial expression of contemporary social problems. Social indicators generally focus on aggregate national conditions rather than on the situation in different regions and localities, and consequently an important dimension of the social system is overlooked. Here the focus is on the notion of "territorial social indicators," bringing together certain concerns of the sociologist and the perspective of the geographer. Furthermore, the book attempts to relate the social indicator research of the past few years to the established methods of geographical inquiry. Tables, charts, bibliographical references are provided with each chapter.

233 Snyder, James C. FISCAL MANAGEMENT AND PLANNING IN LOCAL GOVERNMENT. Lexington, Mass.: Lexington Books, 1977. 306 p.

Local government financial planning requires an understanding of microeconomic theory, the nature and functions of the public sector, and the management process. Budgeting, the last stage in the fiscal planning process, can take two approaches: the leave-it-alone approach or the contemporary, rational approach which requires structural and procedural change. Management of the revenue system includes the improvement of property tax structure and the possible adoption of other tax forms. Other aspects of fiscal management are fiscal relations with state and national governments, debt financing, and the accounting system. Types of fiscal analysis include program or policy evaluation, marginal analysis, and investment analy-sis.

234 Sterne, Richard S.; Phillips, James E.; and Rabushka, Alvin. THE URBAN ELDERLY POOR: RACIAL AND BUREAUCRATIC CONFLICT. Lexington, Mass.: Lexington Books, 1974. 145 p.

This is an empirical study of elderly people living in public housing. The authors found that there are "two worlds of aging";

that is, the experiences and the needs of elderly whites were very different from those of elderly blacks; the whites were richer and better educated, lived longer, more likely to own their home, were less dependent on welfare, and were more self-reliant. Both groups expressed fewer needs than the literature would suggest. Elderly whites had no desire to cooperate with blacks, although elderly blacks were willing to consider the possibility. Most of the elderly poor showed little interest in political activity. Finally, chronological age was a predictor of reduced mobility, but not of social, psychological, or political disengagement.

235   Stinchcombe, Arthur L. CONSTRUCTING SOCIAL THEORIES. New York: Harcourt Brace Jovanovich, 1968. 303 p.

This ambitious book deals with logic of scientific inference, causal structures explaining social phenomena, conceptualization of power phenomena and of environmental effects, and concepts about the structure of activities in a manner accessible to the layman. Technical appendixes and some technical analyses are used.

236   Stone, Richard. "A System of Social Matrices." THE REVIEW OF INCOME AND WEALTH 19 (June 1973): 143-66.

The paper contributes to a United Nations attempt to formulate an integrated system of demographic, manpower, and social statistics through the development of the concept of life sequences. While this article has primarily a sociodemographic focus, the author does indicate how his concept can be linked with economic information on costs and benefits. He asserts that the division of life into definable sequences, such as the learning sequence or the delinquency sequence, is a useful method for cataloging data collected on how individuals are distributed over states at different points in time (called stock information) and how individuals move between states over intervals of time (flow information). Further, the standard matrix framework stores this data conveniently. The author provides examples of his method, for example, by using data pertaining to the educational experience of teenage boys.

237   Stuart, Darwin G. "Urban Improvement Programming Models." In DECISION-MAKING IN URBAN PLANNING, edited by Ira M. Robinson, pp. 343-76. Beverly Hills, Calif.: Sage Publications, 1973.

A programs-objectives matrix is one of the most commonly used methods for evaluating alternative urban plans. This matrix balances alternative public investment programs against specific goals and objectives. Problems arise when different units of measurement are used for different objectives and programs. Urban improvement and public investment programming models

are not the optimal solution to urban decision making. They
do provide one approach, from among many options, that can
be used to determine the allocation of resources.

238 Suchman, Edward A. EVALUATIVE RESEARCH: PRINCIPLES AND
PRACTICE IN PUBLIC SERVICE AND SOCIAL ACTION PROGRAMS.
New York: Russell Sage Foundation, 1967. 186 p.

Suchman has written a handbook for students and practitioners
to use in assessing the impact of action programs. While based
on seminars in the evaluation of public health programs, the
approach which Suchman discusses is transferable to research
on other action programs. He covers the theoretical end of
evaluation; that is, concepts and principles, as well as
evaluative research program design and administration. He
places the whole discussion in the context of the history of
evaluative research and its future.

239 Sullivan, John L. "Multiple Indicators and Complex Causal Models."
In CAUSAL MODELS IN THE SOCIAL SCIENCES, edited by H.M. Blalock,
Jr., pp. 301-34. Chicago: Aldine-Atherton, 1971.

This chapter is a further contribution to the field of empirical
methodology. The author prefers the approach which uses each
indicator separately rather than combining them into an index.
He feels that "the use of the multiple-partial correlation
coefficients allows the researcher to make ample use of multiple
indicators while at the same time retaining a manageable number
of predictions." Unlike factor analysis, the author's approach
assumes a block recursive system and attempts to assess relationships between, but not within, the blocks. An empirical
illustration is included.

240 Taeuber, Karl E. "Toward a Social Report: A Review Article." THE
JOURNAL OF HUMAN RESOURCES 5 (Summer 1970): 354-60.

The author describes a U.S. Department of Health, Education,
and Welfare report entitled "Toward the Evolution of a Regular
System of Social Reporting" (1969). In the report social indicators are defined as "a statistic of direct normative interest
which facilitates concise, comprehensive, and balanced judgments about the condition of major aspects of a society. It
is in all cases a direct measure of welfare and subject to the
interpretation that, if it changes in the 'right' direction,
while other things remain equal, things have gotten better."
Figures on health or crime rates could be social indicators,
but not the number of doctors or policemen. A new indicator
"expectation of healthy life" is analyzed. Other indicators are
also appraised.

241 Thom, Gary C.; and Ott, Wayne R.; in cooperation with the Environ-
     mental Protection Agency. AIR POLLUTION INDICES, COMPENDIUM
     AND ASSESSMENT OF INDICES USED IN THE UNITED STATES AND
     CANADA. Washington, D.C.: Government Printing Office, 1975.
     164 p.

       An extensive survey was conducted of all the air pollution
       indexes that are presently utilized or are available. The data
       were obtained from a literature review; from telephone
       discussions with personnel in state, local, and provincial air
       pollution control agencies; and from material received from
       these agencies. Of the fifty-five metropolitan air pollution
       control agencies surveyed in the United States, thirty-five
       used some form of daily air pollution index. These indexes
       were so varied that it was necessary to develop a system to
       classify indexes according to four criteria: (1) number of
       variables, (2) calculation method, (3) calculation mode, and
       (4) descriptor categories reported with the index. Using the
       classification system, fourteen basically different index types
       were exactly the same. The survey results and agency comments
       were used to identify the general structural characteristics
       and criteria for a candidate for a uniform air pollution index.

242 Todd, Ralph H. "A City Index: Measurement of a City's Attractiveness."
     REVIEW OF APPLIED URBAN RESEARCH 5 (July 1977): 1-16.

       This study relies on objective data to provide a yardstick with
       which to compare conditions in one city with those in other
       cities. The author assumes that these measurable factors do in
       fact determine how well satisfied the residents are with those
       conditions and, by inference, with their city. Eighty quantifi-
       able aspects of a city's economic, demographic, and social en-
       vironment are used and twenty-one cities are thereby ranked
       from most attractive to least attractive major American cities.
       Collected data is included and some interpretive charts also
       appear.

243 Toffler, Alvin. "The Art of Measuring the Arts." ANNALS OF THE
     AMERICAN ACADEMY OF POLITICAL AND SOCIAL SCIENCE 373
     (September 1967): 141-55.

       Toffler proposes a cultural data system to provide additional
       perspectives and information for policymaking. He would
       monitor quantitative and qualitative aspects of cultural change.
       Toffler lists fifteen cultural "quality indicators" that can be
       integrated to form a cultural index.

244 United Nations. Research Institute for Social Development. "The Con-
     cept of Development and Its Measurement." INTERNATIONAL SOCIAL
     DEVELOPMENT REVIEW 2 (March 1970): 1-6.

This brief article was drawn from a lecture on the nature of development given by the director of the United Nations Research Institute. It deals with such topics as the contents of development and measurement of development using per capita national income indexes. Included is a table listing core indicators and a chart noting correspondence points for selected core indicators and per capita gross national product.

245 _____. STUDIES IN THE MEASUREMENT OF LEVELS OF LIVING AND WELFARE. Report no. 70.3. 1970. 103 p.

Studies in this volume include "Measuring Social Variables in Real Terms," "The Level of Living Index: New Versions," and "The Level of Welfare Index." "The Level of Welfare" is conceived as a function of the "Level of Living," but factors other than the flow of goods and services affect the needs of individuals.

246 United Nations. Secretariat. "System of Social and Demographic Statistics: Draft Outlines on Social Indicators." 26 April 1974. 56 p. Mimeo.

See 105.

247 U.S. Bureau of the Census. THE CURRENT POPULATION SURVEY: A REPORT ON METHODOLOGY. Technical Paper, no. 7. Washington, D.C.: Government Printing Office, 1963. 91 p.

This report presents a detailed account of the Current Population Survey with particular emphasis on the sampling and statistical estimation aspects of the survey design. Many illustrative tables and appendixes are included. The report treats the following topics: background of the Current Population Survey, design and rotation of the sample, special design features, survey operations, and sampling errors.

248 _____. NATIONAL DATA NEEDS. FIRE SERVICE STATISTICS. State and Local Government Special Studies, no. 60. Washington, D.C.: Government Printing Office, 1972. 17 p.

The Department of Commerce presents an analysis based upon a conference called to discuss statistical data needs relating to fire services.

249 U.S. National Science Foundation. National Science Board. SEVENTH ANNUAL REPORT: SCIENCE INDICATORS--1974. Washington, D.C.: Government Printing Office, 1975. 242 p.

See 108.

250   U.S. Office of Management and Budget. THE CURRENT POPULATION
SURVEY AS A STATISTICAL INFORMATION SYSTEM. Edited by
Margaret E. Martin. Washington, D.C.: Government Printing Office,
1971. 15 p.

> Martin discusses the Current Population Survey as a statistical
> information system consisting of input, processing of the informa-
> tion, output, and feedback. The input is characterized by
> samples of households on a monthly basis covering a broad
> range of topics. The processing of the data contains a variety
> of classifications and is further characterized by an elaborate
> system of controls. The output from this survey is a series
> of monthly, quarterly, and annual tabulations.

251   Urban Information Systems Inter-Agency Committee. NATIONAL INVITA-
TIONAL CONFERENCE ON COMPUTER ASSISTED INFORMATION AND
REFERRAL SYSTEMS. Proceedings of the National Invitational Conference
on Computer-Assisted Information and Referral Systems, held November
1973. Washington, D.C.: Department of Housing and Urban Development, 1973. 130 p.

> Sponsored by the Urban Information Systems Inter-Agency
> Committee, the conference was held to facilitate the exchange
> of ideas and information among those actively involved in
> planning and operating information and referral systems and
> those involved in human services activities at the federal level.
> Each of eight working groups was assigned the following three
> tasks: (1) to construct an operating definition of information
> and referral, (2) to construct an operating definition of computer-
> assisted information and referral systems, and (3) to identify
> those factors operating for and against such a system. Manage-
> ment topics include the following: how communities can finance
> computer-assisted information and referral, the uses of computer-
> assisted information and referral data, how consumer use of
> information and referral can be increased, and confidentiality
> of data. Technical sessions dealt with data needs, automation
> techniques, classification systems, and data storage and retrieval
> methods.

252   Van Arsdol, Maurice D. "The Generality of Urban Social Area Indexes."
AMERICAN SOCIOLOGICAL REVIEW 23 (June 1958): 277-84.

> Van Arsdol reports on the work of Eshref Shevky, Marilyn
> Williams, and Wendell Bell, who have developed a system
> called social area analysis to analyze census tract populations
> within a framework of a limited number of variables. The
> Skevky group has divided the real structure of an urban com-
> munity into indexes measuring social rank, urbanization, and
> segregation. These indexes are defined in terms of census tract
> measures. Three hypotheses based on the measurements of
> these indexes were tested using data from ten large American
> cities.

The author discusses the capacity for the Shevky indexes to be generalized. The results of factor analyses of the hypotheses indicate that the Shevky indexes appear to have a high capacity for being generalized for the cities studied.

253 Veeder, Nancy W. "Health Services Utilization Models for Human Services Planning." JOURNAL OF THE AMERICAN INSTITUTE OF PLANNERS 41 (March 1975): 101-09.

Planners of urban service delivery systems have relied heavily on mathematical models to predict the behavior of potential clients for these services. The most widely used example of this in planning has been the transportation model. Models of health services utilization currently are sensitive to psychological states, social pressures, motivations and institutional barriers to service utilization. Health services utilization models could be extended to services such as housing, recreation, employment, and education. Social science modeling may help planners expand their understanding in a wide range of human service delivery systems.

254 von Bertalanffy, Ludwig. GENERAL SYSTEM THEORY: FOUNDATIONS, DEVELOPMENT, APPLICATIONS. New York: George Braziller, 1968. 289 p.

See 110.

255 Waller, John D., et al. MONITORING FOR GOVERNMENT AGENCIES. Washington, D.C.: Urban Institute, 1976. 170 p.

Implementation effectiveness is a critical factor in managing public programs. Few agencies secure such information in time to take remedial action. This report suggests procedures to establish an effective monitoring system. The authors draw heavily on the monitoring systems that have been used by state planning agencies for criminal justice programs.

256 Walters, A.; Mangold, J.; and Haran, E.G.P. "A Comprehensive Planning Model for Long-Range Academic Strategies." MANAGEMENT SCIENCE 22 (March 1976): 727-38.

The authors explain a multiperiod linear programming model, which has been devised to aid school administrators in planning and decision making. The technique of goal programming permits evaluations of possible courses of action and the opportunity costs of the various goals. The model includes faculty staffing goals, career constraints, teaching, as well as course loads, tenure constraints, and budget constraints.

257 Warren, Roland L. "The Good Community--What Would It Be?" JOUR-

NAL OF COMMUNITY DEVELOPMENT SOCIETY 1 (Spring 1970): 14-24.

> Agreeing that everyone wants to "live in a good community," this paper suggests nine issues necessary to consider in formulating a model of the "good" community: primary group relationships, autonomy, viability, power distribution, participation, degree of commitment, degree of heterogeneity, extent of neighborhood control, and extent of conflict. Critical questions asked in discussion of each factor are as follows: (1) How much of what we want is actually possible? (2) How much of what seems desirable do we actually want? (3) How much of a price are we willing to pay for it when other values are jeopardized?

258 Webb, Kenneth, and Hatry, Harry P. OBTAINING CITIZEN FEEDBACK: THE APPLICATION OF CITIZEN SURVEYS TO LOCAL GOVERNMENTS. Washington, D.C.: Urban Institute, 1973. 105 p.

> More and more local officials are beginning to use citizen surveys to assess the quality of municipal services. This management tool can provide valuable information on services by age, ethnic group, and income level. The citizen survey can also help explain why citizens are not using certain services, which services are deficient and which are satisfactory, and what types of services are needed. The authors discuss some inherent problems in survey research, offer cost estimates, and illustrate both good and poor techniques in implementing citizen surveys.

259 Webber, Melvin M. "The Roles of Intelligence Systems in Urban Systems Planning." JOURNAL OF THE AMERICAN INSTITUTE OF PLANNERS 31 (November 1965): 289-96.

> This article focuses on the changes in our images of cities, urban problems, and ourselves, all of which are part of the recent developments in urban-policy sciences. The author looks at new images of urban systems, strategies for planning, and the politics involved. The discussion also treats the matter of information gathering and dispersal and its political implications.

260 Weiss, Carol H., and Hatry, Harry P. AN INTRODUCTION TO SAMPLE SURVEYS FOR GOVERNMENT MANAGERS. Washington, D.C.: Urban Institute, 1971. 48 p.

> The authors recommend ways for local officials to use sample surveys to determine the adequacy of public services. The book also includes a useful bibliography.

261 Wertheimer, Richard F. II, and Zedlewski, Sheila R. THE IMPACT OF DEMOGRAPHIC CHANGE ON THE DISTRIBUTION OF EARNED INCOME AND THE AFDC: 1975-1985. Washington, D.C.: Urban Institute, 1977. 96 p.

The authors forecast through 1985 the cost and case load of the federal Aid to Families with Dependent Children (AFDC) program, using the Urban Institute's Dynamic Simulation of Income Model (DYNASIM). This shows how a change in one factor, such as the birthrate, will affect other factors such as age distribution or labor force participation. Alternative forecasts based on different demographic and economic assumptions are indicated.

262 Whiteneck, Gale G. STATE OF THE ART IN DEFINING SOCIAL SERVICES, DEVELOPING SERVICE UNITS, AND DETERMINING UNIT COSTS WITH AN ANNOTATED BIBLIOGRAPHY. Denver: Denver University, Colorado Center for Social Research and Development, 1976. 27 p.

Whiteneck deals with the planning, management, and evaluation of social service delivery systems. The author defines social services in terms of three levels of specificity: broad program, service phase, and task performed by service workers. Whiteneck reviews the Title XX conceptualization of a structured approach to defining services in relation to national goals: self-sufficiency, protection of children and adults, community and home-based care, and institutional care. The author goes on to develop unit cost approaches to costs per case, costs per client receiving a specific service, costs per service output, and costs of service worker time. The volume includes an annotated bibliography on the definition of social services, development of service units, and the determination of unit costs.

263 Willeke, Gene E. "Identifying Public in Social Impact Assessment." In METHODOLOGY OF SOCIAL IMPACT ASSESSMENT, edited by Kurt Finsterbusch and C.P. Wolf, pp. 317-23. Stroudsburg, Pa.: Dowden, Hutchinson and Ross, 1977.

Planners should not be isolated from interested publics. The potential effects of a proposed policy or action should be assessed so that the groups affected can become involved in the planning process. Publics can be identified by the planning staff, through a third party, or by coming together itself. In most cases, the planning staff itself will have to determine what groups will be affected. Methods by which the planning staff may identify publics include analysis of lists of organized groups; geographic analysis; demographic analysis; historical analysis, or reference to correspondence files, newspaper accounts, and so forth; comparative analysis, or reference to studies and projects in closely related fields; and field interviews.

264 Williams, Oliver P. "Life-Style Values and Political Decentralization in

Metropolitan Areas." SOUTHWESTERN SOCIAL SCIENCE QUARTERLY
48 (December 1967): 299-310.

Williams makes a major contribution to the theory of metropolitan politics. He attempts to improve on existing analytical
models as a step toward guiding empirical research and sharp-
ening perceptions of the social values served by the new
metropolitan form. Williams rejects the models of the international relations, market place, and power structure because
they overlook distinctions between centralized and decentralized
services. Instead, he suggests a model incorporating suburban
communities' life-style values and argues that suburbs will
resist integration of life-style services but will accept and
occasionally encourage integration of system-maintenance
services when the issues are perceived correctly. The article
concludes with a discussion of the determining factors and the
social consequences of suburban specialization.

265   . METROPOLITAN POLITICAL ANALYSIS. New York: Free Press,
1971. 118 p.

The author presents a useful introduction to the study of local
and metropolitan politics from the professional's rather than
the student's perspective. Building on economic and geographic
models of the metropolis, Williams argues for the use of "access"
as a central organizing concept in urban studies. Three types
of metropolitan political strategies are outlined: (1) location
change, (2) community formation, and (3) coalition formation.
Thus the politics of metropolitan areas becomes the politics of
homogeneity versus heterogeneity and of accessibility versus
the barriers to accessibility. Zoning, urban renewal (recycling),
incorporation, and annexation become obvious manifestations
of political decision making in this pattern. Four urban problems
are briefly explored within this framework--circulation of
people, waste removal, obsolescence, and growth.

266 Wingo, Lowden. "The Quality of Life: Toward a Microeconomic Definition." URBAN STUDIES 10 (1973): 3-18.

This is a conceptual analysis of the possible contribution of
microeconomics to the measurement of the quality of life.
The technique depends on defining quality of life as composed
of individual preference and external phenomena which engage
that preference. Given this definition, quality of life can be
analyzed into five stages: In stage one, the individual divides
his social productivity between income and leisure; the amount
of leisure produced is the "utility aggregate" for this stage.
In stage two, the money income from stage one (a product of
individual productivity, market characteristics, and labor
service characteristics) is divided between collective and private consumption; collective consumption is the utility aggregate for this stage. In stage three, the disposable income

from stage two is divided between future consumption (savings) and current consumption; savings is the utility aggregate for this stage. In stage four, current consumption is divided between pure private goods and "rent fund," expenditures for pure private goods is the utility aggregate for this stage. Finally, in stage five the rent fund is allocated among a set of accessible, uniquely endowed environments (which involves nonmarket attributes due to the unequal distribution of environmental qualities).

267 Zapf, Wolfgang. "The Polity as a Monitor of the Quality of Life." AMERICAN BEHAVIORAL SCIENTIST (May-June 1974): 651-73.

Zapf advocates use of societal monitoring rather than the traditional approach of an issue-attention cycle. This is necessary in order to provide systematic evaluation of the quality of life as it is being impacted by policy decisions. Societal monitoring improves the statistical infrastructure, incorporates economic analysis, focuses on outputs, and should be operated by both public and private agencies. Monitoring includes review of social trends, comparisons of two or more countries, and the use of social indicators.

268 Ziller, Robert C. "Self-Other Orientations and Quality of Life." SOCIAL INDICATORS RESEARCH 1 (December 1974): 301-27.

This is a phenomenological study of the quality of life. Quality of life is an experience of an individual, and a technique is developed which elicits that experience. The technique involves a limited, verbal cognitive map. This technique is applied to several personal experiences.

Chapter 3

PROBLEMS WITH URBAN INDICATORS

269 Andrews, Frank M. "Social Indicators of Perceived Life Quality."
SOCIAL INDICATORS RESEARCH 1 (December 1974): 279-99.

This paper is a conceptual discussion of the weaknesses of
perceptual indicators of quality of life, especially their validity,
interpretability, completeness, and utility. The author finds
that none of these weaknesses is sufficient to invalidate such
measures. He goes on to suggest other research that is needed
in this area.

270 Austin, Charles J. "Selected Social Indicators in the Health Field."
AMERICAN JOURNAL OF PUBLIC HEALTH 61 (August 1971): 1507-13.

This article concerns social indicators in health services and
contends that programs have failed because indicators are based
on "outdated norms." Austin suggests that a test of relevance
must be applied and offers several models for that purpose,
for example, Blackman and Blum's four approaches to planning
for social change such as goal-oriented development. He suggests
that models be established which are dynamic and responsive
to obvious deficiency and great change.

271 Bauer, Raymond A. "Detection and Anticipation of Impact: The Nature
of The Task." In his SOCIAL INDICATORS, pp. 1-67. Cambridge: MIT
Press, 1966.

See 5.

272 Berry, Brian J.L., ed. CITY CLASSIFICATION HANDBOOK. New York:
John Wiley and Sons, 1972. 394 p.

See 129.

273 Biderman, Albert D. NATIONAL GOALS AND STATISTICAL INDICATORS.
Washington, D.C.: Bureau of Social Science Research, 1963. 38 p.

Biderman discusses the difficulty of formulating indicators

related to consensual goals, such as the national goals stated
by the president's commission. He examines the statistical
abstract of the United States, economic indicators historical
statistics of the United States, space goals, and health, education, and welfare trends. Biderman views the impact of
the U.S. space science program as an example of planned
and unplanned social change.

274 _____. "Social Indicators and Goals." In SOCIAL INDICATORS, edited
by Raymond A. Bauer, pp. 68-153. Cambridge: MIT Press, 1966.

Biderman notes deficiencies in trying to use current data series
and statistics to assess the nature of our social system or to its
current status. He reviews obstacles to an adequate consensual
system of social indicators including invalidity conflicting
indicators, lack of data, incompatible models, inaccuracy,
and value consensus. He uses crime statistics to illustrate the
problem of indicator quality. Valuable appendix data on
national goals is included.

275 Birgersson, Bengt Owe. "The Service Paradox: Citizen Assessment of
Urban Services in 36 Swedish Communes." In COMPARING URBAN
SERVICE DELIVERY SYSTEMS: STRUCTURE AND PERFORMANCE, edited
by Vincent Ostrom and Frances Pennell Bish, pp. 243-67. Urban Affairs
Annual Reviews, vol. 12. Beverly Hills, Calif.: Sage Publications, 1977.

In connection with the 1970 general election in Sweden, data
were collected on citizen attitudes toward government services.
Analysis of these data revealed a paradox; that is, that citizens
receiving higher service levels were more frequently dissatisfied
with the services provided than those receiving lower service
levels. A multivariate analysis of the service standard, personal
attributes, type of commune, and service attitudes was made
to study this paradox. Two possible explanations emerged, although neither was clear-cut: that urbanization is associated
with increased needs for services which cannot be met; and
that an expanded level of services whets the appetite for more
services.

276 Buchanan, James M. PUBLIC FINANCE IN DEMOCRATIC PROCESS:
FISCAL INSTITUTIONS AND INDIVIDUAL CHOICE. Chapel Hill:
University of North Carolina Press, 1967. 307 p.

Buchanan is concerned with the process by which individual
choices are combined to produce collective decisions. He
interprets the fiscal process through an individualistic and democratic framework in which the individual is assumed to be
rational. His purpose is to analyze and predict the effects of
various fiscal institutions on individual behavior in a situation
of collective choice.

In the first part of the book he assumes that fiscal institutions are imposed on individuals and individuals cannot change or alter them. A model of demand for public goods and models of actual tax institutions are examined. Ear marked taxes and the free rider problem with public goods are discussed. Buchanan also introduces some simple decision models and talks about the problems in moving from theory to reality.

In part 2 the individual is assumed to have some power of selection among fiscal institutions. Buchanan analyzes fiscal institutions in the setting of institutional choice.

277 Campbell, Donald T. "Local Indicators for Social Program Evaluation." SOCIAL INDICATORS RESEARCH 3 (September 1976): 237-56.

An important use of social indicators is in evaluating the impact of specific social programs. For successful evaluation, statistics must be available for local areas even though they do not conform to standard administrative units. Subjective social indicators are more flexible and therefore more useful in such cases. If information on lists of specified persons were made available, these records could be used for evaluating ongoing social programs. This could be done without breaching privacy by using code numbers or letters, and no individual data would be released.

278 Carter, Genevieve W. "How Do We Measure the Outcomes of Our Efforts?" PUBLIC WELFARE 29 (Summer 1971): 267-76.

Evaluation and accountability are potential change agents within public welfare organizations. Evaluations usually have political overtones when mandated by legislative bodies. This in turn may change the objectives of the evaluation. With a clarification of ultimate, intermediate, and proximate objectives efficiency and effectiveness studies can begin to determine accountability. Evaluation programs which are flexible and provide for redefinition and regrouping are best. Several evaluation techniques are reviewed: management by objectives; cost-benefit analysis; and planning, programming, and budgeting systems. Evaluation and accountability programs need sound research methodologies, adequate budgets, and a political climate that permits asking the right questions.

279 Cochran, Lilian T., and O'Kane, James M. "Urbanization-Industrialization and the Theory of Demographic Transition." PACIFIC SOCIOLOGICAL REVIEW 20 (January 1977): 113-34.

The article begins with a review of the literature on the "transition theory" and notes some of the problems surrounding the theory. In order to correct these problems the authors present a four-phase framework to interrelate the process of demographic change with urbanization and industrialization.

280 Coleman, James S. "The Methods of Sociology." In A DESIGN FOR
SOCIOLOGY: SCOPE, OBJECTIVES, AND METHODS, edited by
Robert Bierstadt, pp. 86-114. Philadelphia: American Academy of
Political and Social Science, 1969.

> Coleman reviews developments and problems in sociological
> research methods, including social indicators. He deals with
> the need for aggregation and disaggregation of indicators for
> control and for decisions to convert resources.

281 Cowing, Thomas G., and Holtmann, A.G. THE ECONOMICS OF LO-
CAL PUBLIC SERVICE CONSOLIDATION. Lexington, Mass.: Lexington
Books, 1976. 166 p.

> Service districts are forced to change continually due to
> pressures of population movements and urban decay. Consoli-
> dation is difficult and not always desirable. Each service
> should be treated differently, with the appropriate solution
> varying from complete consolidation of the delivery and financing
> of a service by all communities to the provision of the service
> on a purely private basis. Each case should be decided
> separately, depending on the extent of economies of scale and
> the geographic apportionment of the benefits from the service.
> Moreover, in some situations ethical and political judgments will
> have to be made and may even outweigh economic considerations.

282 Datta, Louis-Ellin. "How Bad Was Old? How Good Is New? Reflec-
tions on Evaluating Urban Education." EDUCATION AND URBAN SO-
CIETY 9 (August 1977): 403-28.

> Evaluation of American urban education has received a great
> deal of criticism. Elements of evaluations which have come
> under fire include the following: (1) the measures used,
> especially with regard to ethnic differences; (2) inappropriate
> evaluation designs tending to obscure real differences; (3)
> analytic models working against the likelihood that intended
> program effects might be demonstrated; (4) interpretation of
> evaluation results; and (5) the control of evaluations. After
> discussing these problems, the author analyzed some news
> directions in evaluation methodology.

283 David, Henry. "Assumptions about Man and Society and Historical
Constructs in Futures Research." FUTURES 2 (September 1970): 222-30.

> David analyzes two problems or dangers involved in futures
> research. First, is the character of assumptions the futures
> researcher makes about human behavior. The second problem
> is that futures researchers formulate historical constructs.
> These two concepts are the basis for prediction and forecasting
> and so can distort the results.

284 Davies, Ross. "Using the Census for Planning." PLANNER 62 (January 1976): 15-19.

The British census provides a series of regular indicators that can be used to determine movement patterns and mobility levels at the county and metropolitan level. At the district level, the census is the most inclusive source of housing and migration data. However, the census also has a number of drawbacks: (1) delay in making available more specialized statistics; (2) incompatibility with the stages in the planning process which have divergent information requisites; (3) frequent incompatibility of the spatial units used in the enumerations of traffic, employment, and expenditure; and (4) excessive time lapses between censuses. Therefore, the author views the government's decision to cancel the 1976 midterm census as a serious mistake.

285 Dror, Yehezekal. PUBLIC POLICYMAKING REEXAMINED. San Francisco: Chandler Publishing Co., 1968. 370 p.

The author believes a gap exists between the actual practice of setting policies and the potential best methods that exist today for making policy. The author, because of concern that the gap will expand, has applied to public policymaking various approaches developed in the social sciences, in decision-making analysis, and in systems analysis. He uses his optimal model of public policymaking to identify its weakness in actual practice today and to recommend detailed proposals for improvement.

286 Duhl, Leonard J. "Planning and Predicting: Or What Do You Do When You Don't Know the Names of the Variables." TOWARD THE YEAR 2000, edited by Daniel Bell, pp. 147-56. Boston: Houghton Mifflin, 1968.

Duhl presents a critical analysis of past and present efforts at planning and forecasting as well as an explanation of overall dynamic effects of actions and nonactions and dialogues on the predicting of the future.

The volume itself is a report on activities of the Commission on the Year 2000 of the American Academy of Arts and Sciences in 1965-66. It includes some transcripts of dialogue at working sessions as well as a collection of articles submitted by participants, all of whom are distinguished in various related fields, for example, Eugene Rostow, Daniel Moynihan, and James Q. Wilson.

287 Duncan, Otis Dudley. "Social Stratification and Mobility: Problems in the Measurement of Trend." In INDICATORS OF SOCIAL CHANGE: CONCEPTS AND MEASUREMENTS, edited by Eleanor Bernert Sheldon and Wilbert E. Moore, pp. 675-719. New York: Russell Sage Foundation, 1968.

Duncan discusses problems in the measurement of trends in stratification and mobility for the United States since World War I. He proposes an approach to identifying trends and then to measuring them over time.

288   Duncan, Otis Dudley; Cuzzort, Ray; and Duncan, Beverly. STATISTI-CAL GEOGRAPHY: PROBLEMS IN ANALYZING AREAL DATA. Glencoe, Ill.: Free Press, 1961. 191 p.

Statistical geography refers to a set of methodological problems. The authors recognize that researchers in a variety of disciplines are encountering similar problems in making inferences from statistical data that is ordered by areal units.

This book is an initial investigation of the feasibility of formalizing and codifying the methods of analyzing areal data. It outlines the kinds of quantitative areal data used in various disciplines. The authors discuss the features of areal data that affect the way the data are analyzed. There is an examination of the objectives and problems in manipulating areal data by statistical methods.

289   Eckart, Dennis R., and Durand, Roger. "The Effect of Context in Measuring Anomia." PUBLIC OPINION QUARTERLY 39 (Summer 1975): 199-206.

The authors present an empirical analysis of Srole's anomic scale, a measurement of social disorganization. The authors found that the scale was not measuring a single trait, but did express an intercorrelation of race, social class, and neighborhood. They concluded that "anomic" is not adequately understood or defined.

290   Edwards, John. "Social Indicators, Urban Deprivation and Positive Discrimination." JOURNAL OF SOCIAL POLICY 4 (Fall 1975): 278-87.

Edwards presents a skeptical view of the current usage of social indicators which tend to exaggerate their significance and ignore the underlying realities. Concern for the "arithmetic of woe" has diverted attention from the fundamental assumptions underlying the use of social indicators. There is a need for a clear definition of deprivation with indicators derived from that definition.

291   Elkana, Yehuda, et al., eds. TOWARD A METRIC OF SCIENCE: THE ADVENT OF SCIENCE INDICATORS. New York: John Wiley and Sons, 1978. 354 p.

The editors of this volume have brought together a series of papers which were presented at a 1974 conference sponsored by the Social Science Research Council and the Center for

Advanced Study in the Behavioral Sciences. The conference brought historians, sociologists, and philosphers of science together with physical, life, and social scientists, including specialists in social indicators.

292 Fox, Douglas M. "Methods Within Methods: The Case of Community Power Studies." WESTERN POLITICAL QUARTERLY 24 (March 1971): 5-11

In this conceptual analysis, Fox suggests that the findings of community power studies are closely related to the research methods employed. Depending on how the question is worded, reputational studies may find a monolithic power block of businessmen, or a relatively pluralistic structure. The same differences can be found within the decisional techniques.

293 Friedly, Philip H. "Welfare Indicators for Public Facility Investments in Urban Renewal Areas." SOCIO-ECONOMIC PLANNING SCIENCES 3 (Summer 1969): 291-314.

This work is a reprint of a research paper for the U.S. Department of Housing and Urban Development. The purpose was to evaluate effects of various public investment policies in terms of the people affected. In order to evaluate there must be better information regarding the possible consequences in various areas. A series of benefit-cost measurements related to the categories of the investment are presented along with what the author refers to as welfare indicators.

294 Gastil, Raymond D. "Social Indicators and Quality of Life." PUBLIC ADMINISTRATION REVIEW 30 (November-December 1970): 596-601.

The author explains why we need social indicators. There is a problem of mixed indicators and a lack of communication. Statistics are useful in determining trends. Often, statistics need to be refined. Statistics can be used to describe more than just one category of life. Also there is a difficulty in interpreting statistics. We must (1) consider statistics comparatively, emphasizing trends, (2) measure the quality of services only by output measures, (3) explore the significance of simple statistics and statistical correlations, (4) generally avoid combining statistics information with abstract indexes, and (5) always leave open the significance of a particular statistic. This is an in-depth study of social indicators.

295 Gordon, Ian. "Subjective Social Indicators and Urban Political Analysis: Or, What Do We Need to Know about Who's Happy?" POLICY AND POLITICS 5 (March 1977): 93-111.

See 636.

296 Gross, Bertram M. "The City of Man: A Social Systems Reckoning." In ENVIRONMENT FOR MAN: THE NEXT FIFTY YEARS, edited by William R. Ewald, Jr., pp. 136-56. Bloomington: Indiana University Press, 1967.

See 639.

297 Gross, Bertram M., and Springer, Michael. "A New Orientation in American Government." ANNALS OF THE AMERICAN ACADEMY OF POLITICAL AND SOCIAL SCIENCE 371 (May 1967): 1-19.

See 47.

298 Haran, E.G.P., and Vining, Daniel R., Jr. "On the Implications of a Stationary Urban Population for the Size Distribution of Cities." GEOGRAPHICAL ANALYSIS 5 (October 1973): 296-308.

The authors discuss closed systems in terms of cities, that is, where the aggregate population is stationary in size. The traditional Yule-Simon model, which can be successful in dealing with the observed properties of open systems, breaks down for closed systems. Simon's assumptions about intercity migration produce questionable results in a city with a stable population. There is a need for a more adequate theory for closed systems.

299 Hatry, Harry P. "Issues in Productivity Measurement for Local Government." PUBLIC ADMINISTRATION REVIEW 32 (November-December 1972): 776-84.

See 645.

300 Henriot, Peter J. "Political Questions About Social Indicators." THE WESTERN POLITICAL SCIENCE QUARTERLY 23 (June 1970): 235-55.

Systems of social indicators are not simply a matter of technical skill in gathering and correlating data, but are basically a matter of values, interests and policies (politics). It is important that political scientists examine the various political question that are raised. Criticisms are raised but Henriot's conclusion is that efforts to produce more and better information into the decision-making process are a positive approach. They are part of a wider set of efforts to (1) bridge the gap between social science insights, methods, and skills and public policy formulation and implementation, and (2) to promote concern for value orientations among social scientists. The social indicators movement is seen as presenting a challenge filled with problems and promises.

301 Holleb, Doris. "Social Statistics for Social Policy." In PLANNING, edited by American Society of Planning Officials, pp. 80-85. Chicago:

American Society of Planning Officials, 1968.

> Holleb discusses the difficulties involved in developing adequate and effective urban and social indicators. Social measurements used to record social change and to provide a framework for program evaluation. She deals with the analogy with economic indicators and with the complexities of evaluation.

302 Hoos, Ida R. "Information Systems and Public Planning." MANAGE-MENT SCIENCE 17 (June 1971): B-658-B-671.

> Hoos discusses advanced information systems for public planning and warns of potential threat to individual privacy. She raises the fear of an accumulation of computerized data as an encroachment on the individual's right to privacy.

303 Horowitz, Irving Louis. "Engineering and Sociological Perspectives on Development: Interdisciplinary Constraints in Social Forecasting." INTERNATIONAL SOCIAL SCIENCE JOURNAL 21, no. 4 (1969): 545-57.

> Horowitz discusses the differing attitudes and approaches taken by engineers and sociologists and analyzes the sense of superiority each feels. He views the attempts to draw the sciences together as misdirected. Horowitz suggests various ways the two areas can function together and outlines the reason this is so necessary.

304 _____. "Social Indicators and Social Policy." In his PROFESSING SOCIOLOGY: STUDIES IN THE LIFE CYCLE OF SOCIAL SCIENCE, pp. 328-39. Chicago: Aldine, 1968.

> See 651.

305 Hughes, James W. URBAN INDICATORS, METROPOLITAN EVALUATION, AND PUBLIC POLICY. Rutgers, N.J.: Rutgers-The State University, 1972. 233 p.

> Hughes contends that social accounting has been a matter of counting the countable rather than the essential. He proposes in this highly technical volume how to make better and more meaningful use of existing data. An area of major interest is the Standard Metropolitan Statistical Area and highly populated areas within them. Hughes claims that it is possible to measure the quality of life in each area in spite of great differences. He concludes that his theory of "equifinality" has not been proven true or false and claims more support in existing data to prove it.

306 Katzman, Martin T. "Social Indicators and Urban Public Policy." In PLANNING, edited by American Society of Planning Officials, pp. 85-94. Chicago: American Society of Planning Officials, 1968.

Katzman discusses social indicators in terms of scalability, reliability, and validity. Notes the interaction of social indicators with public policy in the field of education.

307   Kraemer, Kenneth L. "The Evolution of an Information System for Urban Administration." PUBLIC ADMINISTRATION REVIEW 29 (July–August 1969): 389–402.

See 190.

308   Land, Kenneth C. "On the Definition of Social Indicators." THE AMERICAN SOCIOLOGIST 6 (November 1971): 322–25.

The article relates some of the caustic criticism of social indicators. Critics contend the social indicators are not capable of being used as the basis for program planning and implementation. However, national goals and priorities are more dependent upon national objectives and values than on assembled data, and there are too many undefined variables in a social system.

The author agrees that rather extravagant claims have been made on behalf of social indicators yet he maintains that social indicators must be components or variables in a sociological model of a social system. The development of such models is the major unsolved problem of social indicators. Land urges an increasing committment to (1) the construction of appropriate variables and statistics which describe a social system and (2) the analysis of the effects that changes in the input variables have on the output variables. This will enable government to decide which variables can and should be manipulated.

309   Laszlo, C.A.; Levine, M.D.; and Milsum, J.H. "A General Systems Framework for Social Systems." BEHAVIORAL SCIENCE 19 (March 1974): 79–92.

The complexities of post industrial society require the use of models based on a systems framework. Systems models are dynamic because they change with time; systems theory provides a methodical, computer-oriented way of analyzing the behavior patterns of dynamic systems. All human social systems produce feedback pathways. Controllable inputs to the system include general leadership, financial and industrial management, communications media, and the people. Uncontrollable inputs include external influences, acts of God, and ignorance in some cases. Social indicators are measured outputs of the social system. Although a complete set of social indicators cannot be established in the immediate future, it is important that a start be made and productive research be initiated.

310 Lehman, Edward W. "Social Indicators and Social Problems." In HANDBOOK ON THE STUDY OF SOCIAL PROBLEMS, edited by Erwin O. Smigel, pp. 149-76. Chicago: Rank McNally, 1971.

See 71.

311 Long, Norton E. "Indicators of Change in Political Institutions." ANNALS OF THE AMERICAN ACADEMY OF POLITICAL AND SOCIAL SCIENCE 388 (March 1970): 35-45.

See 76.

312 McElrath, Dennis. "Urban Differentiation: Problems and Prospects." LAW AND CONTEMPORARY PROBLEMS 30 (Winter 1965): 103-10.

McElrath sees industrialization and urbanization as the most important processes in transforming society. Industrialization and urbanization yield four dimensions of social differentiation which affect the distribution of a community's resources and rewards to a family or individual: economic status (skills), family status (life-style option), migration status, and ethnic status. Examples of the different problems associated with each dimension separately and in combination with each other are given. Each local area has a unique combination of status dimensions leading to particular problems. McElrath notes the possibility of analysis of mass data to isolate these different kinds of localities.

Dimensions that affect parts of the community are shifting and the divisions that divide localities are changing. McElrath concludes that eventually urban life-style will be limited to those who cannot move and are trapped in the central city.

313 McHale, John. "Science, Technology and Change." ANNALS OF THE AMERICAN ACADEMY OF POLITICAL AND SOCIAL SCIENCE 373 (September 1967): 120-40.

McHale discusses the difficulty of integrating present indicators into new qualitative indicators. He points out that present indicators fail to warn of scientific and technical consequences or express social goals.

314 Morgan, James N., and Smith, James D. "Measures of Economic Well-Offness and Their Correlates." AMERICAN ECONOMIC REVIEW, PROCEEDINGS AND PAPERS 59 (May 1969): 450-62.

This article is a report of some of the initial findings from the first phase of a panel study of the dynamics of economic well-being. It presents some static correlations from the first interview which bear on the way one might measure family well-being. Since it represents only the preliminary findings of the study, little is said of the dynamics. The discussion treats problems of empirical methodology and quantitative analysis.

315   Moynihan, Daniel P. MAXIMUM FEASIBLE MISUNDERSTANDING. New York: Free Press, 1969. 218 p.

This book is an eyewitness account of how an academic solution to poverty was haphazardly transformed into a politically useful program and then grew uncontrollably into a political liability.

The idea germinated from concern in the initial days of the Kennedy term for unemployment and juvenile delinquency into a general concern for poverty. Moynihan asserts the War on Poverty was declared not at the behest of the poor, but for the organized professions who worked with the poor and for those who would benefit. It professed as its objective institutional cooperation, but in actuality it instigated institutional change. This actual objective was wholly unintended by Congress and, because it fostered "dangerous" social change, the War on Poverty became a political liability.

The most important long run impact was the formation of an urban black leadership echelon.

316   Muller, Thomas. ECONOMIC IMPACTS OF LAND DEVELOPMENT: EMPLOYMENT, HOUSING, AND PROPERTY VALUES. Washington, D.C.: Urban Institute, 1976. 148 p.

The author states that assessing the economic impact of land development, on employment, land values, and housing is important, but difficult. However, Muller reviews the technology for measuring employment and housing impact and concludes that it is improving rapidly.

317   _____ . FISCAL IMPACTS OF LAND DEVELOPMENT: A CRITIQUE OF METHODS AND REVIEW OF ISSUES. Lexington, Mass.: Lexington Books, 1975. 60 p.

Private development may have negative or positive effects in terms of public revenues. Muller warns against the bias of the sponsor of the analysis. He evaluates the techniques used for fiscal impact analysis and points out that different committees and even households have different scales for determining service preferences. These differences can yield different fiscal results even if the growth pattern is the same.

318   National Research Council. Urban Information Systems Inter-Agency Committee (USAC). LOCAL GOVERNMENT INFORMATION SYSTEMS-- A STUDY OF USAC AND THE FUTURE APPLICATION OF COMPUTER TECHNOLOGY. Washington, D.C.: 1976. 62 p.

This document assesses the Urban Information Systems Inter-Agency Committee program. Widespread use by larger U.S. cities and counties of computers for routine processing operations is found. However, the potential of computer systems for improving local government management is not being exploited widely by local government. The uses of computer systems in six Urban Information Systems Inter-Agency Committee cities from the standpoint of cost-benefit relationships, transferability of experience between cities, interfaces between computer systems, and private security implications is studied.

319 Olson, Mancur, Jr. "Economics, Sociology, and the Best of All Possible Worlds." THE PUBLIC INTEREST 12 (Summer 1969): 96-118.

See 670.

320 Richardson, Harry W. THE ECONOMICS OF URBAN SIZE. Lexington, Mass.: Lexington Books, 1973. 243 p.

This is a conceptual review of the work in economics on "optimal size" of cities. Richardson presents several theories of city size, particularly those of Tolley and Baumol. He then considers in detail the variables of those theories: the negative externalities a city imposes, the agglomerative economies that can be obtained, the relationship between income and welfare, scale economies in local government, and non-economic social costs. He concludes that "optimal" city size is a myth. He devotes the last part of the book to a consideration of various theories which attempt to explain the distribution of city sizes.

321 Riecken, Henry W. "Social Sciences and Social Problems." SOCIAL SCIENCE INFORMATION 8 (February-June 1969): 101-29.

See 93.

322 Rosenthal, Robert A., and Weiss, Robert S. "Problems of Organizational Feedback Processes." In SOCIAL INDICATORS, edited by Raymond A. Bauer, pp. 302-40. Cambridge: MIT Press, 1969.

The authors discuss problem of feedback defined as the total information process through which primary- and second-order effects of organization actions are spelled out to the organization for comparison with desired objectives. The work draws upon National Aeronautics and Space Administration experiences for illustration and argues need for better understanding and channeling of second-order consequences to reduce social waste.

323 Salamon, Lester M. "Follow-ups, Letdowns, and Sleepers: The Time Dimension in Policy Evaluation." In PUBLIC POLICY MAKING IN A

FEDERAL SYSTEM, edited by Charles O. Jones and Robert D. Thomas, pp. 257–84. Beverly Hills, Calif.: Sage Publications, 1976.

Evaluation researchers must be cognizant of the fact that the impact of a government program may not appear for a considerable amount of time. The author characterizes three types of time-related effects: (1) the "letdown effect," which diminishes over time and is produced by programs aimed at imparting skill or knowledge to program participants; (2) the "latent effect," which increases over time and is produced by programs aimed at changing values or attitudes of program participants; and (3) the "sleeper effect," which does not appear during a program's operation, but shows up later and is produced by programs aimed at changing external social and political conditions.

324   Sametz, A.W. "Production of Goods and Services: The Measurement of Economic Growth." In INDICATORS OF SOCIAL CHANGE: CONCEPTS AND MEASUREMENTS, edited by Eleanor B. Sheldon and Wilbert E. Moore, pp. 76–96. New York: Russell Sage Foundation, 1968.

Sametz questions the accuracy of gross national product as a measure of economic growth or welfare. The basic time-series data should be expanded to cover growth, development, and economic welfare impacts. Population, quality of output, and price changes also do not receive adequate weight.

325   Savas, E.S. "New Directions for Urban Analysis." INTERFACES 6 (November 1975): 1–9.

Quantitative analysis has been applied to many urban service systems. However, its application at the policy level to solve urban problems has been less successful. Some of the difficulties are common to public sector problems, while others are peculiar to local government. Improving the quality of urban life and the management of urban services requires reforms based on accurate data. Quantitative analysis can play an important role in urban change if pursued diligently with an awareness of the limitations.

326   Schneider, Mark. "The Quality of Life in Large American Cities: Objective and Subjective Social Indicators." SOCIAL INDICATORS RESEARCH 1 (March 1975): 495–509.

This paper analyzes the comparison of objective and subjective measures of social indicators across several city areas. The data analysis performed yields the conclusion that there is no statistically significant correlation between objective and subjective social indicators. The author concludes with a cautionary note on the utility of objective social indicators.

327 Sheldon, Eleanor Bernert, and Freeman, Howard E. "Notes on Social Indicators: Promises and Potential." POLICY SCIENCES 1 (Spring 1970): 97-111.

The article is a critical review of the social indicators movement which has promised much and delivered little. Rather than invent new claims for social indicators, the authors urge social scientists to look realistically at the enormity of work needed to transform social indicators into reliable tools of the policy-maker. Shortcomings of social indicators, such as inadequate conceptualization in social theory and lack of an interval measure such as that used in economic indicators (namely money), make their use misleading for setting national goals, for program evaluation, and for social accounting. Goals of the social indicators movement should not be to use indicators for goal setting, program evaluation, or social accounting, but for the improvement of descriptive reporting, for the analysis of social change, and for prediction of future social events.

328 Siegel, Paul M., and Hodge, Robert W. " A Causal Approach to the Study of Measurement Error." In METHODOLOGY IN SOCIAL RESEARCH, edited by Hubert M. Blalock and Ann B. Blalock, pp. 28-59. New York: McGraw-Hill, 1968.

This is a chapter in a textbook of methodology for advanced graduate students in political science, anthropology, sociology, and social psychology. It assumes knowledge of applied statistics and data collection techniques. Blalock discusses topics of measurement and conceptualization problems, use of comparative designs and static analysis and their limitations, and problems of experimental design and dynamic analysis.

329 Singer, Fred S. "Can We Develop an Index for Quality of Life?" SCIENCE 173 (24 September 1971): 1253-54.

Singer raises eight questions on the usefulness of social indicators in evaluating the quality of life.

330 Stringham, Luther W. "Health, Education and Welfare Indicators and Trends." PROCEEDINGS OF THE SOCIAL STATISTICS SECTION, pp. 216-21. Washington, D.C.: American Statistical Association, 1959.

Much effort has been spent by the U.S. Department of Health, Education and Welfare to bring together statistical information. Stringham gives information about the effectiveness of statistical reporting on program developments. There are gaps and delays in the channeling of needed information and better mechanisms are needed to improve the flow of information. Stringham reports that the secretary should receive background information that will provide correct impressions of developments and high-light current and emerging problems. It is revealed that many time-series data have been compiled and are available, but are not being used. Among the services presented are two publications put out by the Department of Health, Education, and Welfare's Office of Program Analysis. They are the HISTORY OF HEALTH, EDUCATION AND WELFARE INDICATORS, a document published monthly in Washington, D.C. by the Government Printing Office, and devised to expose officials to indicators on a regular basis, and a supplement called HEALTH, EDUCATION AND WELFARE TRENDS, which presents long-term annual trend data and is also published in Washington, D.C., by the Government Printing Office.

331   Sullivan, Daniel F. CONCEPTUAL PROBLEMS IN DEVELOPING AN INDEX OF HEALTH. Publication No. 100, Series 2, No. 17. Washington, D.C.: National Center for Health Statistics, Public Health Service, 1966. 32 p.

Sullivan defines morbidity in terms of the total impact of illness or injury. He concludes that mortality rates are not effective health measures when taken alone. Indicators of need and availability of health care are also significant.

332   Taeuber, Karl E. "Toward a Social Report: A Review Article." THE JOURNAL OF HUMAN RESOURCES 5 (Summer 1970): 354-60.

See 240.

333   Terleckyj, Nestor E. "Measuring Progress Towards Social Goals: Some Possibilities at National and Local Levels." MANAGEMENT SCIENCE 16 (August 1970): B765-79.

Terleckyj points to numerous data weaknesses as well as the need for both social indicators and national goals. He proposes six major national goals categories with potential indicators of goals output.

334   Thomas, William A. "Indicators of Environmental Quality." SCIENCE 174 (22 October 1971): 437-38.

Thomas defines "environment" to include biological and sociocultural as well as physical elements. He notes the complexity of constructing indicators of qualitative aspects because there are still no adequate indicators for a quantitative definition of environment.

335   U.S. Bureau of the Census. THE CURRENT POPULATION SURVEY: A REPORT ON METHODOLOGY. Technical Paper, no. 7. Washington, D.C.: Government Printing Office, 1963. 91 p.

See 247.

336   U.S. Environmental Protection Agency. THE QUALITY OF LIFE CONCEPT:
A POTENTIAL NEW TOOL FOR DECISION-MAKERS. Washington, D.C.:
Government Printing Office, 1973. 300 p.

> This book summarizes the results of a symposium in 1972 spon-
> sored by the U.S. Environmental Protection Agency. The pur-
> pose was an attempt to bring various experts from a variety of
> specialties together and to exchange information on the con-
> cept quality of life (QOL). They attempted to explore it in
> general terms; that is, to define it if possible and to make
> effective use of it through development of suggested quantita-
> tive approaches in guiding public policy. The idea was pursued
> from various perspectives, for example, growth, women, blacks,
> and the aged as well as environmental, sociological, and
> psychological perspectives. The book reviews past definitions
> and presents new ones that might help develop indicators of
> QOL. The agency reviews problems of definition, of selecting
> QOL factors, of subjective and objective indicators of quanti-
> fying these selected indicators, and of determining the validity
> of each factor for the individual and applying it to the group
> in aggregate fashion. The last half of the book is an anthology
> of related articles that were either presented to participants
> prior to arrival or were added during the symposium.

Chapter 4

APPLICATIONS OF URBAN INDICATORS

337 Aaron, Henry J. SHELTER AND SUBSIDIES: WHO BENEFITS FROM
FEDERAL HOUSING POLICIES? Washington, D.C.: Brookings Institution,
1972. 238 p.

This book is a review of the distribution of benefits from federal
housing policies. Aaron first reviews the rationale for housing
policies and for housing subsidies. Then he considers the effects
of six policies: taxation, mortgage insurance, federal credit
institutions, public housing, housing assistance, and rural home
loans. He ends by considering the implications of these
policies, pointing out that focusing only on the supply of
housing will not affect the supply of housing service (neighborhood quality, quality of schools, etc.)

338 Adams, Gerald H. AIRPORT DEVELOPMENT: SOCIAL AND ECONOMIC
EFFECTS. Springfield, Va.: National Technical Information Service,
1977. 45 p.

Adams presents an abstract bibliography on airport development
in local regions and communities. He covers physical design,
planning, construction, operations, policies, and impacts.
Included in the book are studies of feasibility, conversion-
utilization of military facilities, economic survival, public
attitudes, and cost effectiveness. Municipal and rural relations, political issues, controversies, and technical assistance
programs are described.

339 _____. BART AND METRO-RAPID TRANSIT FOR THE SAN FRANCISCO
AND WASHINGTON, D.C. AREAS. Springfield, Va.: National Technical Information Service, 1977. 278 p.

Included in this book is a two-section bibliography devoted to
literature on the development of rapid rail mass transportation
in two major metropolitan areas. The first section contains
citations referring to BART, the San Francisco Bay Area Rapid
Transit system in California. Section two refers to the com-

bined subway and surface transit system for the District of
Columbia and outlying areas in Maryland and Virginia. Materials in both sections cover line siting, policies and planning,
cars and power systems, stations and track work, human factors,
travel patterns, and public attitudes. Attention is given to
financing, revenue, maintenance, local impact, and environmental impact as well as fare collection, noise, and legislation.

340 _____. CENTRAL CITY DEVELOPMENT. Springfield, Va.: National
Technical Information Service, 1977. 141 p.

Adams presents an abstract bibliography on the revitalization
and renewal of metropolitan inner city areas. Transportation
planning, housing improvement, community development,
neighborhood upgrading, and industrial programs are documented.
He devotes much attention to the central business district.
Projects are reported for a few specific cities, and discussions
are presented on federal programs, financing, trends, and tax
incentives. Other topics include blighted areas, historic site
preservation, and open space and park studies as well as aban-
doned dwellings, migration problems, slum clearance, and street
maintenance.

341 _____. DUAL MODE TRANSPORTATION. Springfield, Va.: National
Technical Information Service, 1975. 162 p.

Adams has prepared an abstract bibliography on personal rapid
transit systems, intercity networks, rapid transit railways, buses,
and automated guideways. References are made to communication requirements, worst case analysis, freeway transit, dial-
a-ride, airport access, socioeconomic factors, and modal split
and multimodal cargo systems.

342 _____. NEW TOWNS AND NEW COMMUNITIES--PLANNING AND
DEVELOPMENT. Springfield, Va.: National Technical Information
Service, 1977. 124 p.

Adams presents an abstract bibliography on new town developmental programs and projects in various sections of the United
States. Financing, benefits, problems, management, land use,
services, environmental aspects, transportation, housing, aes-
thetics, citizen affairs, industrial relations, employment, community interests, commerce, and public administration are
among the topics covered.

343 Adams, Gerald H., and Lehmann, Edward J. HIGHWAY TRAFFIC NOISE.
Springfield, Va.: National Technical Information Service, 1977. 163 p.

The authors present an abstract bibliography on highway noise
and noise reduction. They include studies on transportation
noise models, environmental aspects, noise sources, tire-

pavement studies, noise barrier design, noise levels, and research in the field. Investigations concerning the central
city are excluded.

344 Adelman, Irma, and Morris, Cynthia Taft. SOCIETY, POLITICS AND
ECONOMIC DEVELOPMENT: A QUANTITATIVE APPROACH. Baltimore:
Johns Hopkins Press, 1967. 307 p.

This book attempts to bridge the gap between the theory and
the practice of economic development. It analyzes systematically the social, political, and economic characteristics of
nations at various stages of economic development. It provides a rigorous demonstration that the applicability of some of
the most commonly held generalizations about economic growth
in fact vary substantially depending on the level of socioeconomic development achieved. Tables and a selected bibliography are included.

345 Aldrich, Howard. "Ecological Succession of Racially Changing Neighborhoods: A Review of the Literature." URBAN AFFAIRS QUARTERLY 10
(March 1975): 327-48.

This is a review of the literature on the expansion of blacks
into previously white neighborhoods. Aldrich divides the literature into three sections: causes and initial conditions for
succession, the process of succession in a neighborhood, and
social and economic consequences of succession.

346 Alker, H.R., Jr., and Russett, B.M. "On Measuring Inequality." BE-
HAVIORAL SCIENCE 9 (July 1964): 207-18.

See 117.

347 Allen, William, and Ginsburg, Leslie B. "Traffic Noise: Some Practical
Implications." JOURNAL OF THE ROYAL TOWN PLANNING INSTITUTE
59 (January 1973): 14-16.

This paper suggests a procedure for determining the impact of
noise for transportation planning. The first step is to create
a noise contour map, taking into account existing background
noise, present noise levels, future traffic flow, and the number
and location of dwellings and open spaces affected. This will
present some problems due to local shielding by buildings, em-
bankments, and so forth. Having predicted noise levels throughout the area, one can then construct a cost-benefit balance
sheet to determine the advisability of a project.

348 Almy, Timothy A., "City Managers, Public Avoidance, and Revenue
Sharing." PUBLIC ADMINISTRATION REVIEW 37 (January-February 1977):
19-27.

Through two mail surveys of 645 U.S. city managers in 1973 and 1974, the author investigated two questions: How influential are city managers in the revenue sharing process, and are managers' values and attitudes obstacles to citizen participation in revenue spending decisions? The results indicate that manager preferences are important predictors of actual spending and that managers generally do not hold public hearings on revenue sharing. City managers' perceptions of community solidarity and satisfaction were an important factor in whether or not to hold public hearings. In those few cities where hearings were held, city managers still were able to exercise considerable discretion in allocating revenue sharing funds.

349 Antunes, George E., and Plumlee, John P. "The Distribution of an Urban Public Service: Ethnicity, Socioeconomic Status, and Bureaucracy as Determinants of the Quality of Neighborhood Streets." URBAN AFFAIRS QUARTERLY 12 (March 1977): 313-32.

This work is based on research supported by a grant from the University of Houston and by computing services at Rice University. It is a study of street quality in Houston, focusing on the variation between predominantly black and predominantly white areas of the city. The authors are interested in the extent to which socioeconomic status, rather than just ethnicity, is related to street quality.

350 Aronson, J. Richard, and Schwartz, Eli. "Determining Debt's Danger Signals." MANAGEMENT INFORMATION SERVICE REPORT 8 (September 1976): 1-16.

Determining financial danger signals before the actual crisis is difficult. However, there are guidelines. Long-term debt should not be used to finance short-term projects. Short-term debt should be related to anticipated tax revenues. The most dangerous trend in urban finance is the use of expanding short-term debt. When the ratio of cash and liquid securities to short-term debt is less than one to five, it is a danger signal. If total local debt exceeds 10 percent of the property tax base or if the debt's growth rate exceeds that of the tax base there is trouble ahead. The MANAGEMENT INFORMATION SERVICE REPORT is published by the International City Management Association.

351 Barabba, Vincent P. "The National Setting: Regional Shifts, Metropolitan Decline, and Urban Decay." In POST-INDUSTRIAL AMERICA: METROPOLITAN DECLINE AND INTER-REGIONAL JOB SHIFTS, edited by George Sternlieb and James W. Hughes, pp. 39-76. New Brunswick, N.J.: Rutgers-The State University, Center for Urban Policy Research, 1975.

This paper presents basic demographic and economic data concerning metropolitan and regional growth and migration patterns in the early 1970's. Certain significant trends are analyzed: nonmetropolitan areas are growing faster than metropolitan areas; a number of large metropolitan areas have had absolute population declines; substantial economic activity and wealth appear to be flowing out of the Northeast; the South is expanding industrially at the expense of other regions; and blacks appear to be reversing their traditional migration pattern from south to north.

352 Barker, Roger G., and Schoggen, Phil. QUALITIES OF COMMUNITY LIFE. San Francisco: Jossey-Bass, 1973. 562 p.

This is an empirical comparison of an American and an English town. Only the public (nonfamily) settings of the towns were studied. The first part of the book is a brief explanation of the methodology used and the research problems addressed. The rest of the book is devoted to presenting and comparing the data on the various settings in the towns and on the behaviors generated in the settings. Barker and Schoggen do not stray very far from their data; as a result the book is strong on data but weak on analysis of the meaning and implications of the data.

353 Baster, Nancy, and Wolf, Scott. LEVELS OF LIVING AND ECONOMIC GROWTH: A COMPARATIVE STUDY OF SIX COUNTRIES 1950-1965. Geneva, Switzerland: United Nations Research Institute for Social Development, 1969. 153 p.

The authors report on the relation of specific social factors to economic growth from 1950 to 1965 in Morocco, Chile, Jamaica, Mexico, Ceylon, and Malaysia. Education and health services had a special impact on economic growth. A set of hypotheses is proposed.

354 Bayer, Kurt Richard. "A Social Indicator of the Cost of Being Black." PhD. dissertation, University of Maryland, 1971. 149 p.

The author develops an overall accounting of the well-being of average black families as compared to average white families. He translates the discriminatory action against blacks into income equivalents to derive this overall accounting or social indicator. Three areas of substantial impairment are measured: public education which ill-prepares blacks for living, residential discrimination which discourages aspirations and opportunity for upward mobility, and inadequate law enforcement in ghetto areas which means high crime exposure. He concludes black well-being is substantially impaired by discrimination. The cost of discrimination as a percent of black family income ranges from thirty to fifty percent.

355 Bell, Roger A. NEEDS ASSESSMENT IN HEALTH AND HUMAN SERVICES. PROCEEDINGS OF THE LOUISVILLE NATIONAL CONFERENCE. Louisville, Ky.: University of Louisville, 1976. 372 p.

See 128.

356 Bhatt, Kiran U. WHAT CAN WE DO ABOUT URBAN TRAFFIC CONGESTION? A PRICING APPROACH. Washington, D.C.: Urban Institute, 1976. 41 p.

Bhatt discusses pricing techniques to secure a more efficient use of city streets in peak traffic situations. He covers its impact on pollution reduction, time savings public transit, urban revenues, and downtown business. He also suggests mechanisms for determining congestion prices and their impact.

357 Black, Gordon S. "Conflict in the Community: A Theory of the Effects of Community Size." AMERICAN POLITICAL SCIENCE REVIEW 68 (September 1974): 1245-61.

This is an empirical analysis of two theories of the relationship between community size and conflict. Black found such a relationship, but found that it is not a simple one. The virtues of "smallness" may be exaggerated by an underlying equating of smallness with homogeneity. Decentralization will encourage citizen participation, but it may also encourage conflict.

358 Blair, Louis H., and Schwartz, Alfred I. HOW CLEAN IS OUR CITY? A GUIDE FOR MEASURING THE EFFECTIVENESS OF SOLID WASTE COLLECTION ACTIVITIES. Washington, D.C.: Urban Institute, 1972. 67 p.

See 134.

359 Bloch, Peter B., and Anderson, Deborah. POLICEWOMEN ON PATROL: A SUMMARY. Washington, D.C.: Police Foundation, 1974. 67 p.

This is an evaluation of the District of Columbia's use of women for regular police patrol duties. The authors use measures including observation of patrol operations, citizen interviews, arrest statistics, disposition of arrests, and attitude measures. For detailed data see the volume with the methodology, tables, and measurement instruments.

360 _____. POLICEWOMEN ON PATROL: FINAL REPORT--METHODOLOGY TABLES, AND MEASUREMENT INSTRUMENTS. Washington, D.C.: Police Foundation, 1974. 258 p.

A technical description of the research on utilization of women for regular police duties in the District of Columbia. For an analytic summary of the findings, see the summary volume (359).

361   Blumenfeld, Hans. "The Urban Pattern." ANNALS OF THE AMERICAN ACADEMY OF POLITICAL AND SOCIAL SCIENCE 352 (March 1964): 74-85.

The metropolis is the result of the dual trends of rural migration to cities and city migration to suburbs. Its reason for
existence is mutual accessibility, primarily of place of residence and of work. The metropolis is unlike the city, for
the metropolis is the center of material production as well as
consumption; the metropolis is larger than the city and dispersed
further; places of work and residence are separated; residential areas are segregated by class and income in order to
assert the last evidence of status in urbanized life--financial
status; and the central area work force is service oriented
with a suburban industrial base.

As a result of these transformations, four types of land use
appeared: central business, industrial, residential, and open
areas. Blumenfeld concludes the metropolis could be arranged
into a better land use pattern through establishment of a
consolidated metropolitan government, a metropolitan authority
for public land ownership, more effective regional taxation,
and more and better housing for the poor. "Better" means
minimal commuting with maximum opportunity for doing so;
easy access to the central and fringe areas; both separation
and integration of function, neighborhood, a regional identification; and room for continuity and change. This improvement will require the public to choose between achieving a
better quality of life and making money off every piece of
property it owns.

362   Bowles, Samuel. "Schooling and Inequality from Generation to
Generation." JOURNAL OF POLITICAL ECONOMY 80 (May-June
1972, part II): 219-51.

Family background has an important direct effect on earnings,
in addition to the important indirect effect on earnings and
occupation reported in previous empirical studies. Its direct
effect on occupation is smaller. Bowles suggests on this basis
that substantial inequity of economic opportunity exists in the
United States and that schooling is a major transmitter of
economic status from one generation to the next. He develops
in his statistical analysis a model involving concepts of schooling,
income, and socioeconomic family background; an explanation
of how he operationalizes his concepts; an analysis of measurement errors; and conclusions based on the discovered correlations.

363 Brail, Richard K., and Chapin, F. Stuart, Jr. "Activity Patterns of Urban Residents." ENVIRONMENT AND BEHAVIOR 5 (June 1973): 163-90.

See 140.

364 Broady, Maurice. "The Sociology of the Urban Environment." EKISTICS 29 (March 1970): 187-90.

Broady is concerned with urban quality of life as affected by the planning of towns and cities in attempting to achieve social ideals through physical means. He sees a change in current insights which are leaning towards a concern with people as human beings, not only as shoppers, employees, and residents. Broady raises the question of how one describes, develops, or changes the social ethos of a town? There are case study references to Harlow, England.

365 Browne, Robert S. "The Constellation of Politics and Economics." REVIEW OF BLACK POLITICAL ECONOMY 2 (Fall 1971): 44-45.

Blacks have attained political power without having economic power. This is a reversal of the normal process, but their current problem is to secure increased capital investment in black neighborhoods. To date their political power has not been sufficient to achieve this end.

366 Bruvold, William H. "Belief and Behavior as Determinants of Environmental Attitudes." ENVIRONMENT AND BEHAVIOR 5 (June 1973): 202-18.

Using the results from a survey of environmental attitudes, beliefs, and behaviors, Bruvold found that there is a moderate relationship between beliefs and attitudes, and that the relationship could be strengthened by including a measure of behavior. In other words, environmental attitudes were found to be a function of two variables, information and experience; modifying beliefs will not be as effective as modifying both beliefs and experience.

367 Bryce, Herrington J.; Erber, Ernest; and Clay, Phillip. "Minorities and the Future of the Cities." In URBAN GOVERNANCE AND MINORITIES, edited by Herrington J. Bryce, pp. 3-13. New York: Praeger, 1976.

The year 1970 was a turning point in black settlement patterns. With the peaking of the struggle for civil rights in the 1960's, the impetus for social change had come to an end by 1970. Blacks began to choose their place of residence for reasons that did not differ essentially from those of whites. There are two noneconomic factors which significantly affect settlement patterns: the desire of blacks to live in areas of black population concentration and continued discriminatory housing practices. The passage of laws against discrimination in housing has increased housing opportunities for blacks somewhat and may lessen the tendency toward concentration. However, such laws are difficult to enforce. It is probable that urban blacks will continue to be concentrated in central cities for some time, but areas of the cities that they occupy will change.

368 Bunge, Mario. "What Is A Quality of Life Indicator." SOCIAL INDI-CATORS RESEARCH 2 (June 1975): 65-79.

This article defines and illustrates the concepts of indicators, social indicators, and life quality indicators. A bibliography is included.

369 Butler, Edgar W., and Kaiser, Edward J. "Prediction of Residential Movement and Spatial Allocation." URBAN AFFAIRS QUARTERLY 6 (June 1971): 477-94.

This is an ecmpirical study of residential movement. The authors found that there were two stages in the moving process: the decision to move (mobility) and the selection of a location (choice). The best predictor of mobility was the age of the head of the household, followed by family size and age of children, race, tenure at current location, and satisfaction with current housing. Twenty-eight percent moved within the same neighborhood, 57 percent moved within the metropolitan area but to a new neighborhood, and 15 percent left the metropolitan area. Choice was primarily a function of race and income.

370 Butterworth, Douglass. "Rural-Urban Migration and Microdemography: A Case Study from Mexico." URBAN ANTHROPOLOGY 4 (Fall 1975): 265-83.

Age data from the Mexican national censuses show that the community of Tilantongo, Oaxaca has a high fertility ratio, relatively large cohorts in the young adult ages, and a balanced sex ratio, which might suggest a growing population. Yet, after examing vital data and data from previous censuses, it is obvious that the community has been experiencing an intense out migration. A special census conducted by the author provides some leads about the selectivity of the migration patterns which resulted in the observed age-sex structure.

371 Cebula, Richard J., and Vedder, Richard K. "A Note on Migration, Economic Opportunity, and Quality of Life." JOURNAL OF REGIONAL SCIENCE 13 (August 1973): 205-11.

This is an empirical study of thirty-nine SMSA's to determine why people migrate. It was hypothesized that migration is an investment decision, that is, people move if there are positive net benefits over time as a result. The authors found a strong relationship between net migration and economic growth in the same period. They conclude on the basis of their analysis of economic, social, and environmental factors that migrants are interested in explicit economic considerations and implicit environmental considerations.

372 Chapin, F. Stuart, Jr. "Free Time Activities and Quality of Urban Life." JOURNAL OF THE AMERICAN INSTITUTE OF PLANNERS 37 (November 1971): 411-17.

This is an empirical study of the use of time allocation as an indicator of the quality of life. On the basis of a comparison of an activity survey for Washington, D.C., and an activity survey for entire nation, Chapin suggests that the amount and the variety of discretionary time are indicators of the quality of life.

373 "City Hall's Approaching Revolution in Service Delivery." NATION'S CITIES 10 (January 1972): 9-40.

This special report summarizes a federally sponsored, six-city study of the development and implementation of an integrated municipal information system. The six cities discussed are Charlotte, North Carolina; Dayton, Ohio; Long Beach, Calif.; Reading, Pennsylvania; St. Paul, Minn.; and Wichita Falls, Texas. The six cities are researching the various ways an integrated approach to the development of information systems can be used to support the operation of municipal governments. The summary discusses the research efforts, the concepts used, and the past experiences of local officials.

374 Cobb, James C. "Urbanization and the Changing South: A Review of Literature." In SOUTH ATLANTIC URBAN STUDIES 1, edited by Jack R. Censer, N. Steven Steinhert, and Amy M. McCandless, pp. 253-66. Columbia: University of South Carolina Press, 1977.

Most scholars have felt that the South's peculiar social and political traditions would face a serious challenge as urbanization and industrialization weakened old thought and behavior patterns. Several recent studies have verified this presumption. In his famous essay, Louis Wirth argued that an urban environment could remake or alter human behavior. Scholars who utilized the New Deal model expected urbanization to play a central role in making the region's politics more rational and interest oriented. While the evidence does not show a total loss of old customs and traditions, urban growth is definitely decreasing the South's distinctiveness.

375 Coleman, James S.; Kelly, Sara D.; and Moore, John A. TRENDS IN SCHOOL SEGREGATION, 1968-73. Washington, D.C.: Urban Institute, 1975. 133 p.

> By studying the changes in the degree of segregation and inter-racial contact in various urban conditions and relationships, this report provides reasons for the phenomenon of resegregation of education.

376 Colley, Donald G. "A Social Change Index--An Objective Means to Discern and Measure the Relative Current Social Condition of Cities, Towns, and Their Sub-Communities." SOCIAL INDICATORS RESEARCH 2 (June 1975): 91-118.

> This article develops a social change index derived from a combination of social indicators which are reported by the state of Rhode Island census taken on an annual basis. It is intended as a means to identify social needs and problem areas and may also be used for priority ranking of need, and for program monitoring and evaluation. The article includes a bibliography.

377 Collins, John N., and Downes, Byran T. "The Effects of Size on the Provision of Public Services: The Case of Solid Waste Collection in Smaller Citiers." URBAN AFFAIRS QUARTERLY 21 (March 1977): 333-48.

> This study analyzes two main questions: first, the cost advantage of cooperating with neighboring communities in order to increase the scale of garbage collection operations; and second, the cost effects of providing this service through a municipally operated system rather than a private one. St. Louis County is the study site.

378 Connolly, Harold X. "Black Movement into the Suburbs: Suburbs Doubling Their Black Population during the 1960's." URBAN AFFAIRS QUARTERLY 9 (September 1973): 91-111.

> This is an empirical study of the statistical evidence that black people are moving to the suburbs in increasing numbers. Connolly found that most of the increase was due to the expansion of the ghetto to contiguous areas and to the expansion of already existing black suburban areas. The blacks who moved to the suburbs were more like suburban whites than central-city blacks: they were middle-class homeowners who held white-collar jobs and had a high educational level.

379 Dawson, Grace. NO LITTLE PLANS: FAIRFAX COUNTY'S PLUS PROGRAM FOR MANAGING GROWTH. Washington, D.C.: Urban Institute, 1977. 168 p.

Fairfax County, Virginia's PLUS program was a major growth management effort. The Planning and Land Use System was an eighteen-month program aimed at revamping land use control in a large and rapidly growing suburb of Washington, D.C. This summary is for citizens, decision makers, and local government staff involved in planning and land use control. It explains what Fairfax County achieved with its $1.5 million program; what Fairfax County's experience can tell other local governments about what to do; and what not to do in future growth management programs.

380   De Abuquerque, Klaus; Mader, Paul D.; and Stinner, William F. "Modernization, Delayed Marriage and Fertility in Puerto Rico: 1950 to 1970." SOCIAL AND ECONOMIC STUDIES 25 (March 1976): 55-65.

This study finds that no necessary relationship exists between modernization, including urbanization, and delayed marriage. It also finds a much less effective intervening role for delayed marriage between modernization and lowered fertility. When a significant relationship exists as between female education and delayed marriage in Puerto Rico in 1970, the relationship deviates from expectations. The author thus found no direct effect of urbanization on fertility in any of the time periods. The authors felt that this was due to the ruralization of the cities and the development of subsistence urbanization. They used the data from the U.S. Censuses of Puerto Rico for 1950, 1960, and 1970 on fourteen subnation units (municipios), with multivariate regression analysis as the primary technique.

381   de Graft-Johnson, K.T. "Some Economic and Social Indicators to Measure Development in West Africa." INTERNATIONAL SOCIAL SCIENCE JOURNAL 27, no. 1 (1975): 78-86.

De Graft reviews various definitions of developments and points out deficiencies particularly with use in West Africa. He reviews areas where there is available data and then explains the selection of "social indicators" for West Africa. He also reviews economic indicators and their relationship to development, that is, their use as measures of development.

382   de Leeuw, Frank; and Struyk, Raymond J.; with Schnare, Ann B.; Oxanne, Larry; and Marshall, Sue A. THE WEB OF URBAN HOUSING. Washington, D.C.: Urban Institute, 1975. 231 p.

The authors present a model of a miniature housing market applied to six metropolitan areas--Durham, North Carolina; Austin, Texas; Portland, Oregon; Pittsburgh; Washington, D.C.; and Chicago. The model predicted the implications of various housing policies for low and middle income people. Surprisingly, the same policy had different results in different metropolitan areas.

383   de Torres, Juan. "The West: Footloose, But Not All Fancy-Free."
ACROSS THE BOARD 14 (June 1977): 26-33.

> This is an essay in U.S. economic geography. In treating the
> West, the author has divided his analysis into three areas: the
> Northwest, the central West and the Southwest. Part of the
> comparative analysis rests on the reliance, or lack of reliance,
> on the natural resource base of the three areas. In the South-
> west, however, a clear development toward reliance on human
> resources is evident. The article provides interesting insight
> into the clear differences in living patterns between East and
> West.

384   Dorfman, Robert, and Dorfman, Nancy S., eds. ECONOMICS OF THE
ENVIRONMENT: SELECTED READINGS. New York: W.W. Norton
and Co., 1972. 426 p.

> A series of twenty-six articles concerned with the economic
> aspects of current environmental problems is presented. The
> volume provides a detailed analysis via contributions by twenty-
> six authors representing various fields and assessments of the
> current state of the economy and environment and suggested
> changes. It also outlines, in economic terms, divisions relating
> to the environment and how they interrelate. Included are
> various types of pollution, social costs, waste disposal, and
> many others.

385   Doty, Robert W., and Peterson, John E. "The Federal Securities Laws
and Transactions in Municipal Securities." NORTHWESTERN UNIVERSITY
LAW REVIEW 71 (July-August 1976): 283-412.

> State and local governments have increasingly turned to borrowing
> as a financial tool. The municipal securities market is charac-
> terized by a large number of issues, including many of small
> size. The credit-risk record of municipal bonds has been superior
> to that of corporate securities. Federal antifraud provisions
> apply to municipal securities transactions, although, histori-
> cally, there have been few defaults and consequently little
> concern for disclosure. But since the difficulties of New York
> City, New York State, and a few other bond issuers have
> become public knowledge, disclosure has ceased to be a
> luxury. There are some differences, of course, but many
> principles developed under the securities laws for corporate
> securities serve as valuable precedents for protecting investors
> in municipal securities.

386   Duncan, Beverly. FAMILY FACTORS AND SCHOOL DROPOUT: 1920-
1960. Final Report, Cooperative Research Project No. 2258. U.S.
Office of Education. Ann Arbor: University of Michigan, 1965. 47 p.

> The author examines the effect of time period, geographic

area, and family background on male schooling. Factors examined in schooling itself included entry age into schooling, age-grade retardation, age upon leaving school, age upon re-entry, and the final point--the ultimate educational attainment.

The immediate family context accounted for about 30 percent of the variance in school years completed. Individual abilities confused the effect of a family background. Classification of families by the region of the country and by rural-urban status of their place of residence revealed only about a 2 percent effect on the educational level attained. Finally, there is a clear upward trend in educational attainment levels for successive cohorts of teenage males since the turn of the century.

387   _____. "Trends in Output and Distribution of Schooling." In INDI-CATORS OF SOCIAL CHANGE: CONCEPTS AND MEASURES, edited by Eleanor B. Sheldon and Wilbert E. Moore, pp. 601-72. New York: Russell Sage Foundation, 1968.

This essay explains the quantification of how available schooling is distributed among members of society. It concentrates on identifying a few basic data sets that bear on twentieth-century trends in the output and distribution of schooling in America. Almost all of this type of information is collected by the U.S. Bureau of the Census. Significantly, the bureau has pioneered the use of the demographer's concept of cohort; information collected for a group of people who have in common the timing of an event defining their membership, such as birth in a common year.

388   Duncan, Beverly, and Duncan, Otis D. "Minorities and the Process of Stratification." AMERICAN SOCIOLOGICAL REVIEW 33 (June 1968): 356-65.

This paper discusses the rate of upward social mobility of ethnic minorities. Using data from a 1962 sample of native American non-Negro males, age twenty-five to sixty-four whose family head had a nonfarm occupation when the respondent was sixteen, the authors look at the influence of social and national origin on educational and occupational achievement. Social origin is measured by the number of school years completed by the family head and the status of the family head's job. Achievement of the respondent is measured by the number of school years he has completed and the status of his job.

The data shows that the education and occupational achievement of family heads is more important than national origin in explaining the difference among respondents with respect to education and occupational attainment.

The authors conclude that discrimination does not usually take place on ethnic grounds. This conclusion about discrimination against ethnic minorities contrasts sharply with the evidence on discrimination against black Americans.

389   Duncan, Otis D.; Schuman, Howard; and Duncan, Beverly. SOCIAL CHANGE IN A METROPOLITAN COMMUNITY. New York: Russell Sage Foundation, 1973. 126 p.

This work reports on the authors' effort in a 1971 "Replication of Baseline Studies" which had been done from 1953 through 1959 in Detroit (known as the Detroit Area Studies). An attempt was made to measure changes during the intervening period (1959 to 1971) in various areas such as marriage; women and work; rearing children; social, political, and religious participation; and racial attitudes. The authors' purpose was to demonstrate, in simplified form, the potential usefulness of the survey method and replication.

390   Duncan, Otis D., et al. METROPOLIS AND REGION. Baltimore: Resources for the Future, Johns Hopkins Press, 1960. 587 p.

This book provides a view of the American metropolis around 1950. The authors use an ecological approach to study the metropolis relying on disciplines such as economics, geography, and sociology.

The first part of the book looks at the nature of the metropolis and suggests criteria for the metropolis and analyzes problems using the criteria. Part 2 studies the metropolis-region relationship and notes the varying kinds of metropolitan dominance over regions in manufacturing and agriculture. The third section explains how the material in part 4 was compiled and also summarizes the conclusions of the study. Industrial profiles of the Standard Metropolitan Areas and regional relationships are explained. A single classification of Standard Metropolitan Areas is developed. Part 4 consists of individual Standard Metropolitan Area studies of fifty major cities which support the conclusions of the study.

391   Dunn, Edgar S., Jr. ECONOMIC AND SOCIAL DEVELOPMENT: A PROCESS OF SOCIAL LEARNING. Baltimore: Johns Hopkins Press, 1971. 327 p.

Dunn examines current approaches to prediction and planning based mainly on growth and development. He presents highly theoretical ideas based on the theory that evolution is the cause of social learning. Dunn examines the process of biological and sociological evolution and how this same type of system functions as the development system we experience. The inference is that close examination of the evolutionary process will yield the basis for predictions.

392 Edmonston, Barry. POPULATION DISTRIBUTION IN AMERICAN CITIES.
Lexington, Mass.: Lexington Books, 1975. 156 p.

This is an analysis of a model of population concentration
in major metropolitan areas. Using a negative exponential
function of the population density gradient, Edmonston studies
the procedures for measuring population concentration, describes
urban population concentration both historically and comparatively,
and analyzes the causes of urban population concentration.
Given data for the population, land area, and degrees of land
excluded from a hypothetical circular city as well as for both
the central city and the suburbs, Edmonston found he could
adequately estimate the negative exponential function for any
city.

393 Edwards, John D. "Community Growth and the Land Development Process: An Hypothesis." CONTACT 9 (Summer 1977): 55-72.

Edwards examines the economic, employment, and population
factors which influence the rate of growth in metropolitan
areas. To maintain a high rate of growth, a community must
engage in major housing production, which in turn influences
land investment practices. Rapid growth is the primary influence
on land development trends. Rapid growth encourages specialization in land development because demand is sufficient to
support it, but high demand encourages speculative building
for a mass market.

394 Eggleston, Ann. "Economic Indicators: Purchasing's Perspectives on
Tracking the Economy." PURCHASING 78 (4 March 1975): 44-51.

This article deals with the present state of the economy along
with various "subarticles" on the state of specific parts of the
economy and how changes will affect it. It provides an example
of how economic indicators have become useful. Eggleston
discusses inventory, sales ratios, auto sales, housing starts,
interest rates and business expansion, and so forth.

395 Eklund, Kent E. "A Social Access Explanation for Community Land-Use
Evaluations." LAND ECONOMICS 53 (February 1977): 78-96.

Developing community land use controls generates two sets of
evaluative criteria: social composition of community and tax
base consideration. The first reflects the importance of specific social networks such as church, school, and play groups for
younger children. The second involves the problem of insuffi-
cient tax revenues for meeting municipal costs. A partial solution is a supplement in the form of land uses which generate
revenues, such as commercial and industrial developments.
Where multiple dwellings predominate, tax base stability can
be enhanced by restricting the number of bedrooms of each unit,

which prevents an increase in educational burdens and other
density factors such as solid waste control.

396   Elazar, Daniel J. "Variations in State-Local Relations." In his AMERI-
      CAN FEDERALISM: A VIEW FROM THE STATES, pp. 180-86. New
      York: Thomas Y. Crowell Co., 1966.

      Seven variables affecting state-local government relationships
      are identified: (1) political culture, (2) general culture, (3)
      sectionalism, (4) urban-rural areas, (5) metropolitan-nonmetro-
      politan areas, (6) localism, and (7) intermetropolitan areas.
      These variables are then applied to the fifty states.

397   Elgin, Duane; Thomas, Tom; Logothetti, Tom; and Cox, Sue. CITY
      SIZE AND THE QUALITY OF LIFE: AN ANALYSIS OF THE POLICY
      IMPLICATIONS OF CONTINUED POPULATION CONCENTRATION.
      Washington, D.C.: U.S. National Science Foundation, 1974. 142 p.

      This is a collection of seven papers which review the research
      on the relationship between city size and quality of life. The
      papers find that, for many people, city size is inversely corre-
      lated with quality of life (as measured by noneconomic dimensions).
      Although people have freedom of movement, economic forces
      which press for agglomeration constrain the ability of people
      to act on that freedom. Thus while there may be popular
      support for policies of population redistribution, such policies
      to be successful, must take into account the economic forces.

398   Farley, Reynolds. "The Changing Distribution of Negroes Within Metro-
      politan Areas: The Emergence of Black Suburbs." AMERICAN JOURNAL
      OF SOCIOLOGY 75 (January 1970): 512-29.

      In this paper, Farley argues that central cities and suburbs
      are becoming increasingly dissimilar in social composition and
      that the out-migration of blacks from the central city will not
      change this process. Until 1960, central city blacks had pro-
      portionally more prestigious jobs and more education than blacks
      in the suburbs: Farley claims that suburbs are now attracting
      higher status young black families. Three types of suburbs
      are experiencing growth of the black population: older, denser
      suburbs with employment centers; new suburban developments;
      and the suburban ring of larger cities.

399   Fava, Sylvia F. "Beyond Suburbia." ANNALS OF THE AMERICAN
      ACADEMY OF POLITICAL AND SOCIAL SCIENCE 422 (February 1975):
      10-24.

      Fava predicts that in the near future the majority of Americans
      will be suburbanites. She discusses the implications of this
      trend.

400 Feldman, Kerry D. "Demographic Indices of the Squatter Problem in Davao City, Philippines." URBAN ANTHROPOLOGY 4 (Winter 1975): 365-86.

> The phenomenon of urban squatting has diverse cross-cultural dimensions. This study looks at families who live in squatter suburbs rather than in inner-city housing. The men are wage-earners rather than peddlers. Families do have potential to become self-supporting. High fertility behavior is a constant for all squatters and the birthrate in Davao City is predicted to rise as the marriage age is decreasing. The number of mis-carriages and deceased children per mother is also declining.

401 Ferriss, Abbott L. INDICATORS OF CHANGE IN THE AMERICAN FAMILY. New York: Russell Sage Foundation, 1970. 145 p.

> Ferriss uses time-series data or measurement of factor(s) over a period of many years and plots this data on graphs and puts it into tables. The methodology pertains specifically to statis-tical data on critical trends in the family within acknowledged constraints of available information and information which re-veals significant trends. Ferriss uses data from all over the United States and builds his time series with this information and to illustrate the need for and the utility of analyzing changes via times series. Some of the family trends covered are marriage rate, divorce rate, family size, fertility rate, illegitimate birthrate, income, and poverty. The book includes a multitude of graphs, figures, and tables on these subjects.

402 _____. INDICATORS OF TRENDS IN AMERICAN EDUCATION. New York: Russell Sage Foundation, 1969. 454 p.

> Using data from the U.S. Bureau of the Census and U.S. Office of Education, Ferriss develops statistical time series of educational trends. He provides data and analysis on enrollment, teachers, quality of education, graduates, trends in educational organi-zation and finance, and educational attainment. Ferriss ana-lyzes thirteen of the twenty-five goals and objectives proposed for education by the 1960 President's Commission on National Goals.

403 _____. INDICATORS OF TRENDS IN THE STATUS OF AMERICAN WOMEN. New York: Russell Sage Foundation, 1971. 451 p.

> Building on the framework presented in the Foundation's first volume--INDICATORS OF SOCIAL CHANGE (1968)--Abbott Ferriss has collected, analyzed and assessed data on particular subject matter bearing on social trends. Focusing on the changing status of women in the United States, he asks whether changes in the objective status of women might account for the rise of protest movements and related feminist endeavors.

The vast array of trend data presented covers a variety of life situations in which women are involved: education, marital status and fertility, labor force status, employment and income, health, and recreation. On these data alone, he finds little cause for the reemergence of feminists' activities and refers to other plausible hypotheses.

404   Fischer, Claude S. "The City and Political Psychology." AMERICAN POLITICAL SCIENCE REVIEW 69 (June 1975): 559-71.

This is a study of the effects of urban life on the psychology of political involvement. Previous research suggested that the rate of participation is higher in larger communities, although there has been some conflicting evidence. Fischer found that the urban context is not a very important determinant of political involvement. There was some evidence of a weak relationship between urbanism and political behavior. While there is a slight relationship between urbanism and involvement, the mobilization is on the national level rather than the local level; further, very large cities may generate a sense of inefficacy.

405   Flax, Michael. BLACKS AND WHITES: AN EXPERIMENT IN RACIAL INDICATORS. Washington, D.C.: Urban Institute, 1971. 79 p.

Flax selects sixteen socioeconomic indicators including income, education, health, housing, family conditions, and employment. He compares the relative rates of change during the 1960's by whites and blacks, and summarizes the gaps and trends in terms of these indicators.

406   _____. A STUDY IN COMPARATIVE URBAN INDICATORS: CONDI-TIONS IN 18 LARGE METROPOLITAN AREAS. Washington, D.C.: Urban Institute, 1972. 144 p.

Flax analyzes eighteen metropolitan areas--New York City, Los Angeles-Long Beach, Chicago, Philadelphia, Detroit, San Francisco-Oakland, Washington, D.C., Boston, Pittsburgh, St. Louis, Baltimore, Cleveland, Houston, Minneapolis-St. Paul, Dallas, Milwaukee, Cincinnati, and Buffalo--in terms of fourteen indicators of quality of urban life. The indicators are: poverty, income, health, mental health, community concern, educational attainment, citizen participation, social disintegration, air quality, unemployment, housing, public order, racial equality, and transportation. He also analyzes fire protection indicators in the central cities and in the suburbs, viewing each separately to provide a basis for comparison.

407 Foner, N. "Women, Work, and Migration: Jamaicans in London."
URBAN ANTHROPOLOGY 4 (Fall 1975): 229-49.

This article examines the changed status of female Jamaican
migrants in London, focusing on two new aspects of their
lives; the superior wage-earning opportunities in the city
and the separation from kin and close relatives. These changes
have improved the lives of these women, but their effects are
not entirely positive. The ability to earn a decent salary
appears to strengthen their claims to power and respect in
relationship to their husbands and gives them the feeling that
they are more independent in England than in Jamaica. The
absence of kin tends to enhance women's power in the home,
but adds to the burden of child rearing. The concluding
section delves into the implications of this study for the
analysis of urban migrant women generally.

408 Friedly, Phillip H. "Welfare Indicators for Public Facility Investments
in Urban Renewal Areas." SOCIO-ECONOMIC PLANNING SCIENCE
3 (Summer 1969): 271-314.

See 293.

409 Gans, Herbert J. PEOPLE AND PLANS: ESSAYS AND SOLUTIONS
ON URBAN PROBLEMS. New York: Basic Books, 1968. 395 p.

This collection of essays includes a number of previously pub-
lished selections including: "Urbanism and Suburbanism as
Ways of Life," "Planning and Social Life," and "The Balanced
Community." In addition there are four previously unpublished
pieces on suburbs: "The Suburban Community and Its Way of
Life," "Planning for the Everyday Life and Problems of Sub-
urban and New Town Residents," "Suburbia Reclaimed," and
"The Disenchanted Suburbanite."

410 Garn, Harvey A.; Tevis, Nancy L.; and Snead, Carl E. EVALUATING
COMMUNITY DEVELOPMENT CORPORATIONS. Washington, D.C.:
Urban Institute, 1976. 148 p.

This is a case study of three community development corporations (CDC)--the Bedford-Stuyvesant Restoration Corporation in
Brooklyn, the Woodlawn CDC in Chicago, and the Zion
Investment Associates in Philadelphia. The authors and the
CDC managers jointly developed goals which were identifiable
and quantifiable and the performance record of the CDC's is
evaluated in light of these goals. Some of the goals were
to increase the number of housing units rehabilitated and
number of trainees finding employment after completing their
training programs. The three case studies highlight the advantages and disadvantages of the CDCs.

411 Garn, Harvey A., and Wilson, Robert H. A CRITICAL LOOK AT
     URBAN DYNAMICS. Washington, D.C.: Urban Institute, 1970.
     38 p.

> The authors provide a critical analysis of some of the assump-
> tions of Jay Forrester's book, URBAN DYNAMICS (Cambridge,
> Mass.: MIT Press, 1969), in light of new developments.
> They question whether important aspects of urban structure
> have been adequately treated. They also express doubt re-
> garding Forrester's conclusions on housing and subsidy programs
> and on the effectiveness of urban job training.

412 Gerbner, G. "Cultural Indicators: The Case of Violence in Television
     Drama." ANNALS OF THE AMERICAN ACADEMY OF POLITICAL
     AND SOCIAL SCIENCE 388 (March 1970): 69-81.

> There has been a cultural transformation due to the revolu-
> tionized the message-production system. The messages reflect
> the structure and functions of the institutions that transmit
> them. These messages impose their own forms of collective
> consciousness upon other social relationships. The consequences
> for the quality of life, for the humanness of society, and for
> government are far-reaching. Informed policymaking and valid
> interpretation of social behavior require systematic indicators
> of the prevailing climate of the changing symbolic environ-
> ment. A central aspect of cultural indicators would be the
> periodic analysis trends in the structure of message systems
> producing conceptions of life relevant to socialization and
> public policy. Findings of studies of violence on network TV
> illustrate the terms of such analyses and demonstrate the need
> for more comprehensive, cumulative, and comparative informa-
> tion on mass cultural trends and patterns.

413 Gertler, Leonard O., and Crowley, Ronald W. CHANGING CANADIAN
     CITIES: THE NEXT 25 YEARS. Toronto: McClelland and Stewart, 1977.
     474 p.

> Analyzing Canada's dramatic urban growth reveals a pattern
> which reflects the historical forces that have shaped Canada's
> destiny: the ties to powerful neighbors and partners, the
> evolution of the Canadian economy, and the various economic
> forces and technologies that have fostered urbanization. The
> Canadian urban scene is extremely diverse--the cities are often
> widely different, not only physically but also socially and
> economically. The future of urban Canada will be determined
> by a number of interacting forces: the historical institutional
> framework, the impact of external forces, and the internal
> interaction of forces that comes into play every time a public
> or private decision is made.

414 Gibson, J.E. DESIGNING THE NEW CITY: A SYSTEMIC APPROACH.
New York: John Wiley and Sons, 1977. 28 p.

Gibson applies systematic, nonmathematical methodology to
the problem of urban revitalization. Eight alternative solutions
to this problem are posed: (1) eliminate the cities, (2) avoid
the problem through legal measures which would change the
attitudes and behavior patterns of all citizens, (3) maintain
the status quo, (4) revitalize at the household or neighborhood
level, (5) promote controlled but rapid growth in selected towns,
(6) develop new towns within dense urban areas, (7) develop
satellite communities around urban areas, and (8) design and
build freestanding new cities (FSNCs). Three factors are of
primary importance in analyzing FSNCs: optimum city size,
urban form, and site location. FSNC planning would of
course include the three traditional planning components:
physical, economic, and social.

415 Glaser, Daniel. "National Goals and Indicators for the Reduction of
Crime and Delinquency." ANNALS OF THE AMERICAN ACADEMY OF
POLITICAL AND SOCIAL SCIENCE 371 (May 1967): 104-26.

Glaser provides a definition of crime and describes four different
types. He presents some historical background and present con-
notations. Glaser reviews past efforts to tabulate crime and
to identify trends and establish and assess indicators. He gives
possible explanations for shifts in crime rates and points out
difficulties involved in the absolute determinations based on
raw statistics. He also pursues the problem of unreported
crime and methods to be used to correct it and thus make
better indicators. In addition, Glaser pursues the effect of
judicial and correctional decisions on recidivism and crime
rate as well as the interrelationship between various elements
of government involved with crime.

416 Glenn, Norval D. "Massification Versus Differentiation: Some Trend
Data From National Surveys." SOCIAL FORCES 46 (December 1967):
172-80.

This is a study to see if the common assertion that homogenity
and massification are taking place among different segments of
American society can be supported by empirical evidence.
First, Glenn attempts to assess trends by looking at differences
in ages in different categories of responses to national survey
questions. Second, he uses available trend study data.

The data indicate that differences between South and non-
South, low education-high education, manual-nonmanual,
white-nonwhite, and Protestant-Catholic have probably increased
rather than decreased. Differences between male-female and
urban-rural seem to have diminished moderately but "the rural-
urban convergence that almost all observers claim to perceive
is real but not as marked as many people believe."

417   Goeke, Joseph R. "Some Neglected Social Indicators." SOCIAL INDI-
CATORS RESEARCH 1 (May 1974): 85–105.

Goeke feels that social indicators have been good predictors
of social change and its direction. Specifically discussed are
public opinion indicators, political indicators, and demographic
indicators. The author cites several examples of use of social
indicators that were erroneous and duplicate other work in the
field. Goeke concludes with a call for a "clearinghouse" to
monitor and evaluate social indicator research. His rationale
is that this system would prevent resource waste, duplication
and neglect of existing information.

418   Goldfield, David R. "A Reply to Professors Zikmund and Hadden."
URBAN AFFAIRS QUARTERLY 12 (September 1976): 112–16.

Goldfield attempts to predict the limits of suburban growth
with a case study of the Washington, D.C., metropolitan area.
He analyzes four related growth factors--fertility and family
formation trends, housing, transportation, and central city
rehabilitation. In their comments, Zikmund and Hadden cast
doubt on the strength and direction of the trends as interpreted
by Goldfield and caution against generalizing the experience
of the Washington area to the national scene. Goldfield
responds that Washington's atypicality makes it a prototype of
a new national trend in the revitalization of central cities
and retrenchment of suburban areas.

419   Goode, R. Ray. "Dade County Moratorium Strategy." PUBLIC MANAGE-
MENT 56 (May 1974): 24–25.

In the 1970's, Dade County, Florida, began to reassess its
policy of support for uncontrolled growth. Of particular concern were protection of the natural environment and provision
of adequate municipal services. County-wide zoning, a professional planning department, an adopted land use master
plan, subdivision regulations, and other planning tools were
not adequate to control the pace of development. Moratoriums
were introduced to halt water and sewer expansion, new
building starts, and zoning changes. Legal decisions have
supported the constitutionality of the moratorium procedure,
and community acceptance has been widespread. However,
there has been criticism from affected property owners and
developers, and a substantial increase in staff workloads.

420   Gottmann, Jean. "The Evolution of Urban Centrality." EKISTICS 39
(April 1975): 220–28.

Gottmann presents a discussion of the concept of centrality:
a multiplicity of central functions gathered in one urban place
that rests on one or several transportation networks that con-

verge on that place. Gottmann claims that there is a new
centrality emerging, one of movement and complementariness
between distant places.

421 Greer, Scott A.; McElrath, Dennis; Minar, David; and Orleans, Peter.
THE NEW URBANIZATION. New York: St. Martin's Press 1962. 384 p.

> The authors assert that two new types of urbanization are oc-
> curring which are distinct from the past industrial urbanization
> of Europe and the United States. One occurs in the new
> cities of new nations; the other in the mature cities of the
> United States and Europe. These new urban processes create
> fresh demands, hierarchies, ecologies of settlement, and resource
> distributions, thus transforming society.

> New cities in developing nations do not have a strong economic
> base, a supportive hinterland, organizational power, or social
> and family links which characterize the older urbanization.

> New urbanization in older industrial nations is distinguished
> by expansion of the urban population, the development of the
> horizontal city, and development of a different life-style.

> Articles selected substantiate this assertion and include com-
> parative urbanism to discover propositions about urban differen-
> tiation, political integration and urbanism, spatial patterns
> and economic activities in cities based on von Thunen, a
> truer and more objective version of the social reality of urbani-
> zation and suburbanization, urban-suburban psychological
> differences, various local community types among different
> population types, community power, educational policy develop-
> ment, political integration, urban politics and nonpartisanism,
> decision making, political disorganization of metropolitan areas,
> political economies, and citizenship and consumership in metro-
> politan areas.

422 Guest, Avery M. "Population Suburbanization in American Metropolitan
Areas, 1940-1970." GEOGRAPHICAL ANALYSIS 7 (July 1975): 267-83.

> This is an empirical study of the changes in American metro-
> politan areas since 1950. Guest found that the process of
> suburbanization has led to general deconcentration in metro-
> politan areas (including central cities), so that in many of
> these areas there is no clear distinction between the core
> city and suburbs in terms of density of other population charac-
> teristics.

423 Gurr, Ted Robert. ROGUES, REBELS AND REFORMERS: A POLITICAL
HISTORY OF URBAN CRIME AND CONFLICT. Beverly Hills, Calif.:
Sage Publications, 1976. 192 p.

> Gurr compares crime and civil strife in four cities (London,
> Stockholm, Sydney, and Calcutta) between 1800 and 1970.

He shows a general decline in crimes of theft and violence throughout most of the nineteenth century, following a crime wave that peaked about 1830. Since 1950 there has been a dramatic rise in crime. Reaction to the disorder produced by the early nineteenth-century crime wave resulted in reforms in the institutions of criminal justice. These institutions appeared to successfully contain disorder in the nineteenth century, but probably only because they coincided with societal changes that led in the same direction. Their inability to deal with the crime wave of the later twentieth century suggests that the amount of crime and civil strife in a society depends on factors beyond the justice policies, whether reformist or repressive.

424 Gurr, Ted Robert, and Ruttenburg, Charles. "A Causal Model of Civil Strife: A Comparative Analysis Using New Indices." AMERICAN POLITICAL SCIENCE REVIEW 62 (December 1968): 1104-24.

The authors use cross-sectional analyses of data collected for 114 cities to develop a model of civil strife.

425 Gustely, Richard D. "The Allocational and Distributional Impacts of Governmental Consolidation: The Dade County Experience." URBAN AFFAIRS QUARTERLY 12 (March 1977): 349-64.

The literature on governmental consolidation has generally stressed cost savings as the main justification for consolidation. However, in Dade County, Florida, expenditures actually rose after consolidation. This rise can possibly be explained by restrictions on the elimination of municipal jobs and adjustment of municipal wages to the higher levels of the metropolitan government.

426 Guttman, Joel. "Measuring the Quality of Life." DISSENT 20 (Fall 1973): 470-72.

Guttman presents a conceptual analysis of a quality-of-life index that would combine all effects into a single measure of net gain or loss. The index would be specific to the project in question, reflecting the priorities and interests of the community. While the index has its shortcomings, the author claims it is superior to the alternatives: interest-group bargaining and cost-benefit analysis.

427 Guttman, Louis. "Social Problem Indicators." ANNALS OF THE AMERICAN ACADEMY OF POLITICAL AND SOCIAL SCIENCE 393 (January 1971): 40-46.

This articles serves as a progress report on the development of a theory for and research on social problem indicators in Israel with particular emphasis on the so-called "mapping sentence" approach for determining proper observations. The approach was designed and actually used in Israel and a portion is devoted to historical background. The article contains a "mapping sentences" table. The author explains results thus far as well as hoped-for future uses.

428 Hadden, Jeffrey K. "Use of Ad Hoc Definitions." In SOCIOLOGICAL METHODOLOGY, edited by Edgar F. Borgatta, pp. 276-85. San Francisco: Jossey-Bass, 1968.

Hadden presents a critical examination of the concept of "suburb." He illustrates the difficulties with various U.S. Bureau of the Census definitions and their implications for alternative research strategies. The author suggests that "suburbia" can rest within the political boundaries of the central city and that not all places outside those political boundaries ought to be considered suburban.

429 Hadden, Jeffery K., and Borgatta, Edgar F., eds. AMERICAN CITIES: THEIR SOCIAL CHARACTERISTICS. Chicago: Rand McNally, 1965. 193 p.

The objective of this study is to promote an alternate method of classifying cities and to provide a source book of urban data. The method of classifying cities is based on factor analysis. The main research involved eight parallel factor analytic studies of 1960 census data for cities. The study involves all cities in the United States with twenty-five thousand or greater population evaluated on sixty-five variables.

The analysis is done separately for each city and for the following groups: central cities, suburbs, and independent cities.

430 Hamilton, Edward K. "Productivity: The New York City Approach." PUBLIC ADMINISTRATION REVIEW 32 (November-December 1972): 784-95.

The New York City productivity program was designed to maintain and improve the quality of service to citizens at a time when the work force was being reduced. Public reports are issued quarterly to inform public officials and citizens of what types and quality of service is being provided. Several obstacles to implementing a productivity program are discussed and the evolution of New York's program from 1965 to 1972 is recounted. New York set four major goals in their productivity program--reducing unit costs, improving the deployment of resources, improving government organization processing and procedures, and technological innovations. Within each major goal area programs are outlined such as rat control,

park cleaning, sanitation vehicle maintenance, fire response,
police dispatch, sanitation deployment, capital construction,
and computer use. While problems still need to be resolved,
the public has come to expect a periodic, detailed statement
of the output and input factors in service delivery.

431 Hanushek, Eric A. EDUCATION AND RACE: AN ANALYSIS OF THE
EDUCATIONAL PRODUCTION PROCESS. Lexington, Mass.: D.C.
Health and Co., 1972. 162 p.

The central concern of this book is the education of minorities
in the United States--past, present, and future. Quantitative
analysis using statistical modes is employed to study existing
schools and to compare educational possibilities facing school
systems. Sample analyses are made of urban schools in the
Great Lakes and the Northeast.

432 Harrison, Bennett. URBAN ECONOMIC DEVELOPMENT: SUBURBANI-
ZATION, MINORITY OPPORTUNITY, AND THE CONDITION OF THE
CENTRAL CITY. Washington, D.C.: Urban Institute, 1974. 200 p.

Harrison relates the urban economic condition to national
economic cycles and concludes that central cities can reverse
or at least survive the out-migration of industry. He proposes
attention be paid to public ownership and management of
strategic central city land. He also questions the reliability
of traditional economic measures.

433 Harvey, Robert O., and Clark, W.A.V. "The Nature and Economics of
Urban Sprawl." LAND ECONOMICS 41 (February 1965): 1-9.

A general "think piece" on the topic of suburbanization and
urban sprawl. Among the topics briefly addressed are the
physical pattern, causes, and costs of sprawl.

434 Hatry, Harry P. "Issues in Productivity Measurement for Local Government." PUBLIC ADMINISTRATION REVIEW 32 (November-December 1972):
776-84.

See 645.

435 Hauser, Philip M., and Duncan, Otis Dudley, eds. "Human Ecology and
Population Studies." In their STUDY OF POPULATION: AN INVENTORY
AND APPRAISAL, pp. 678-716. Chicago: University of Chicago Press,
1969.

The volume provides an exhaustive statement on the status of
the science of demography. Parameters of human ecology are
defined and within that framework population is examined.
The book contains material of thirty different authors.

436 Hauser, Robert M., and Featherman, David L. "Trends in the Occupational Mobility of U.S. Men, 1962-1970." AMERICAN SOCIOLOGICAL REVIEW 38 (June 1973): 302-10.

> The experience of the period 1962 to 1970 demonstrates the historical tendency toward upward mobility among U.S. men, but that tendency is neither uniform nor inevitable. These changes consisted of a shift from the manual to nonmanual occupations combined with a shift from lower to higher status occupations within the manual and nonmanual groups.

437 Hawes, Mary H. "Measuring Retired Couples' Living Costs in Urban Areas." MONTHLY LABOR REVIEW 92 (November 1973): 3-16.

> This is a summary of the U.S. Bureau of Labor Statistics' report of a low, medium, and high budget for a retired couple. It includes a summary of component cost levels and how the figures were derived for thirty-nine metropolitan and four non-metropolitan areas in the United States. Indexes of comparative costs on the three levels are given as well as dollar figures.

438 Hayes, Charles R. THE DISPERSED CITY: THE CASE OF PIEDMONT, NORTH CAROLINA. Research Paper No. 173. Chicago: University of Chicago, Department of Geography, 1976. 157 p.

> The term "dispersed city" describes a group of closely spaced interdependent municipalities. The North Carolina Piedmont Dispersed City consists of Winston-Salem, Greensboro, High Point, Burlington, Asheboro, and Lexington. The author argues that this group of cities actually functions as a single urban unit. Evidence for this position includes the overlap of downtown trade areas, by cross-commuting for shopping purposes, by the number of people who live in one city and work in another, and by patterns of media consumption and wholesale distribution. The area developed as it did because of the level of transport technology during the formative stage of settlement, the rotation of manufacturing location, and the importance of the county seat to county residents.

439 Herrick, Neal Q., and Quinn, Robert P. "The Working Conditions Survey as a Source of Social Indicators." MONTHLY LABOR REVIEW 94 (April 1971): 15-24.

> Workmen's compensation in America remains inadequate. Tragically, government action in this field often occurs only after publicity surrounding major disasters. These authors feel strongly that as economic indicators are used to formulate fiscal and monetary policy, so should working conditions indicators be developed to help shape worker-related laws and programs. While considerable data has existed for years, it does not

include sufficient reflection of workers' viewpoints. Worker experience and evaluation are essential to the accurate measurement of working conditions problems, and this survey, conducted by the University of Michigan's Survey research center in late 1969, is an effort to overcome this data deficiency. Using a national probability sample of 1,533 employees, ages sixteen years or more, who worked at least twenty hours a week, the survey inquired into the extrinsic and intrinsic elements of their work and attempted to evaluate their job satisfaction based on the responses.

440 Hill, Richard C. "Separate and Unequal: Governmental Inequality in the Metropolis." AMERICAN POLITICAL SCIENCE REVIEW 68 (December 1974): 557-68.

Hill seeks to determine the factors associated with metropolitan fiscal disparities by conceptualizing the metropolis as a social stratification system. The analysis of data from the Milwaukee Standard Metropolitan Statistical Areas (SMSA) shows that (1) governmental inequality is rooted in income inequality among families in the SMSA and varies directly with residential segregation of social classes, and (2) racial discrimination and SMSA size, age, and population density are also important indicators of fiscal differentiation.

In his comment Max Nieman ("Social Stratification and Governmental Inequality." AMERICAN POLITICAL SCIENCE REVIEW 70 [March 1976]: 149-54.) contends that Hill's use of family income to measure fiscal capacity is deficient as a test of his complex social stratification model. Nieman proposes several other measures which he uses to analyze governmental inequality in thirty-nine Milwaukee suburbs and draw conclusions different from those of Hill. In his rejoinder ("The Social Stratification and Governmental Inequality Hypothesis: A Rejoinder." AMERICAN POLITICAL SCIENCE REVIEW 70 [March 1976]: 154-59.) Hill questions the validity of Nieman's measures, presents additional data to support his findings, and discourses on the normative perspectives of "public choice theorists" such as Nieman.

441 Hinday, Virginia Aldise. "Parity and Well-Being among Low-Income Urban Families." JOURNAL OF MARRIAGE AND THE FAMILY 37 (November 1975): 789-97.

The number of children (parity) has a strong negative relationship to the well-being of a poor family. Poverty is caused by factors other than parity, but the author maintains that policy should be directed at limiting the number of births to avoid further depressing socioeconomic well-being. Income level, public assistance, and number of months of maternal employment were correlated with parity. These relationships were not a function of changed welfare status, changed marital status, or recency of last birth. Additional children reduced a mother's ability to organize and run a household and limited a family's ability to save, although it showed no obvious effect on the ability to purchase durable goods.

442 Hirsch, Gary B., and Riccio, Lucius J. "Measuring and Improving the Productivity of Police Patrol." JOURNAL OF POLICE SCIENCE AND ADMINISTRATION 2 (June 1974): 169-84.

See 181.

443 Hoel, Lester A. PUBLIC TRANSPORTATION: PROBLEMS AND OPPOR-TUNITIES. Charlottesville: University of Virginia, Department of Civil Engineering, 1977. 89 p.

A collection of papers on urban transportation solutions relevent to North American cities. Designed as a general overview of public transportation issues: deficiencies in existing systems, relative use of urban transportation modes, characteristics of transit riders, the peaking problem, categories of alternatives for improvement, and options for meeting urban transportation needs.

444 Hoover, Edgar M., and Vernon, Raymond. ANATOMY OF A METROPOLIS: THE CHANGING DISTRIBUTION OF PEOPLE AND JOBS WITHIN THE NEW YORK METROPOLITAN REGION. New York: Doubleday, 1959. 338 p.

This book is one of the first--and still one of the very best--attempts to provide a total social and economic picture of a major metropolitan area in geographic perspective. Based largely on data from the 1950 census, the book remains only marginally useful as a description of the New York region today. By contrast, the general patterns and trends described are still operative both in and around New York City and other metropolitan areas. The book is important now as a model of a good metropolitan study and as a theoretical discussion of metropolitan development generally.

After delineating the areas of study and the primary subregions within, the authors focus on economic activity as a major determinant of regional growth and metropolitan geography. Changing spatial needs of various economic activities influence locational decisions which in turn affect the geographic distribution of jobs, local tax bases, and the locational needs of other economic activities. Consequently, people tend to live where they have satisfactory access to jobs, and commercial establishments follow their customers.

445 Howard, William A. "City-Sized and Its Relationship to Municipal Efficiency: Some Observations and Questions." EKISTICS 28 (November 1969): 312-15.

See 652.

446 Hughes, James W. "Dilemmas of Suburbanization and Growth Controls." ANNALS OF THE AMERICAN ACADEMY OF POLITICAL AND SOCIAL SCIENCE 422 (February 1975): 61-76.

This is a conceptual analysis of the forces and implications of widespread resettlement processes. Hughes found that a growing concern for the quality of life and for environmental protection is leading to a reconsideration of the benefits of growth. He explains why these forces are focusing on the suburbs and analyzes the control mechanisms that have been developed. He ends with a discussion of the criterion of reasonableness of growth control ordinances.

447 Isler, Morton; Sadacca, Robert; and Drury, Margaret. KEYS TO SUCCESSFUL HOUSING MANAGEMENT. Washington, D.C.: Urban Institute, 1974. 70 p.

Research has established that the type of ownership is not the major variable in the quality of housing management. In each type of multifamily housing--cooperative, nonprofit, and limited dividend projects--there are high, low, and medium performance categories. Certain variables are identified which are related to successful housing management. These variables are: maintenance of physical conditions, tenant satisfaction with services and management, and reasonable costs of maintenance. Where tenant concern and responsiveness by management are found together successful management often follows. The data are drawn from surveys and analyses of sixty multifamily projects.

448 Jackson, Kenneth T. "Urban Deconcentration in the Nineteenth Century." In THE NEW URBAN HISTORY, edited by Leo F. Schnore, pp. 110-42. Princeton, N.J.: Princeton University Press, 1975.

Jackson explores the concept of "urban deconcentration" primarily through an analysis of patterns in Philadelphia during the nineteenth century. Five definitions of deconcentration are proposed and illustrated historically: (1) proportion of people living outside the central city, (2) lowering of area-wide population densities, (3) decline in core population, (4) outward movement of higher socioeconomic status level urban residents, and (5) increasing residence-work distances. The author concludes that urban deconcentration, if not suburbanization, is certainly an urban phenomenon with long historical roots.

449 Johnson, David Richard, and Booth, Alan. "Crowding and Human Repro-
duction." MILBANK MEMORIAL FUND QUARTERLY 54 (Summer 1976):
321-37.

> The authors examined 470 urban Toronto women to determine
> the effect of neighborhood and household crowding on fertility
> and infant mortality. Crowding did not retard fertility nor
> did it influence fetal-infant survival. The authors contended
> that if crowding influences fertility, it would be best studied
> elsewhere than in North America.

450 Johnston, Denis F. "The OMB Report, SOCIAL INDICATORS, 1976."
Paper presented at the 136th annual meeting of the American Statistical
Association, 12 p.

> This is a comprehensive explanation of the format and content
> of SOCIAL INDICATORS, 1976, published by the U.S. Govern-
> ment Printing Office in 1977. SOCIAL INDICATORS, 1976
> is the second report of its kind to be prepared by the Statisti-
> cal Policy Division of the U.S. Office of Management and
> Budget and its format is similar to that of its predecessor,
> SOCIAL INDICATORS, 1973, issued in February 1974.
>
> It features graphic presentation of summary descriptive data
> on the socioeconomic characteristics of the U.S. population,
> with limited geographic detail and considerable disaggregation
> by age, sex, color, and other factors.

451 Kania, Richard R.E., and Mackey, Wade C. "Police Violence as a
Function of Community Characteristics." CRIMINOLOGY 15 (May 1977):
27-48.

> The authors examine the variation among the states in the
> rates of police use of deadly force. They find significant
> correlations between police violence and cultural attributes
> such as incidence of riots, crude birthrates, number of families
> receiving food stamps or welfare aid, homes without television,
> and the like. The strongest correlation is with a variable
> termed "public rates of violence." Where public violence is
> slight, police violence is also low. However, where the inci-
> dence of violence reveals that force is a common means of
> conflict resolution, the police will adopt its use. Thus, the
> authors hypothesize that the police use of violence is a cultur-
> ally determined characteristic, reflecting the characteristics
> of the communities served, and not a matter of individual or
> collective police pathology.

452 Karp, David A.; Stone, Gregory P.; Yoels, William C. BEING
URBAN: A SOCIAL PSYCHOLOGICAL VIEW OF CITY LIFE. Lexington,
Mass.: D.C. Heath and Co., 1977. 242 p.

This book examines what it is that actually makes a city.
For one thing, it has a large population which occupies a
relatively large space. For another, its functions extend over
a territory larger than that defined by the legal boundaries.
Economic factors are also important. Money and its exchange
for goods and services capture symbolically an important aspect
of urbanism. Moreover, a sense of community is an important
aspect of urbanism. A city consists of many small communities
in various stages of cohesion. Urban life is a well-controlled
blend of indifference and involvement.

453 Kasarda, John D. "The Structural Implications of Social System Size:
A Three-Level Analysis." AMERICAN SOCIOLOGICAL REVIEW 39
(February 1974): 19-28.

This is an empirical study of the relationship between size
and social system change, at three levels of analysis: institution, community, and society. Kasarda found that the larger
the organization the more effort is expended on communication components. Thus, larger organizations show increases in
the professional and technical component and a decreased
share to the management component. This calls into question
the presumption that larger organization size promotes economies
of scale.

454 _____. "The Theory of Ecological Expansion: An Empirical Test."
SOCIAL FORCES 51 (December 1972): 165-75.

Kasarda analyzes the relationship between population size and
organizational structure in 157 Standard Metropolitan System
Areas in order to empirically support the theory of ecological
expansion, which holds that population growth in the periphery
of a system is matched by administrative growth in the nucleus
to insure coordination of all activities.

455 Kemp, Michael A. REDUCED-FARE AND FARE-FREE URBAN TRANSIT
SERVICES: SOME CASE STUDIES. Washington, D.C.: Urban Institute,
1974. 37 p.

Kemp shows the sensitivity of mass transit ridership to fares.
He explores reduced fare and free fare programs in Rome,
Atlanta, San Diego, Boston, Cincinnati, and Stockholm. He
concludes that service improvements are more significant than
fare reductions in attracting transit users and expanding transit
revenues.

456 King, Leslie J. "Cross Sectional Analysis of Canadian Urban Dimensions:
1951 and 1961." CANADIAN GEOGRAPHER 10 (December 1966):
205-24.

King reports on the empirical findings of a study on the structure
of Canadian cities and how such findings relate to theories of
urban systems. The empirical findings were based on the comparison of data taken for 1951 and 1961. The data was generated
from "urban components" such as youthfulness of the female
population, frontier location and economic orientation, suburban occupational and housing structure, high socioeconomic
residential status, metropolitan socioeconomic structure, and
urban depression. The study demonstrates the sensitivity of
urban models, based on some of the components, to changes
in the urban structure over time.

457 King-Hele, Desmond. THE END OF THE TWENTIETH CENTURY. New
York: St. Martin's Press, 1970. 206 p.

In his chapter on the "Quality of Living," King-Hele divides
the quality into sections of pollution, systems of misgovernment, social groups, and leisure. Air pollution is a critical
problem in developed countries. The author gives a history
of pollution, a description of pollutants, and a survey of the
different types and describes the effects of pollution on plants,
animals, and humans. He then paints a very frightening
picture of city living, enumerating the enormous problems
cities face. He describes cities as "obsolete" and suggests
that further development be restricted to new towns, with no
more than one hundred thousand people. However, most
people "prefer 'bronchitis' in the city to boredom in the
country." Further, in the author's view, most governments
are out of date, and the best government would be a world
government. With regard to the family, King-Hele sees it
as continuing to decline in influence. And finally, he sees
affluent countries headed towards shorter work weeks with
machines producing more leisure time. Education for leisure
time should become an integral feature of schooling.

458 Kirby, Ronald F., and Bhatt, Kiran U. GUIDELINES ON THE OPERA-
TION OF SUBSCRIPTION BUS SERVICES. Washington, D.C.: Urban
Institute, 1975. 76 p.

The report discusses the planning and operation of subscription
bus services, which are tailored to serve urban travelers. It
presents ten detailed case studies of such services, covers
guidelines for developing riders, securing vehicles and drivers,
meeting legal requirements, and establishing routes, schedules,
and fares. It goes on to discuss the relationship of such
approaches to congestion, pollution, and energy.

459 Kirby, Ronald F.; de Leeuw, Frank; and Silverman, William; assisted
by Dawson, Grace. RESIDENTIAL ZONING AND EQUAL HOUSING
OPPORTUNITIES: A CASE STUDY IN BLACK JACK, MISSOURI. Washington, D.C.: Urban Institute, 1972. 34 p.

The authors document the differential impact of a zoning ordinance prohibiting multiunit housing on housing opportunities for blacks in metropolitan St. Louis. Findings indicate that the city of Black Jack, Missouri prohibited the construction of multiunit housing that had the support of the U.S. Department of Housing and Urban Development. The impact analysis methodology used should be transferrable to other metropolitan areas.

460   Kirby, Ronald F., et al. PARA-TRANSIT: NEGLECTED OPTIONS FOR URBAN MOBILITY. Washington, D.C.: Urban Institute, 1975. 319 p.

The authors explore the range of urban passenger systems which lie between mass transit systems and the private automobile. These paratransit systems include taxis, jitneys, and dial-a-ride services, as well as ride-sharing through car and van pools, and subscription buses. Since paratransit forms use existing roadways, their expanded use would not involve the massive expenditures required for subways.

461   Klecka, William R. "Applying Political Generations to the Study of Political Behavior: A Cohort Analysis." PUBLIC OPINION QUARTERLY 35 (Fall 1977): 358-73.

The author uses a new application of cohort analysis to determine the separate effects of "point in the life cycle" and "generational grouping" on political behavior and opinions. Four opinions were included, each sampled a number of times over a sixteen-year period. A generational effect appeared in attitudes about federal aid to education. Voter turnout was related more to one's point in the life cycle, that is, middle age or young twenties, and so forth. The issue of isolationism showed a generational effect which was supplanted by a life cycle effect over time. Party identification was not linked strongly to either life cycle or generational effects. The author concludes that neither aspect of aging--one's generation cohort group or one's position in the life cycle--is significantly linked to political behavior.

462   Kormondy, Edward J. "The Nature of Ecosystems." In SOCIETY AND ENVIRONMENT: THE COMING COLLISION, edited by Rex R. Campbell and Jerry L. Wade, pp. 40-45. Boston: Allyn and Bacon, 1972.

Kormondy's brief chapter in this book of approximately fifty chapters is devoted to a wide range of ecological, biological, and sociological factors. The purpose is to acquaint the layman with the scope of environmental problems. This chapter is devoted mainly to ecosystems. It explains briefly the various types and divisions of ecosystems and the interdependence of the systems.

463 Krendel, Ezra S. "Social Indicators and Urban Systems Dynamics." SOCIO-ECONOMIC PLANNING SCIENCES 5 (August 1971): 387-93.

See 191.

464 Kulash, Damian J. INCOME DISTRIBUTIONAL CONSEQUENCES OF ROADWAY PRICING. Washington, D.C.: Urban Institute, 1974. 32 p.

Kulash explores the costs and benefits of congestion pricing for different income groups. He uses data from Boston, San Francisco, and Washington, D.C., to predict specific impacts.

465 Lancaster County, Pa. PHASE THREE RECOMMENDATIONS: A COMPRE-HENSIVE PLAN FOR SERVICES COORDINATION. Vol. 9. Human Services Information System Project of Lancaster County: 1974. 101 p.

This report on the Human Services Information System (HSIS) Project of Lancaster County includes recommendations that cover coordination of forty-two program areas within the following major areas of agency involvement: direct services as well as service-supportive, planning, administrative, and information programs and activities. The findings and recommendations concerning each program are based on four components of the HSIS: program inventory findings of 158 agencies, systems design plans developed by HSIS teams, interviews with approximately 40 agencies, and proposed policies. All of these components are detailed in other volumes of the report. Appendixes contain planning reports required for comprehensive planning and program review, a data elements checklist, a list of HSIS project reports, and the 1974 Allied Services Act.

466 Larson, Richard C. URBAN POLICE PATROL ANALYSIS. Cambridge: MIT Press, 1972. 289 p.

This study develops a model for the allocation of urban police patrol forces. The ability of police forces to improve their use of resources through better technology is considered by many to be a major step forward in improving police-community relations. Citing fragmentation as a major problem in criminal justice agencies, the author suggests a closer working relationship between agency administrators and quantitatively trained experts. The police response system and the difficulties of processing calls for service are discussed and some of the technical suggestions for overcoming police allocation problems are presented by using a hypothetical city of two hundred thousand.

467 Lehmann, Edward J. FINANCING AND TAXATION FOR URBAN CON-TROL OF POLLUTION. Springfield, Va.: National Technical Information Service, 1977. 183 p.

Lehmann has put together an abstract bibliography on urban and regional planning that stresses means of financing pollution abatement programs and of taxing sources as a means of pollution reduction. The reports are divided into three sections: air pollution studies, solid waste disposal studies, and water pollution and sewage treatment studies.

468   Lehmann, Edward J., and Adams, Gerald H. FINANCING URBAN TRANSPORTATION. Part I: General Studies. Springfield, Va.: National Technical Information Service, 1977. 121 p.

Financing methods are presented to show the various ways in which urban transportation systems can be supported by communities, metropolitan areas, and regions. Systems such as bus lines, subways, rapid rail, and taxis are discussed as well as dial-a-ride operations and transit for the elderly. Some attention is given to urban airports, fare structures, and ridership.

469   _____. FINANCING URBAN TRANSPORTATION. Part II: Local Studies. Springfield, Va.: National Technical Information Service, 1977. 164 p.

This volume is an abstract bibliography on the financing of urban transportation in local areas. Cities covered include Atlanta, New York City, Washington, D.C., Philadelphia, Houston, Baltimore, San Francisco, Minneapolis, Milwaukee, and many smaller localities. Among the systems involved are rapid transit rail, bus, shared taxicab, dial-a-bus, dial-a-ride, and subway. Some attention is also given to metropolitan airports.

470   Leonard, Karen. "Women and Social Change in Modern India." FEMINIST STUDIES 3 (Spring-Summer 1976): 117-30.

This study of the Kaysath caste attempts to locate indicators of political and social change for women. The Kaysath are an urbanized caste. The author presents seven variables useful in measuring changes in both women's behavior and expectations: patterns of naming women; age at marriage; amount and type of education; employment outside the home, before and after marriage and motherhood; the ratio of never-married women to all women; and marriage across caste and subcaste lines.

471   Levin, Melvin R., and Rose, Jerome G. "The Suburban Land Use War: Skirmish in Washington Township, New Jersey." URBAN LAND 33 (May 1974): 14-18.

This article reports a legal battle over land use in Washington Township, N.J.--a small, single-family residential community which has virtually no commercial development, no industry, and no multifamily dwellings. The controversy began when the

owner of a small tract of land appealed the denial of a zoning
variance to construct some apartment units. The courts ordered
the township to amend its ordinance to make provision for
multiple-family and rental housing, but the township resisted.
The Urban Land Institute, appointed as an advisor to the court,
recommended that the site owned by the plaintiff be rezoned
for multiple-dwelling use, citing the need for apartment housing
by young and elderly couples. A generation of litigation is
predicted, as judicial determinations in exclusionary zoning
cases strive for socioeconomic balance between central cities
and the suburbs.

472   Levine, Arnold J. ALIENATION IN THE METROPOLIS. San Francisco:
      R and E Research Associates, 1977. 111 p.

      This is a study of alienation, put together by a team from the
      Department of Social Psychiatry of Cornell Medical College
      as part of a major mental health survey. The area studied
      was Yorkville, a section of New York City. A major finding
      of the study was that certain groups were more prone to cer-
      tain types of alienation than others: for example, those of
      Italian and Czechoslovakian ancestry have larger percentages
      in both the highly cynical and highly pessimistic groups and
      fully a third of the Lutherans were pessimistic.

473   Levy, Frank; Meltsner, Arnold J.; and Wildavsky, Aaron. URBAN OUT-
      COMES: SCHOOLS, STREETS AND LIBRARIES. Berkeley and Los Angeles:
      University of California Press, 1972. 271 p.

      This is one of a series of books to emerge from the Oakland
      Project. It examines the government's distribution of goods
      and services to local citizens. Agencies concerned with
      schools, streets, and libraries are examined to see how they
      allocate services and what makes them allocate these in a
      particular way. The authors also discuss how organizational
      decisions lead to particular outputs. School budgets are analyzed,
      as are the allocations to major traffic routes and the resources
      allocated to the central library. The final chapter examines
      the comparative analysis of outcomes by focusing on patterns
      of resource distribution, redistribution dilemmas, and ways of
      judging outcomes.

474   Ley, D.F., and Anderson, G. "The Delphi Technique in Urban Fore-
      casting." REGIONAL STUDIES 9 (November 1975): 243-49.

      Adequate urban planning requires futures research. The Delphi
      technique has been used by planners to help determine the
      physical, social, and political dimensions of urban development.
      This technique was used in Nanaimo, British Columbia where
      government, business, political, community, and professional

groups participated in developing scenarios for the years 1980
and 2000. The projections helped the various groups see their
future needs more clearly and allowed for some preliminary
collective planning.

475   Lineberry, Robert L. "On the Politics and Economics of Urban Services."
URBAN AFFAIRS QUARTERLY 21 (March 1977): 267-72.

Lineberry discusses four aspects of urban public services: jurisdictional size, institutional arrangements, responsiveness, and
equity. These issues are highly interrelated, each posing
specific policy problems. With regard to jurisdictional size,
the question deals with fragmented and small-scale jurisdictions
on the one hand versus metropolitan-wide jurisdictions on the
other. Institutional arrangements are a matter of "who should
provide what to whom?" Responsiveness to citizen demands
is hampered by bureaucratic sluggishness. Questions of equity
pertain to who gets what and are approached differently from
community to community and from service to service.

476   Liu, Ben-Chieh. "Quality of Life Indicators: A Preliminary Investigation."
SOCIAL INDICATORS RESEARCH 1 (1974): 187-208.

An overall quality of life (QOL) social indicator is developed
by Liu for the U.S. Nine separate indicators are combined:
individual status, equality, living conditions, agriculture,
technology, economic status, education, health and welfare,
and state and local governments. The QOL indicator was
compiled using over one hundred variables for all fifty states
and Washington, D.C. Sources of the data are given and
all states were ranked.

477   _____. QUALITY OF LIFE INDICATORS IN U.S. METROPOLITAN
AREAS: A STATISTICAL ANALYSIS. New York: Praeger, 1976. 315 p.

This study is an effort to measure and compare the quality of
life in the fifty states. The study was launched in April 1974
through a grant awarded by the Washington Research Center
of the Environmental Protection Agency to the author, who
was an economist of the Midwest Research Institute. Its purpose is to quantitatively assess the quality of urban life throughout the United States. This publication is limited to a summary
of empirical results for only one point in time, 1970.

478   Louis, Arthur M. "The Worst American City." HARPER'S, January 1975,
pp. 67-71.

The author proceeds with the assumption that "there are no
good cities in America today--only bad and less bad." He
limits the inquiry to fifty of America's largest cities and evaluates them on the basis of twenty-four categories of data,

involving crime, health care, affluence, housing, education, atmosphere, and available amenities. The data, as the author admits, is old. Nevertheless, he concludes that the old north-western cities are among the least attractive, while western and southwestern cities generally rank among the most desirable.

479 McCalla, Mary Ellen. LOCAL COMMUNITY OR METROPOLITAN COMMUNITY: SOCIAL INTERACTION IN THE SELF-SUFFICIENT SUBURB. Environmental Policies and Urban Development Thesis, Series no. 18. Chapel Hill: University of North Carolina, Center for Urban and Regional Studies, 1976. 40 p.

"Loss of community" is a concept around which disagreement continues. Some writers argue that the scale and complexity of modern cities discourages social interaction among individuals, thus diminishing their sense of identity with the local spatial community. Others argue that the spatial areas in which indi-viduals engage in social interaction have expanded into the metropolitan community. A path analysis was employed to determine the relative effects of "self-sufficiency" of twelve suburban new towns and travel patterns of new town residents in metropolitan areas on the use of local facilities, local social interaction, sense of identity with local community, and on life satisfaction. Effects from the majority of variables are quite small, except for social interaction, which has a moderate positive effect on community identity. The study concludes that the building of self-sufficient new towns may be an inefficient way to affect local social interaction intended to develop an identity with the local community.

480 McLennan, Kenneth, and Seidenstat, Paul. NEW BUSINESSES AND URBAN EMPLOYMENT OPPORTUNITIES. Lexington, Mass.: Lexington Books, 1972. 250 p.

This is an empirical study of industrial structure, population distribution, and labor supply for an entire metropolitan area, with an eye to determining solutions to ghetto unemployment. It was found that the greatest increase in employment occurred in nonghetto areas; central-city nonghetto areas were even able to thwart some manufacturing firms, although ghetto areas did not. When firms did locate in the ghetto, they tended to employ fewer people, to offer fewer high-skilled jobs, and to grow at a slower rate. The ghetto seemed to provide no locational advantages for any firm. The most likely improve-ment for ghetto unemployment would be to improve transportation to other sectors of the city where there are better employment opportunities, and to provide training for ghetto residents in types of occupations which are expanding in the core of the city. Minority enterprises in the ghetto were not considered to be of much help to the unemployment problem.

481 Maher, C.A. "Urban Form and City Size: An Ontario Example." In
THE FORM CITIES IN CENTRAL CANADA: SELECTED PAPERS, edited
by L.S. Bourne, R.D. MacKinnon, and J.W. Simmons, pp. 37-46.
Toronto: University of Toronto Press, 1973.

Maher reports on a study of fifty-one Ontario cities, which
analyzed relationships between city size and the following
factors: population and land use densities, size of developed
area, and land use composition. The basic method of analysis
used was correlation and linear regression. A high correlation
was found between developed area and population size, and
between population density and city size. A low correlation
was found between proportions of area devoted to the various
major land uses and city size.

482 Malenbaum, Wilfred. "Progress in Health: What Index of Progress?"
ANNALS OF THE AMERICAN ACADEMY OF POLITICAL AND SOCIAL
SCIENCE 393 (January 1971): 109-21.

Malenbaum asserts that in poor countries there is ample evidence
to suggest a positive correlation between increased health inputs and growth productivity along with increased population
growth. He also asserts that increased population and productivity result in higher rates of health input. Malenbaum
sees as a possibility that measures of health inputs, that is,
indicators, could function as an index of economic and social
progress, and he attempts to analyze data seeking the solutions.

483 Marcum, John P., and Bean, Frank D. "Minority Group Status as a
Factor in the Relationship Between Mobility and Fertility: The Mexican
American Case." SOCIAL FORCES 55 (September 1976): 135-48.

This paper examines two contrasting approaches to understanding
the influence of minority group membership on the relationship
between mobility and fertility of urban Mexican Americans,
based on 1969 data from Austin, Texas. One approach emphasizes
minority group status, while the other emphasizes economic
underdevelopment. According to the former view, major
fertility changes take place with the greater integration of the
group into the larger society. The latter view suggests that
fertility changes are greater where the minority group is less
integrated into the larger society. These ideas were tested
on Mexican-American couples, split according to generational
distance from Mexico. The results tended to support the minority
group status approach, revealing lower than average expected
fertility on the part of couples removed from Mexico for at
least three generations.

484 Margolis, Julius. "The Demand for Urban Public Services." In ISSUES
IN URBAN ECONOMICS, edited by Harvey S. Perloff and Lowden Wingo,
Jr., pp. 527-65. Baltimore: Johns Hopkins Press, 1968.

The author starts from the assumption that urban public services
are poorly supplied. He examines the scope of public expenditures and some of the characteristics of local government
relevant to the analysis of public services. This includes per
capita expenditures, intergovernmental relations, fragmentation,
decision-making opportunities and constraints, and the lack
of quantitative measures for public services. An analysis of
public goals and externalities is presented. Urban political
processes are examined with respect to how well they reflect
consumer preferences. Also, some political economy models
are discussed. The author concludes that the economic model
of choice as applied to public services is the optimal way to
determine consumer demand. The technique for achieving this
is benefit-cost analysis which has been used extensively in
water supply and urban transportation but is being extended to
a much wider range of urban public services.

485   Masotti, Louis H., and Hadden, Jeffrey K., eds. SUBURBIA TRANSITION.
New York: New Viewpoints, 1974. 239 p.

Masotti and Hadden have put together a carefully selected
collection of articles from the NEW YORK TIMES on suburbia.
Most of the items included first appeared in the 1960s or
early 1970s and thus remain highly relevant descriptions of
suburban life and problems today. Among the topics are the
suburban myth, the suburbs and race relations, the dispersal
of commerce and industry, the politics of exclusion, crime
and other suburban problems, the politics of suburbia, and
suburban development past and future. Although a number
of articles focus on the suburbs around New York, others
pinpoint Black Jack, Missouri; Warren, Michigan; Dayton,
Ohio; and other areas.

486   _____. THE URBANIZATION OF THE SUBURBS. Beverly Hills, Calif.:
Sage Publications, 1973. 600 p.

This is a major collection of original articles on suburbia.
While not systematically structured to reflect a single point of
view or theoretical perspective, the most common theme of
these articles is the gradual evolution of suburbia into one
integrated urban whole with the central city. Thus, political
boundaries are the most significant, and perhaps the only,
difference between the suburbs and the central city. Where
differences appear, they are manifestations of population
characteristics and development stage rather than geography
or some inherent special attributes of the suburban environment.

The essays included cover a wide range. Only a few topics--
education, crime, mental health, personal behavior, religion,
and the arts--are conspicuously absent.

487 Meyer, David R. "Classification of U.S. Metropolitan Areas by Charac-
teristics of Their Nonwhite Populations." In CLASSIFICATION OF CITIES:
NEW METHODS AND EVOLVING USES, edited by Brian Berry, pp. 61-94.
New York: John Wiley and Sons, 1972.

> This essay sets up a multidimensional analysis of Standard Metro-
> politan Statistical Areas (SMSAs) based on the characteristics of
> their nonwhite inhabitants. Factors include socioeconomic
> status, age, housing, unemployment, and position in urban
> hierarchy. The author proposes classifying SMSAs based on
> these characteristics.

488 Miller, Herman P. INCOME DISTRIBUTION IN THE UNITED STATES:
A 1960 MONOGRAPH. Washington, D.C.: U.S. Bureau of the Census,
Government Printing Office, 1966. 306 p.

> This is a study of the changes in income distribution in the
> United States during a twenty-year period between 1940 and
> 1960. It is based primarily on the information collected in
> three censuses. The study provides a great deal of statistical
> data on both families and individuals. Statistical tables
> include wage trends by occupation and lifetime earnings by
> education, color, and region.

489 Miller, S.M. "Comparative Social Mobility." CURRENT SOCIOLOGY
9 (1960): 1-89.

> This is an investigation into social mobility, that is, upward
> or downward movement of a family in the social structure, in
> eighteen different nations. It examines the influence of social
> mobility on attitudes and behavior and on the social structure
> in those countries. Social mobility is studied in terms of
> frequency, direction, causes, and consequences. Statistical
> data include the percentage of families whose sons have
> moved out of their fathers' socioeconomic class to another,
> making comparisons among the countries. The author suggests
> that mobility research in the future should consider additional
> political and social factors.

490 Mills, Edwin S. STUDIES IN THE STRUCTURE OF THE URBAN ECONOMY.
Baltimore: Johns Hopkins Press, 1972. 151 p.

> Cities have higher population densities than their surrounding
> jurisdictions. The size of cities is often determined by public
> and private decisions consisting of a trade off between low
> transportation and exchange costs on the one hand and diminishing
> returns to the ratio of nonland inputs to land inputs on the other.
> Several models are discussed showing how market forces affect
> employment and housing, forecasting growth and the effects
> of zoning, taxation, and other public policies. A model is
> presented showing the effects of urban transportation costs on

location decisions. Improvements in transportation may increase central business district employment slightly; this in turn will reduce the urban area's density.

491   Ministry of Industry, Trade and Commerce. PERSPECTIVE CANADA II: A COMPENDIUM OF SOCIAL STATISTICS 1977. English ed. Ottawa: Minister of Supply and Services, 1977. 335 p.

This volume provides a compilation of salient social indicators in Canada attempting to define a more precise delineation as to what constitutes a social indicator. The volume includes many charts, maps, and histograms comparing data among Canada's provinces and cities and between Canada and other countries.

492   Mitchell, Joyce M., and Mitchell, William C. "The Changing Politics of American Life." In INDICATORS OF SOCIAL CHANGES: CONCEPTS AND MEASUREMENTS, edited by Eleanor B. Sheldon and Wilbert E. Moore, pp. 247-94. New York: Russell Sage Foundation, 1968.

See 82.

493   Moos, Rudolf H., and Insel, Paul M., eds. ISSUES IN SOCIAL ECOLOGY: HUMAN MILIEUS. Palo Alto, Calif.: National Press Books, 1974. 616 p.

This is a collection of forty-four articles on the effect of the environment on human behavior. The articles are organized into ten sections: theory and design, physical forces and social behavior, population density and the use of space, man-made designs and psychosocial consequences, behavior settings and psychosocial interactions, organizational structure and social behavior, characteristics of the milieu of inhabitants, psycho-social climate and environmental press, reinforcement contin-gencies and social behavior, and person-environment fit. This collection includes several articles that are difficult to locate elsewhere.

494   Morgenstern, Oskar. ON THE ACCURACY OF ECONOMIC OBSERVA-TIONS. 2d ed., rev. Princeton, N.J.: Princeton University Press, 1963. 322 p.

This second edition appeared thirteen years after the first and has been almost completely rewritten. The later work is an important contribution to the study of national economic statistics. Fortunately it has been written for both the general reader and the professional economist.

Part 1 examines the nature of economic data--errors, accuracies, sources, and uses. Part 2 describes specific types of govern-ment statistics (foreign trade, agricultural, employment, and so forth) in an attempt to indicate various levels of accuracy one may expect to find when using each. The book includes over thirty tables, a dozen figure displays as well as a bibliography.

495 Moriyama, Iwao M. "Problems in the Measurement of Health Status." In INDICATORS OF SOCIAL CHANGE: CONCEPTS AND MEASUREMENTS, edited by Eleanor B. Sheldon and Wilbert E. Moore, pp. 573-99. New York: Russell Sage Foundation, 1968.

See 200.

496 Morrey, C.R. 1971 CENSUS: DEMOGRAPHIC, SOCIAL AND ECONOMIC INDICES FOR WARDS IN GREATER LONDON. 2 vols. London: Greater London Council, 1976. 210 p.

This report draws from the 1971 census to present data at the ward level on some of the social, economic, and demographic characteristics of the population of London and its housing. A total of 105 indexes were used covering such areas as resident status; age and sex structure of the population; small, pensioner, and large households and families; tenure and overcrowding; density of occupation; housing conditions; tenure and facilities; car ownership, socioeconomic groups; activity and unemployment rates; birthplaces; new commonwealth ethnic groups; one-year immigrants; mode of transport to work; and industry.

497 Morrison, Peter A. "Demographic Trends That Will Shape Future Housing Demand." POLICY SCIENCES 8 (June 1977): 203-15.

Morrison presents four important demographic influences that will shape housing demand in the United States: first, the population's changing age profile; second, the trend toward marriage at a later age; third, the widening mortality differential between the sexes, which has increased the tendency for women to outlive men; and fourth, the slowing down and even reversal of traditional rural to urban and urban to suburban migration patterns.

498 National Wildlife Federation. 1971 ENVIRONMENTAL QUALITY INDEX. Washington, D.C.: 1971. 16 p.

Sets out the components of the third annual environmental quality (EQ) index for water, air, soil, living space, wildlife, timber, minerals, recycling wastes, and population. The EQ for 1971 was 55.5, a 15 point loss from 1970, which showed an even larger loss from 1969. Increased environmental awareness has not been able to stem the tide of decline.

499 Orr, Larry L. INCOME, EMPLOYMENT, AND URBAN RESIDENTIAL LOCATION. New York: Academic Press, 1975. 140 p.

This is an empirical study of five hypotheses about residential location, especially of low-income households. Orr found that the location of low-income households is sensitive to employment opportunities and housing costs, and the location of high-income households is sensitive to educational and recreational expenditures (although the causal relationship may be that higher income results in higher quality service). He found that restrictive-density zoning does not radically change residential land use because it is usually set at the free-market optimum. The distribution of manufacturing and employment opportunities was found to be sensitive to land and tax costs. Orr also found that the elastic demand and inelastic supply of rental housing results in the capitalization of property taxes.

500 Ostrom, Elinor, and Smith, Dennis C. "On the Fate of 'Lilliputs' in Metropolitan Policing." PUBLIC ADMINISTRATION REVIEW 36 (March–April 1976): 192–200.

The authors cite three negative assumptions about small police departments and examine several studies which helped to frame these assumptions. Then they report on police performance in a number of jurisdictions in the St. Louis metropolitan area. Data was obtained from 4,000 respondents in forty-four neighborhoods served by twenty-nine jurisdictions to assess the performance of small, medium, and large police departments. Some of the findings were that the size of police departments are negatively related to performance on most indicators, most small police departments are performing at higher levels than the largest departments in the St. Louis area, and larger departments do not necessarily have better-educated policemen. Some small departments might be consolidated but no recommendation for consolidation of all the small departments seems warranted based upon the data.

501 Otis, Todd. "Measuring 'Quality of Life' in Urban Areas." EVALUATION. 5 (Fall 1972): 35–38.

The social-environment audit system of the First National Bank of Minneapolis, Minnesota, is described in order to encourage the generation of data useful in evaluating the quality of life of an institution affecting that area.

502 Ottensman, John R. THE CHANGING SPATIAL STRUCTURE OF AMERICAN CITIES. Lexington, Mass.: Lexington Books, 1975. 207 p.

This is a longitudinal study of urban patterns, particularly the spatial distribution of housing and population in Milwaukee over the past fifty years. The purpose of the study is to determine which models of spatial patterning are most able to deal with historical change. Population distribution is examined for both static and dynamic models: exponential models, gravity models, and intervening opportunity models, Residential differentiation is examined using concentric models, sector models, gradient models, factorial models, Muth's housing-market model, and Hoover and Vernon's neighborhood evolution model. Ottensman found that the static models of population performed quite well, although care must be taken to correctly ascertain the changing values for the parameters. He found that models of residential differentiation have more descriptive than predictive usefulness.

503 Pachon, Harry P., and Lovrich, Nicholas P. "The Consolidation of Urban Public Services: A Focus on the Police." PUBLIC ADMINISTRA-TION REVIEW 37 (January-February 1977): 38-47.

In the context of the "public choice" perspective, some writers have argued against metropolitan consolidation, especially police consolidation. The primary assertions of these anticon-solidationists are as follows: (1) that larger police departments are not more efficient or economical; and (2) that citizen satisfaction with urban police services varies inversely with the size of the city. The authors of this article contest these assertions. They claim that evidence concerning efficiency is inconclusive and that citizen satisfaction is actually more a function of a city's socioeconomic characteristics than its size. Finally, the authors state that, all other factors being equal, larger cities can provide more satisfying police services.

504 Palisi, Bartolomeo J. "Wife's Statuses and Husband-Wife Companionship in an Australian Metropolitan Area." JOURNAL OF MARRIAGE AND THE FAMILY 39 (February 1977): 185-91.

Family companionship functions have been greatly expanded with industrialization and urbanization. The study here assumes that the level of companionship varies according to the wife's social status. The author predicts that a couple's joint partici-pation increases with socioeconomic status and as urban resi-dence increases, but that it decreases with age and with length of marriage. Suburban Australians were sampled and the hypothesis was supported. Recently married couples, high socioeconomic status couples, highly urbanized couples, and young couples demonstrated the most companionship.

505 Palley, Howard A., and Palley, Marian Lief. "Social Policy Analysis--The Use of Social Indicators." WELFARE IN REVIEW 9 (March-April 1971): 8-14.

The results of this study indicate that on the basis of social indicator-generated information along, it is not possible to predict the probability of a social disorder in a black ghetto. However, there are some inferences that can be drawn from this analysis. Since there are no instances where the aggregate black welfare indicators are equal to, or higher than, the corresponding white indicators, it may be that lower welfare indicators are the conditions sufficient to produce racial disorders. It is possible that when these disparities are corrected there may be no more racial disorders. If the source of racial disorders is somewhere else, these disparities may still contribute to social strain which leads to social disorders. The study illustrates the fact that social indicators can be used to produce findings with important public policy implications in social welfare. It also raises questions requiring the further development of social indicators.

506   Parsons, Talcott. SOCIETIES: EVOLUTIONARY AND COMPARATIVE PERSPECTIVES. Foundation of Modern Sociology Series, vol. 1. Englewood, Cliffs, N.J.: Prentice-Hall, 1966. 120 p.

This volume deals with the total society as a social system using a comparative analytic perspective. This book involves a survey of the principal societies classified as "advanced intermediate": primitive, ancient Egypt and Mesopotamia, China, India, Islam, Rome, and the two "seed-bed" cultures of Israel and Greece. The introductory chapter treats the concept we term "society."

The approach is not merely evolutionary, but rather reconsiders the idea of social evolution in the context of the major theoretical and empirical advances that have accumulated since the earlier evolutionists first wrote their ideas. A selected bibliography is included.

507   Peirce, David; Garbosky, Peter N.; and Gurr, Ted Robert. "London: The Politics of Crime and Conflict, 1800 to the 1970s." In THE POLITICS OF CRIME AND CONFLICT: A COMPARATIVE HISTORY OF FOUR CITIES, edited by Ted Robert Gurr, Peter N. Grabosky, and Richard C. Hula, pp. 33-214. Beverly Hills, Calif.: Sage Publications, 1977.

Common crimes against persons and property peaked in London in the 1830s and then declined steadily, reaching a low in the 1920s. This early nineteenth-century crime wave spurred comprehensive reforms in criminal law, police institutions, and penal practices. After 1950 there was a sharp resurgence in public disorder, which by 1970 exceeded the level of 1830. The earlier crime wave was probably the result of poverty and destitution, while the contemporary one seems more the result of affluence and opportunity. The earlier crisis spurred widespread institutional reforms chiefly because the elites identified disorder with the threat of revolution; the contemporary crime wave carries no such threat and has caused no comparable official concern.

508 Peskin, Henry M. "Accounting for the Environment (A Progress Report)."
SOCIAL INDICATORS RESEARCH 2 (September 1975): 191-210.

This article examines a relatively recent research effort to
measure environmental assets and to place them into national
accounting. It presents the accounting principles used in the
project which was undertaken at the National Bureau of Economic
Research and reports some of the preliminary results of the
work. In addition, the article briefly discusses the policy and
research implications of the preliminary findings.

509 Phares, Donald. "Racial Change and Housing Values: Transition in an
Inner Suburb." SOCIAL SCIENCE QUARTERLY 52 (December 1971):
560-73.

This article along with Phares's "Racial Transition and Residential Property Values" (ANNALS OF REGIONAL SCIENCE 5
[December 1971]: 152-60.) challenges the conventional
assumption that residential property values decline as racial
integration proceeds. Phares found no significant relationship between housing prices and racial transition in his study
of University City, Missouri, a St. Louis suburb. Any differences observed among areas were eliminated in the long run.

510 Powell, Dorian L. "Female Labor Force Participation and Fertility: An
Exploratory Study of Jamaican Women." SOCIAL AND ECONOMIC
STUDIES 25 (September 1976): 234-58.

The author notes that Jamaica has a high level of working
women and also a high level of fertility. The data suggests
a strong positive relationship between urban residence and female
work force participation. This is true for both eastern and
western Jamaica. The author also looked at various types of
female unions with men, including marriage. Women with no
union have higher rates of work than those with unions. Dis-
rupted unions generally lead to female labor force participation.

511 Rabinovitz, Francine F., and Siembieda, William J. MINORITIES IN
SUBURBS: THE LOS ANGELES EXPERIENCE. Lexington, Mass.: Lexington Books, 1977. 100 p.

Research shows that the suburbanization of blacks has proceeded
faster in Los Angeles than in any other metropolitan area. Nevertheless, black suburbanization clearly takes place in a ghetto-
related corridor and the distribution of black population is much
more concentrated than black-white income distribution would
predict. Communities in which blacks and whites are of similar
class have the same kinds of problems as those where blacks and
whites are of different class. Thus far, government policy has
not affected the situation much. Blacks generally feel that they
are treated fairly by public officials, yet they are pessimistic
about the future of the communities into which they have moved.

512   Real Estate Research Corporation. THE COSTS OF SPRAWL. 3 vols.
       Washington, D.C.: Government Printing Office, 1975. 331 p.

       These three volumes contain the most thorough theoretical
       analysis of the costs of low density residential construction
       published to date. Cost estimates are generated for six
       hypothetical communities and then compared--high density
       planned, low density planned, and unplanned (sprawl) plus
       three of medium density. Each community is tested on the
       basis of four factors--energy consumption, environmental impact,
       capital cost, and operating cost. The most significant findings
       are those contrasting the high density planned case versus the
       low density unplanned. Sprawl was judged to be clearly the
       least desirable in relation to all four factors. While the con-
       clusions of the study are subject to criticism, on the whole it
       represents an important break-through in the study of suburban
       sprawl and community planning generally.

       See also Alan Altsluter's review of this study in the JOURNAL
       OF THE AMERICAN INSTITUTE OF PLANNERS 63 (April 1977):
       207-9.

513   Redfearn, George V. "Differential Patterns of City and Suburban Growth
       in the United States." JOURNAL OF URBAN HISTORY 2 (November 1975):
       43-66.

       This is an analysis of longitudinal and cross-sectional compari-
       sons of aggregate central-city and suburban growth rates. The
       authors found that annexation has played a large part in the
       growth of cities throughout history, especially younger cities.
       This has tended to obscure the suburban growth that had
       occurred, and causes measures of the percentage of population
       increase to be unreliable for longitudinal studies.

514   Redick, Richard. "1970 Census Data Used to Indicate Areas with Dif-
       ferent Potentials for Mental Health and Related Problems." In MENTAL
       HEALTH STATISTICS: NATIONAL INSTITUTE OF MENTAL HEALTH
       SERIES. Public Health Service Publication 2171 no. 3 of Series C.
       Washington, D.C.: Government Printing Office, 1971.

       Redick points out that the need for mental health services for
       certain area populations can be predicted. Indicators include
       economic, social, and educational, status; life, style, extent
       of familism; and ethnicity. Residential area analysis factors
       include residential instability, feminine careerism, and area
       homogeneity. Dane County, Wisconsin, is analyzed as an
       example.

515   Rindfuss, Ronald R. "Fertility and Migration: The Case of Puerto Rico."
       INTERNATIONAL MIGRATION REVIEW 10 (Summer 1976): 191-203.

The effect of urban migration on fertility is particularly inter-
esting when the areas of origin and destination differ drama-
tically in reproductive norms. Typically, areas of origin have
a higher level than areas of destination. It is expected that
urban migration would produce a lowered fertility compared to
nonmigrating contemporaries in the place of origin. It is
supposed generally that migration itself and exposure to lower
fertility norms will cause a lowering of fertility among the
urban migrants. The author compares the census records of
Puerto Ricans in the United States with Puerto Ricans in Puerto
Rico. The supposition is not borne out, and the author found
that there was essentially no difference between current
fertility of urban island residents and of recent immigrants to
the mainland. Nor do these groups differ significantly from
long-time United States residents. What might have been
originally attributed to the migratory process is actually a
function of urban residence.

516   Rose, Harold. "The All Black Town: Suburban Prototype or Rural Slum."
In PEOPLE AND POLITICS IN URBAN SOCIETY, edited by Harlan Hahn,
pp. 397-431. Beverly Hills, Calif.: Sage Publications, 1972.

Rose attributes most black migration to the suburbs to a desire
to improve education and employment opportunities. He indicates
that much of the black increase is actually spillover from adjoining
black areas within the central city.

517   Russett, Bruce M., and Bunselmeyer, Robert. WORLD HANDBOOK OF
POLITICAL AND SOCIAL INDICATORS. New Haven, Conn.: Yale
University Press, 1964. 373 p.

The authors present data on 133 countries in terms of the human
rights proclaimed in the Universal Declaration of Human Rights.
The data includes human resources, government and politics,
communications, wealth, health, education, family and social
relations, distribution of wealth, and income and religion.

518   Ruth, Henry S. RESEARCH PRIORITIES FOR CRIME REDUCTION EFFORTS.
Washington, D.C.: Urban Institute, 1977. 140 p.

The former Watergate Special Prosecutor covers a research
agenda designed to eliminate the knowledge gaps in the
criminal justice system. He uses crime statistics and presents
personal views as to describe the kinds of indicators that
would be most useful.

519   Ryder, Norman B. "The Cohort as a Concept in the Study of Social
Change." AMERICAN SOCIOLOGICAL REVIEW 30 (December 1965):
843-61.

With a focus on structural transformation, this essay presents a demographic approach to the study of social change. The author views each new cohort as defined by age and time, as a possible intermediary in the process of transforming society. Consequently this sociological essay directs the reader's attention toward the study of various cohorts in time series. Such an approach contrasts with conventional period-by-period analyses.

The author recognizes and explains some of the methodological problems inherent in this approach. He remains firm, however, in his belief that transformations of the social world modify people of different ages in different ways and that the effects of these transformations are persistent.

520 Salaff, Janet W. "The Status of Unmarried Hong Kong Women: The Social Factors Contributing to the Delayed Marriage." POPULATION STUDIES 30 (November 1976): 391-412.

The Dixon model which assesses the factors responsible for a rise in the age of marriage has been applied to Hong Kong women, ages twenty to twenty-four in 1973. Of these, twenty-eight were interviewed in depth. Of these, four delayed marriage because of the unavailability of suitable mates. Twenty-one felt that marriage was economically unfeasible. Three felt that early marriage would jeopardize opportunities and only one felt that an early marriage would be advantageous. The author concluded that the age structure contributes to a woman's participation in the labor force and early marriage would hinder their chances to meet personal and family obligations. The author observed that delayed marriage enhances women's status and is a good policy to be pursued by developing nations.

521 Scammon, Richard M. "Electoral Participation." ANNALS OF THE AMERICAN ACADEMY OF POLITICAL AND SOCIAL SCIENCE 371 (May 1967): 59-71.

Scammon provides indicators of voter participation based upon the work of the Kennedy Commission on Registration and Voter Participation. He proposes more emphasis on maximizing access to voting.

522 Schaenman, Philip S., and Swartz, Joe. MEASURING FIRE PROTECTION PRODUCTIVITY IN LOCAL GOVERNMENT: SOME INITIAL THOUGHTS. Washington, D.C.: Urban Institute, 1974. 97 p.

This volume contains guidelines on measures of how well an urban government provides fire protection. It includes measures for the prevention as well as the suppression of fires.

523 Schiltz, Timothy, and Moffitt, William. "Inner-City/Outer-City Relationships in Metropolitan Areas." URBAN AFFAIRS QUARTERLY 7 (September 1971): 75–108.

> The authors present a lengthy bibliographic essay covering much of the suburban literature published before 1971. They put primary emphasis, however, on those materials directed to city-suburban contrasts and interactive relationships. Among the topics covered are central-city and suburban disparities, governmental fragmentation, and metropolitanism. A long bibliography of sources is included.

524 Schmandt, Henry. "Municipal Decentralization: An Overview." In URBAN ADMINISTRATION: MANAGEMENT, POLITICS, AND CHANGE, edited by Alan Edward Bent and Ralph A. Rossum, pp. 287–315. Port Washington, N.Y.: Kennikat Press, 1976.

> The main theoretical arguments for municipal decentralization are (1) an extended version of the concept of federalism and (2) the idea of the neighborhood as a focus for program and service administration. Those who support decentralization point to the unresponsiveness of large bureaucratic structures, citizen alienation, different social problems among neighborhoods, and the importance of citizen influence and control. The author describes various forms decentralization can take: services provided through neighborhood offices; neighborhood advisory groups established; political authority delegated to individual communities; or community development corporations established. The form decentralization takes will depend on such factors as population size, territorial boundaries, community needs, problem-solving capabilities, and finance capabilities.

525 Schwartz, Edward E., ed. PLANNING-PROGRAMMING-BUDGETING SYSTEMS AND SOCIAL WELFARE. Paper presented at a Workshop on Evaluating the Delivery of Social Welfare Services held 25 May 1968. in San Francisco. Chicago: University of Chicago, School of Social Service Administration, 1970. 58 p.

> Schwartz describes the federal planning, programming, and budgeting system and its application to social welfare programs.

526 Seligman, Lee, and Karnig, Albert K. "Black Representation in the American States: A Comparison of Bureaucracies and Legislatures." AMERICAN POLITICS QUARTERLY 4 (April 1976): 237–45.

> Seligman and Karnig question the views held by some other scholars that the American civil service bureaucracy is more representative of the population than is the legislative branch of government. They cite civil service data for the years 1970 to 1972 to support their position. The racial composition of bureaucracies and legislatures in the thirty-eight states

studied indicates that the black population is underrepresented
in both bureaucracies and legislatures. Blacks were underrepresented in both areas in most states as well as in the
federal government, and there is little difference in the ratio
of black representation between the legislative and bureaucratic
areas.

527 Shariff, Zahid. "Social Information and Government Sponsored Development." A Case Study from West Pakistan." ANNALS OF THE ACADEMY
OF POLITICAL AND SOCIAL SCIENCE 393 (January 1971): 92-108.

Greater governmental participation in economic organization
in the developing countries is increasingly an irreversible trend
and increasingly accomplished fact. In Pakistan Industrial
Development Corporation (PIDC) was selected for this study.
The extent of governmental participation in Pakistan's economic
organization is rather limited. Achievements include: development of areas avoided by private industry, control of excessive
concentrations of industry, investment in heavy industry, good
labor relations, and training of scientists and managers. There
has been a lot of waste, inefficiency, corruption, and loss of
funds; social information should not be used to justify waste-
ful projects. The author stresses the danger of misusing social
indicators.

528 Skogan, Wesley G. "The Changing Distribution of Big-City Crime. A
Multi-City Time-Series Analysis." URBAN AFFAIRS QUARTERLY 13
(September 1977): 33-48.

This article analyzes the relationships between the aggregate
demographic characteristics of cities, their investment in
policing, and officially reported crime rates. Data from the
thirty-two largest cities during 1946 to 1970 were used. The
most recent data support the contention that crime rates are
highest in large, dense, heterogeneous cities. However,
data from earlier years suggest that this is a relatively recent
phenomenon and is due to the process of suburbanization.
Before the flight of the middle classes out of the cities,
there was no such stratification between relatively crime-free
suburbs and crime-ridden central cities. Rather, during earlier
periods, stratification took place among neighborhoods within
the city.

529 Smelser, N.J., and Lipset, S.M., eds. SOCIAL STRUCTURE AND
SOCIAL MOBILITY IN ECONOMIC DEVELOPMENT. Chicago: Aldine,
1966. 323 p.

This book is a collection of papers on the relations between
social structure and social mobility under conditions of economic
development. The papers are organized into the following
groups: theoretical and methodological issues in studying the

relationships between development and social mobility, traditional and modern stratification, the effects of economic development on social mobility, noneconomic influences on mobility, and political aspects of social mobility.

In the introduction Smelser and Lipset define and discuss social
structure, social mobility, stratification, and the consequences
of rapid development on social structure and the pattern of
social mobility. Smelser and Lipset introduce research areas
that relate to mobility such as education, rates of growth,
tradition and modernity, and value orientations which are
elaborated in the other papers.

530   Smith, Joel. "Another Look at Socioeconomic Status Distribution in
Urbanized Areas." URBAN AFFAIRS QUARTERLY 5 (June 1970): 423-53.

This is a retest of Schnore's hypothesis that suburban populations
will show a higher average than central-city populations on
any measure of socioeconomic status, regardless of size or age
of urbanized area. Smith, however, defines suburb only as
incorporated places, while Schnore considered the whole urban
fringe. Smith also failed to find support for the hypothesis.

531   SOCIAL INDICATORS: PROBLEMS OF DEFINITION AND OF SELECTION.
New York: UNESCO, Methods and Analysis Division, 1974. 28 p.

The purpose behind this volume is to establish an order of
countries ranked according to development levels and to measure
progress towards "objectives of the United Nations Second Development Decade." It emphasizes the need for "human resources
indicators" and the potential such indicators would have for
monitoring social change. The publication reviews the great
difficulties in defining indicators and offers solutions on international level that they feel could be applied within the
various countries as well. The publication also reviews the
next problem of determining which indicators are to be selected
to measure social change or specific area within general category. UNESCO suggests certain criteria for selection and explains utility via formulas and tables. The volume ends with
a description of UNESCO's prescribed method of establishing
a list of development indicators.

532   Stallings, C. Wayne. "Local Information Policy: Confidentiality and
Public Access." PUBLIC ADMINISTRATION REVIEW 34 (May-June 1974):
197-204.

This article discusses a model policy developed in Charlotte,
North Carolina which regulates the collection, storage, use,
and dissemination of information. The policy which can be
adopted by any local government protects privacy while pro-
moting reasonable public access to public documents. The

author discusses the administrative structure for decision making
and the procedures and techniques for implementing the plan
as well as a classification system for information and the
varying degrees of access permitted for each classification.
The plan can only work if all public officials are committed
to privacy and access and are willing to exert pressure on
all parties concerned to achieve the twin goals.

533   Stanback, Thomas M., and Knight, Richard. SUBURBANIZATION AND
THE CITY. Montclair, N.J.: Universe Books, 1976. 230 p.

The authors examine the process of suburbanization and its
impact on the labor markets of cities and their outlying areas.
They draw upon census of population materials and the Social
Security Continuous Work History file to show how central
cities have experienced job gains in office activities and
losses in manufacturing and local consumer-oriented activities.
The trend includes an increase in female office jobs in the
city and expanded suburb-to-city commuting, which provides
a supply of white collar workers. The suburban job market
consists of two sharply contrasting types of employment: low-
skill, low-wage jobs in local services and relatively well-paid
manufacturing employment, along with selected managerial
and professional positions. The suburban economy benefits
from income generated by the large numbers of commuters to
the city.

534   Stephan, G. Edward, and Tedrow, Lucky M. "A Theory of Time Mini-
mization: The Relationship Between Urban Area and Population."
PACIFIC SOCIOLOGICAL REVIEW 20 (January 1977): 105-12.

Density and market potential are well-known factors in the
determination of city size; another important factor is travel
time to and from the city center. A gigantic city in terms of
space would solve problems connected with the first two factors.
But the larger the city, the greater the average travel time.
Since there are ultimate limits to travel time, there will be
a time cost in space acquisition.

535   Sutton, Richard J.; Korey, John; Bryant, Steve; and Didson, Richard.
"American City Types: Toward a More Systematic Urban Study."   URBAN
AFFAIRS QUARTERLY 9 (March 1974): 369-401.

This is an empirical illustration of a method for classifying
cities. The authors use a cluster-analysis methodology with
forty-one variables measured for 669 cities. They found that
nine components described most of the cities, and that sociocultural characteristics were more important to the components
than economic function.

536   Sweetser, F.L. "Ecological Factors in Metropolitan Zones and Sectors."
      In QUANTITATIVE ECOLOGICAL ANALYSIS IN THE SOCIAL SCIENCES,
      edited by Mattei Dogan and Stein Rokkan, pp. 431-58. Cambridge:
      MIT Press, 1961.

> This article is concerned with the relative stability of metro-
> politan ecological factors. Sweetser compares and analyzes
> the ecological structure of Boston and Helsinki. He performs
> factor analysis of certain variables first for the total metropolis
> and then for each of the sectors and zones into which he
> divides the metropolis. Metropolitan ecological differentiation
> is classified as either universal or special.
>
> Sweetser's analysis supports his belief that the universal dimension
> of metropolitan ecological differentiation in Boston and Helsinki
> would be more stable than the special factors. Sweetser also
> discusses technical and substantive classification of metropolitan
> ecological factors and the importance of setting proper boundaries
> of metropolitan communities for factorial ecological analysis.

537   Szelenyi, Ivan. "Urban Sociology and Community Studies in Eastern
      Europe: Reflections and Comparisons with American Approaches." COM-
      PARATIVE URBAN RESEARCH 4, nos. 2-3 (1977): 11-20.

> Rapid industrial development in Eastern Europe and the urgent
> need for industrial investments has created a situation in which
> there are more jobs available than housing. Part of the labor
> force has been kept outside the city because housing is unavail-
> able. Housing needs in socialist societies are determined by
> social "needs" as opposed to consumer demands. However,
> there is still a positive correlation between quality of housing
> and high income.

538   Taeuber, Conrad. "Population: Trends and Characteristics." In INDI-
      CATORS OF SOCIAL CHANGE: CONCEPTS AND MEASUREMENTS,
      edited by Eleanor B. Sheldon and Wilbert E. Moore, pp. 27-76. New
      York: Russell Sage Foundation, 1968.

> Taeuber presents a basic analysis of American population growth
> since 1790, along with indications of the weaknesses of the
> data. Population characteristics including age, sex, race,
> migration, ethnic origin, education, religion, economic activity,
> household, and other vital statistics are discussed.

539   Taylor, Charles L., and Hudson, Michael C. WORLD HANDBOOK OF
      POLITICAL AND SOCIAL INDICATORS. 2d ed. New Haven, Conn.:
      Yale University Press, 1972. 443 p.

> The purpose of the volume was to collect data which would
> facilitate quantitative cross-national research. It is an attempt
> to compare nations on a great variety of politically relevant
> indexes. While the authors do not test hypotheses, they do

make data available and interpretable to those who would do so. The book was sponsored by the World Data Analysis Program at Yale University and a great deal is owed to the eminent behavioralist theoretician there, Karl W. Deutsch, one of many notable scholars connected with this work.

540   Terleckyj, Nestor E. IMPROVEMENTS IN THE QUALITY OF LIFE: ESTIMATES OF POSSIBILITIES IN THE UNITED STATES, 1974-1983. Washington, D.C.: National Planning Association, 1975. 281 p.

This study develops an analytical system for the understanding of changes in the quality of life and attempts some empirical estimates within the framework. The stress is on results rather than resource input and consequently this brings the object of analysis closer to the objectives of families and individuals. The volume represents the findings of two research projects undertaken by the author at the National Planning Association over a seven-year period beginning in the late 1960's. Part 1 consists of the "multi-output productive relationships formulated in the activity-output and activity-cost matrices," while part two provides a detailed discussion of particular fields of social concerns. Tables and charts are included.

541   Thurow, Lester. "The Occupational Distribution of Returns to Education and Experience for Whites and Negroes." In FEDERAL PROGRAMS FOR THE DEVELOPMENT OF HUMAN RESOURCES, vol. 1. pp. 267-84. Washington, D.C.: Government Printing Office, Subcommittee on Economic Progress for the Joint Economic Committee, 1968.

Thurow considers the effects of education and on-the-job training on income. He develops a human capital function that considers the joint impact of these two factors, using 1960 census data for males between eighteen and sixty-four years of age. Thurow applies the human capital function to comparisons between whites and blacks, between the North and the South, and among ten occupations. He concludes that when education and experience increase together, the impact is greater than the sum of the separate impacts. He recommends that educational programs and training programs be coordinated to obtain the maximum benefit.

542   _____. POVERTY AND DISCRIMINATION. Washington, D.C.: Studies in Social Economics, Brookings Institution, 1969. 214 p.

Thurow discusses the relationship between poverty and discrimination and shows that programs to change the distribution of income will not benefit blacks to the same extent as whites unless racial discrimination can be eliminated. Thurow quantifies the causal factors of income distribution at the bottom of the scale by developing an econometric model. He examines factors such as resource utilization, human capital, market imperfections, and racial discrimination.

Thurow concludes that if everything else is equal, poverty is greater for blacks. He sees the need for programs which address the problems of both poverty and discrimination.

543 Toffler, Alvin. FUTURE SHOCK. New York: Random House, 1970. 505 p.

In looking at changes in societal behavior the author attempts to point out where society is heading. Although lacking in quantitative statistics, Toffler skillfully uses everyday examples as social indicators to make his point clear.

544 Tucker, C. Jack, and Reid, John D. "Black Urbanization and Economic Opportunity: A Look at the Nation's Large Cities." PHYLON 38 (Spring 1977): 55-64.

Black population has grown steadily in metropolitan areas since World War II. Migration patterns reaffirm that blacks continue to concentrate in the largest cities. In 1970, 45 percent of all urban blacks were living in twenty-six American cities. On the other hand, whites have exhibited a mass exodus to the suburbs and to smaller cities. In central cities of all sizes, black population growth exceeds white, and the number of blacks living in the suburbs is negligible.

545 Turner, F.C., and Davis, Harmer E. A COMPARATIVE ANALYSIS OF URBAN TRANSPORTATION REQUIREMENTS. Vol. 1. Washington, D.C.: International Road Federation, 1977. 53 p.

Turner and Davis present a study of urban transportation systems in thirty-one urban areas located in fourteen countries including nine American cities.

546 _____. A COMPARATIVE ANALYSIS OF URBAN TRANSPORTATION REQUIREMENTS. Vol. 2. Washington, D.C.: International Road Federation, 1977. 134 p.

The authors examine thirty urban areas in fourteen countries. Volume 2 contains detailed comments and statistics pertaining to the mass transit situation and experience in each urban area studied. It is a support document for volume 1.

547 Unfug, Charles S., and Schwartz, Lewis. "Development Pains." ENVIRONMENT 19 (January-February 1977): 28-34.

This article points out that land use has traditionally been a matter for local concerns and that state input has been problematical. Colorado and Vermont provide good examples of the

practical limits and problems that affect comprehensive attempts
at state zoning legislation. Local land-use controls have not
been effectively superseded by state controls in either state,
and the result is a mixture of local and state controls. The
lesson of the Colorado and Vermont experiments is that there
will have to be a combination of state and local land use
control in order for it to be effective.

548 United Nations. COMPENDIUM OF SOCIAL STATISTICS: 1963. New
York: 1964. 586 p.

This is a collection of tables displaying statistical indicators
of the quality of life in nations throughout the world. Organized
into eight sections, the compendium describes the major aspects
of the social situation in the world by nation and by region.
It also indicates trends or changes in the levels of living.

549 _____. COMPENDIUM OF SOCIAL STATISTICS: 1967. New York:
1969. 662 p.

This is a revised and updated edition of the 1963 compendium.
Like its predecessor, it provides basic statistical indicators
which describe the major aspects of world and regional social
situations as well as changes and trends in the levels of living.
A total of sixty-two tables are included showing analytical
rates, index numbers, and rations.

550 U.S. Advisory Commission on Intergovernmental Relations. TRENDS IN
METROPOLITAN AMERICA: AN INFORMATION REPORT. Washington,
D.C.: Government Printing Office, 1977. 79 p.

The Advisory Commission on Intergovernmental Relations studied
population and economy in the eighty-five largest Standard
Metropolitan Statistical Areas, concentrating on changes since
1960. Results indicate that central cities that have not annexed
their suburbs are in a dangerous condition of decline in economic
and political importance. More than half the central cities
lost population between 1960 and 1973. Most of these are in
the East and Midwest, where central cities have not annexed
suburban territory and taxes are highest. Central cities in the
South and West are growing in population. In the South,
where annexation is most common, the proportion of the metro-
politan-area population found in the central city has steadily
increased over the last two decades. Generally, in all areas
of the country, population density and white population have
declined in central cities, and per capita income, share of
job locations, and growth of retail volume are lower than in
the suburbs.

551 U.S. Bureau of the Census. CURRENT POPULATION REPORTS, Series

P-60, no. 53. "Income in 1966 of Families and Persons in the United States." Washington, D.C.: Government Printing Office, 1967. 51 p.

Part of an ongoing series begun in 1948 to monitor consumer income changes between the census years, this pamphlet contains both text and forty-eight tables which note and interpret change. This particular report was based on a survey of 52,000 households in 449 sample areas. Numerous similar reports are published annually in this continuing series.

552 _____. CURRENT POPULATION REPORTS. Series P-23, no. 58. "A Statistical Portrait of Women in the United States." Washington, D.C.: Government Printing Office, 1976. 90 p.

This is another official document prompted by the U.N. General Assembly's designation of 1975 as International Women's Year. It presents a statistical portrait of women's changing role in the United States during this century. It brings together data, most of which has been published previously, from various government documents and professional journals. Most of the time-series data postdates 1950 when such information became more generally available. Areas of study include population growth and composition, longevity, mortality, health, residence and migration, marital and family status, fertility, education, participation in the labor force, income and poverty status, voting and public office holding, and crime and victimization. Recent information concerning black and Spanish women is also included.

553 _____. CURRENT POPULATION REPORTS: POPULATION CHARACTER-ISTICS-GEOGRAPHICAL MOBILITY: MARCH 1975 TO MARCH 1976, by Kristin A. Hansen, Celia G. Boertlein, and Larry H. Long. Washington, D.C.: Government Printing Office, 1977. 6 p.

This volume presents information on the mobility of the United States population for the twelve-month period ending March 1976. Data is provided for four types of mobility: general (nonmovers within and between counties, states, and regions; and movers from abroad), detailed (movers within, into, and from Standard Metropolitan Statistical Areas [SMSAs]; their central cities; and areas outside central cities in SMSAs), metropolitan (nonmovers and movers within, between, from, to, and outside SMSAs), and central city (metropolitan data plus additional information on the central city of the SMSA). Statistics on the region of residence and inter- and intrastate and regional mobility are also included. Mobility data is presented by one or more of the following social and economic characteristics: sex, age, race, Spanish origin, relationship to head of household, type of residence, number and age of children, years of school completed, marital status, major occupational group, income, receipt of public assistance, and poverty status.

554 _____. LOCAL GOVERNMENT FINANCES IN SELECTED METROPOLITAN AREAS AND LARGE COUNTIES: 1974-75. Series GE-75, no. 3. Washington, D.C.: Government Printing Office, 1976. 103 p.

This document presents statistics on local government finances in seventy-four Standard Metropolitan Statistical Areas (SMSAs) and large counties in the United States during fiscal year 1974-75. Data are shown concerning the finances of local government in major SMSAs and the county areas outside the SMSAs.

555 U.S. Department of Commerce. Office of Federal Statistical Policy and Standards, and Bureau of the Census. SOCIAL INDICATORS, 1976. Washington, D.C.: Government Printing Office, 1977. 564 p.

This is the second report of its kind, and the format is similar to that of its predecessor, SOCIAL INDICATORS, 1973. It features color graphic presentations of summary descriptive data on the socioeconomic characteristics of the population of the United States, with limited geographic detail but with considerable disaggregation by age, sex, race, and other variables. The contents of this volume are organized into twelve chapters: "Population," "The Family," "Housing," "Social Security and Welfare," "Health and Nutrition," "Public Safety," "Education and Training," "Work," "Income, Wealth, and Expenditures," "Cultural Activities," "Leisure and Time Use," and "Social Mobility and Participation."

556 U.S. Department of Health, Education, and Welfare. ROLES OF CITIES IN HUMAN SERVICES. Rockville, Md.: 1976. 42 p.

An abstract bibliography on thirty-four documents concerned with the roles of cities in the planning, management, and delivery of human services. Project Share is a clearinghouse for a number of sources, including U.S. Department of Health, Education, and Welfare-funded demonstration projects, universities, and public interest groups. Topics range from administration of services and policy analysis to service delivery experiences. Some of the reports describe the development of municipal information systems, while others are concerned with the interrelationships among various governmental units and levels.

557 U.S. Department Of Health, Education, and Welfare. Children's Bureau. CHILD WELFARE IN 25 STATES--AN OVERVIEW. Washington, D.C.: Government Printing Office, 1976. 208 p.

This document reviews the child welfare service delivery systems of twenty-five selected states based on a survey of all management and program components of the child welfare service delivery system. Data was obtained from an advance questionnaire sent to state child welfare delivery systems as well as a series of structured interviews with state and local agency representatives. This data was compiled into twenty-five profiles highlighting the strengths, weaknesses, and exemplary features of each state's system. Among the important issues identified in the survey were child welfare in competition with other services, the scope of child welfare services and clients, organization, competence of personnel, financing and the economy, advocacy for child welfare, management, planning, and needs assessment and evaluation.

558 U.S. Department of Justice. Law Enforcement Assistance Administration. CRIMINAL JUSTICE AGENCIES IN THE UNITED STATES. Washington, D.C.: National Institute of Law Enforcement and Criminal Justice, Statistics Division, 1970.

This report is a statistical summary compiled from the 1970 National Criminal Justice Directory survey by the U.S. Bureau of the Census. Included are all state, county, city, township, and special district governments with a 1960 population of 1,000 or more. Figures are given for enforcement agencies, courts, prosecutor's offices, defender's offices, adult and juvenile correction agencies, probation offices, and other agencies. They are also given for each state by level of government.

559 _____. EXPENDITURE AND EMPLOYMENT DATA FOR THE CRIMINAL JUSTICE SYSTEM 1968-69. National Criminal Justice Information and Statistics Service, Series SC-EE no. 1, Special Studies no. 56. Washington, D.C.: Government Printing Office, 1970. 55 p.

This official document includes financial and employment data concerning criminal justice activities of federal, state, and local governments. Unlike the previous two reports, this one also includes new data collected concerning expenditure and employment data on prosecution and indigent defense activities of the various governments.

560 U.S. Department of Labor. Bureau of Labor Statistics. EMPLOYMENT AND UNEMPLOYMENT IN SELECTED CITIES (JANUARY-DECEMBER 1976). Washington, D.C.: Government Printing Office, 1977. 16 p.

The report contains labor force and unemployment estimates for selected cities for use in administration of economic assistance programs of the U.S. Department of Commerce.

561 U.S. Department of Labor. Workplace Standards Administration. STATE
ECONOMIC AND SOCIAL INDICATORS. Bureau of Labor Standards,
Bulletin no. 328. Washington, D.C.: Government Printing Office,
1970. 28 p.

This pamphlet contains charts indicating rankings by states in
assorted categories, including family income, wages, and educational attainment. A section on social indicators includes
several commonly used indicators which suggest the scope and
severity of social problems.

562 U.S. Federal Bureau of Investigation. CRIME IN THE UNITED STATES
1976: UNIFORM CRIME REPORTS. Washington, D.C.: Government
Printing Office, 1976. 304 p.

The Uniform Crime Reporting Program is the outgrowth of a
need for a national and uniform compilation of law enforcement
statistics. The 1976 report includes a "Crime Index of Reported
Offenses" and a "Crime Index of Offenses" cleared by arrest.
It also contains statistics and comments concerning persons
arrested, persons charged, and law enforcement personnel.
While the factors which cause crime are many and vary throughout the country, some of these factors are discussed in the
report along with trends and features of criminal acts.

563 U.S. National Goals Research Staff. TOWARD BALANCED GROWTH:
QUANTITY WITH QUALITY. Washington, D.C.: Government Printing
Office, 1970. 228 p.

The report, prepared at the president's behest, discusses some
of the problems related to the growth of America's economy,
population, wealth, technology, and education. It outlines
the current debates concerning preferred policy objectives
and ways to achieve "balanced growth." The appendix includes
graphic charts with analyses of social, economic, and technical
trends and projections, for example, gross national product,
size of the labor force, educational characteristics of the
population, relative difference in per capita income among
national regions, options for future population growth, and
educational enrollment.

564 Van Dusen, Roxann A., ed. SOCIAL INDICATORS, 1973: A REVIEW
SYMPOSIUM. Washington, D.C.: Social Science Research Council,
Center for Coordination of Research on Social Indicators, 1974. 87 p.

This volume is a review of SOCIAL INDICATORS, 1973, published by the Statistical Policy Division of the U.S. Office of
Management and Budget (OMB). The OMB work, which included eight major areas of social study--health, public safety,
education, employment, income, housing, leisure and recreation, and population--was the first government chartbook of

social conditions and trends in the United States. Its contribution to the field of social indicators could not be overestimated and the SSRC conveyed a review symposium in February 1974, immediately following publication of the OMB report, to summarize and evaluate the value and the quality of the government's effort. This publication includes several articles prepared for or about the symposium and written by member scholars of the SSRCs Advisory and Planning Committee on Social Indicators, both foreign and American.

565 Vipond, Joan. "City Size and Unemployment." URBAN STUDIES 11 (February 1974): 39-46.

This article reports on a study done to test the hypothesis that there are economies of scale in British urban labor markets which influence unemployment rates. The hypothesis was tested for both men and women workers by measuring the association between city size and unemployment. Data from the sample census of 1966 was used. In each case there was a correlation found, but it was a positive one for women and a negative one for men.

566 Ward, J.D. TOWARD 2000: OPPORTUNITIES IN TRANSPORTATION EVOLUTION. Washington, D.C.: U.S. Department of Transportation, Office of the Secretary, 1977. 46 p.

Ward describes possible directions for the nation's transportation system and identifies research and development strategies to take advantage of the most promising opportunities. The book contains a brief examination of population and demographic trends. It analyzes transportation opportunities in several major areas, such as urban transportation, the private automobile, freight-systems, as well as cross-cutting issues such as decision making. The report also includes general discussions of the relationships among transportation changes in the spatial organization of the nation (land use) and the use of resources, energy, labor, and capital.

567 Warner, Sam Bass, Jr., and Fleisch, Sylvia. MEASUREMENTS FOR SOCIAL HISTORY. Beverly Hills, Calif.: Sage Publications 1977. 232 p.

Current planning strategies can be greatly enhanced by placing historical case studies in the context of useful modern knowledge. An historical approach will help explain national, regional, and urban changes--such as population growth, racial distribution, industrialization, urbanization, migration, and fertility-- and thus aid policymakers.

568 Wasylenko, Michael J. "Some Evidence of the Elasticity of Supply of Policemen and Firefighters." URBAN AFFAIRS QUARTERLY 12 (March 1977): 365-82.

In this study, a model was constructed which includes supply and demand equations for eleven public functions. These equations cover such areas as salary, education, unionization, intergovernmental grants-in-aid, and unemployment. The model was tested for wages and employment of police and firefighters for the fiscal year 1968 and included cities with a population of 50,000 or more. The results show that, in general, there is a less than perfectly elastic supply of public employees. Given this situation, differences in the level of demand for public services can be expected to lead to differences in public employment and also wage levels.

569   Webber, Melvin M. "The Post City Age." DAEDALUS 97 (Fall 1968): 109-110.

This is an essay in which the author presents his thoughts on national development in an age of urbanization beyond the city. We have a national urban society which has not touched all Americans equally. Under these circumstances the city can no longer serve as the central organizing idea behind public efforts to develop a national strategy which would accelerate human development and prosperity. This is an introductory chapter to an issue in which a number of scholars set forth a series of targets for the nation's development. References are included.

570   Weicher, John C. "A Test of Jane Jacobs' Theory of Successful Neighborhoods." JOURNAL OF REGIONAL SCIENCE 13 (April 1973): 29-40.

This is an empirical study of the hypothesis put forward by Jane Jacobs that diversity is a generator of successful neighborhoods. Weicher expresses this theory in a quantitative fashion and tests it using multiple regression analysis. He finds that the relationship between density and diversity is the opposite of that predicted by Jacobs. He further finds that diversity has a negative effect on the success of neighborhoods.

571   "Where the Grass is Greener." ECONOMIST 241 (25 December 1971): 15;   242 (22 January 1972): 17-8.

This British periodical attempts to rate several countries in order of pleasantness according to social indicators. A critical evaluation of the statistics used raises many questions as to the reliability of the figures. Points are assigned or subtracted based on: population density, divorce, early marriage, population per doctor, traffic fatalities, murders, infant mortality, ratio of cars to people, proportion of seventeen year olds in school, proportion of dwellings with baths, ratio of telephones to people, and taxes. The United States comes out at the top of the list.

572 White, Michelle J. "Firm Suburbanization and Urban Subcenters." JOURNAL OF URBAN ECONOMICS 3 (October 1976): 323-43.

This presents a mathematical model of firm location in which jobs are located both at the urban center and at a suburban subcenter. White quantifies and discusses several issues: a firm's locational decision when both suburban and central business district export terminals exist; problems in ensuring an adequate labor supply in the suburbs, the effects of a firm's move on a suburb; and the public policy influences on a firm's suburban location decision.

573 Willmott, Peter. "Population and Community in London." NEW SOCIETY 30 (October 1974): 206-10.

Willmott sees an increased "gentrification" of the inner areas of London, resulting not only in the traditional "pull" migration as upwardly mobile working-class households move it, but also "push" migration as the middleclass outbids the lower classes for "historical" housing. This is destroying the traditional kin-network base of the British working-class community to be replaced by middle-class associational forms of community. Willmott suggests that housing policy should be adjusted to permit greater choice of housing for people in their district of residence.

574 Winthrop, Henry. "Social Costs and Studies of the Future." FUTURES 1 (December 1969): 488-99.

Winthrop decries the neglect of social costs be decision makers and even futurists. He applies a systems analysis approach to nuclear power to show the indifference to and the need for systematic treatment of taking account of social costs.

575 Zody, Richard E., and Enlow, Ronald E. AN OPERATIONAL URBAN INFORMATION SYSTEM. Urban Affairs Paper No. 1. Washington, D.C.: National Association of Schools of Public Affairs and Administration, December 1976. 26 p.

The authors pose the need for uniform and stable information systems among the various divisions of metropolitan governments. In 1971 an information system called Wichita-Sedgwick County Intergovernmental Enumeration (WSCIE) was set up to fulfill the data needs for the Wichita urban area of 340,000. The system has generated mixed results, but, according to the authors, it has shown the need for a centralized independent authority to deal with questions of data access and control.

Chapter 5

INDICATOR-RELATED PROGRAM EVALUATIONS

576 Blair, Louis H., and Schwartz, Alfred I. HOW CLEAN IS OUR CITY?
A GUIDE FOR MEASURING THE EFFECTIVENESS OF SOLID WASTE
COLLECTION ACTIVITIES. Washington, D.C.: Urban Institute, 1972.
67 p.

See 134.

577 Bloch, Peter B. EQUALITY OF DISTRIBUTION OF POLICE SERVICES:
A CASE STUDY OF WASHINGTON, D.C. Washington, D.C.: Urban
Institute, 1972. 27 p.

This study compares the equality of police services in two areas
of Washington, D.C. The study was prompted by a lawsuit
filed by a black community in Washington, D.C., alleging an
inequality in the distribution of police services. The author
concludes the allegation cannot be supported either by the
amount of police services or their effectiveness in dealing
with crime. The comparative measures include property crime
rates and trends, violent crime rates, citizen satisfaction,
service calls per officer, police per one hundred robberies,
average police per ten thousand residents, number of service
requests per police car, and daily average police per square
mile. This study can be implemented in other cities.

578 Bloch, Peter B., and Specht, David I. EVALUATION OF OPERATION
NEIGHBORHOOD. Washington, D.C.: Urban Institution, 1973. 148 p.

New York City adopted a program of assigning 10 percent of
its police to neighborhood teams. This study provides data on
community response, police reactions, crime statistics, and
other indicators.

579 Burt, Marvin R., and Blair, Louis H. OPTIONS FOR IMPROVING
THE CARE OF NEGLECTED AND DEPENDENT CHILDREN IN NASHVILLE,
TENNESSEE: PROGRAM ANALYSIS APPLIED TO LOCAL GOVERNMENT.
Washington, D.C.: Urban Institute, 1971. 136 p.

The study describes a methodology for evaluating a human services function of local government--the care of children whose parents have neglected them. The costs and effectiveness of different approaches to processing such cases through the foster homes, welfare organizations, and courts are discussed based on the Nashville experience.

580 Christensen, Kathleen. SOCIAL IMPACTS OF LAND DEVELOPMENT: AN INITIAL APPROACH FOR ESTIMATING IMPACTS ON NEIGHBORHOOD USAGES AND PERCEPTIONS. Washington, D.C.: Urban Institute, 1976. 144 p.

Christensen provides a methodology for determining social impacts of physical development. She stresses the impact of public recreation facilities usage; shopping; pedestrian mobility; environmental quality, personal safety, and privacy; and cultural values. She also suggests ways of measuring impacts on different population subgroups.

581 Dajani, Jarir S.; Vesilind, P. Aarne; and Hartman, Gerald. "Measuring the Effectiveness of Solid Waste Collection." JOURNAL OF URBAN ANALYSIS 4 (1977): 181-219.

The authors provide a conceptual framework for evaluating the effectiveness of solid waste collection. Effectiveness is composed of a user satisfaction component and community effects are measured by visual inspection of streets and vacant lots. By combining these two measures, decision makers can gain a better picture of needs for planning purposes.

582 Derthick, Martha. NEW TOWNS IN-TOWN: WHY A FEDERAL PROGRAM FAILED. Washington, D.C.: Urban Institute, 1972. 103 p.

Derthick reviews seven projects to build low income housing communities on central city sites. The projects at San Antonio; New Bedford, Massachusetts; San Francisco; and Louisville had already failed. The Atlanta, Detroit, and Washington, D.C., projects were still in progress.

583 Dickey, John W., and Fustely, Richard D. A GUIDE FOR ANALYZING LOCAL GOVERNMENT SERVICE PRICING POLICIES WITH SPECIAL REFERENCE TO THE EFFECTS ON URBAN DEVELOPMENT. Blacksburg: Virginia Polytechnic Institute and State University, Center for Urban and Regional Studies, 1975. 68 p.

This guide attempts to help local governments identify and assess means for controlling growth through various service pricing mechanisms. A twelve-step process was created and detailed. The authors use Fairfax County, Virginia, as an example.

584 Fisk, Donald M., and Lancer, Cynthia A. EQUALITY OF DISTRIBUTION OF RECREATION SERVICES: A CASE STUDY OF WASHINGTON, D.C. Washington, D.C.: Urban Institute, 1974. 46 p.

Focusing on a lawsuit charging discrimination against blacks in one section of Washington, D.C., the authors seek to determine if predominantly black communities are receiving inferior public recreation services. The technique developed can be used to measure inequality in recreation services in other communities. The study advances several measurement criteria including capital expenditures, operating expenditures, and quantity and quality of opportunities and utilization. The authors conclude that in Washington, D.C., the determination of equity in distribution of recreation services depends upon the measures chosen for comparison.

585 Greiner, John M.; Dahl, Roger E.; Hatry, Harry P.; and Miller, Annie P. MONETARY INCENTIVES AND WORK STANDARDS IN FIVE CITIES: IMPACTS AND IMPLICATIONS FOR MANAGEMENT AND LABOR. Washington, D.C.: Urban Institute, 1977. 94 p.

This volume summarizes productivity improvement programs in Kansas City, Missouri; Harrisburg, Pennsylvania; Flint, Michigan; Philadelphia; and Orange, California. These case studies deal with work standards for street maintenance personnel, work standards and "productive hours" records for vehicle maintenance staff, wage incentives tied to work standards for water meter repair and installation personnel, performance bonuses for waste collectors, and performance incentives for police department employees. This publication is useful for designing work standards and performance incentives for public employees.

586 Harrison, Bennett. PUBLIC EMPLOYMENT AND URBAN POVERTY. Washington, D.C.: Urban Institute, 1971. 63 p.

The author evaluates the impact of public service jobs on the economic status of the urban poor and points out that public sector jobs often require little experience or skill. These jobs are usually located in central cities where the poor are located.

587 Hatry, Harry P., et al. MEASURING THE EFFECTIVENESS OF BASIC MUNICIPAL SERVICES: INITIAL REPORT. Washington, D.C.: Urban Institute, 1974. 118 p.

This study is the result of a joint effort between the Urban Institute and the International City Management Association in St. Petersburg, Florida, and Nashville, Tennessee. The project developed procedures by which local public officials can receive regular feedback on citizen satisfaction on a range of basic services. Effectiveness criteria have been developed for solid

waste collection and disposal, recreation, library services,
police and fire protection, local transportation, water supply,
and complaint processing. Objectives and data collection
methods and sources are provided for each of the services.
Citizen surveys and questionnaires are discussed from the perspective of implementation and interpretation.

588 Holahan, John. FINANCING HEALTH CARE FOR THE POOR: THE
MEDICAID EXPERIENCE. Lexington, Mass.: Lexington Books, 1975.
176 p.

Holahan reviews the operation of Medicaid. Equity, efficiency,
and rising costs are explored in detail. Eligibility requirements permit many nonpoor to be covered in some states while
in others many of the poor are not covered. Benefits vary
from state to state, and major disparities are found in the
expenditures per eligible person. There are few incentives
for hospitals, physicians, or patients to make efficient use of
services.

589 Illinois Department of Local Government Affairs. EXPERIMENTAL HOUS-
ING ALLOWANCE PROGRAM: THE FINAL REPORT. Springfield: Illinois
Department of Local Government Affairs, 1976. 99 p.

The state of Illinois was one of the eight agencies participating
in the Administrative Agency Experiment (AAE). The AAE is
a major component of the Experimental Housing Allowance
Program (EHAP). It was designed to evaluate different techniques of administering an allowance program for housing. This
report provides the perspective of the agency personnel who
ran the experiment in Peoria, Illinois. It includes a description of the experimental site, highlights, successes, and impact
of the experiment in the community.

590 Koltis, Athena P. "Effects of Income Maintenance on the Economics of
Communities." URBAN AFFAIRS QUARTERLY 8 (June 1973): 465-87.

This is a discussion of the short-run effects of an income maintenance plan on the economies of different communities. The
effects are discussed under several headings: consumer expenditures, housing, labor demand and supply, unemployment, wages,
and prices. Both favorable and unfavorable effects are discussed.

591 Kulash, Damian J., and Silverman, William. DISCRIMINATION IN
MASS TRANSIT. Washington, D.C.: Urban Institute, 1974. 53 p.

The authors deal with allegations that racial minorities or lower
income people in cities are discriminated against in the provision of mass transit. This volume reviews methodological
inadequacies in cost approaches to evaluating the service distribution questions.

592 Lineberry, Robert L. EQUALITY AND URBAN POLICY: THE DISTRIBU-
TION OF MUNICIPAL PUBLIC SERVICES. Beverly Hills, Calif.: Sage
Publications, 1977. 205 p.

This is an analysis of the distribution of urban services. It
poses and then tests five hypotheses about service distribution.
Three of the hypotheses concerning race, socioeconomic status,
and power position fall under the umbrella of an "underclass"
explanation; that is, that the quantity and/or quality of urban
services are positively related to the proportion of Anglo, upper-
class, or powerful persons in a neighborhood. A fourth hypothesis is that the distribution of urban services is a function of
ecological aspects of a neighborhood such as population density
or geographical character. The fifth hypothesis is that urban
services are distributed according to the bureaucratic rules
and regulations in force in the jurisdiction. A case study of
San Antonio casts doubt on the "underclass" explanation and
suggests that bureaucratic decision rules are more critically
linked to service delivery than any neighborhood attributes.

593 McGranahan, Donald V. "Analysis of Socio-Economic Development
Through a System of Indicators." ANNALS OF THE AMERICAN ACADEMY
FOR POLITICAL AND SOCIAL SCIENCE 393 (January 1971): 65-81.

An attempt is made to find indicators for measuring the components of an international definition of levels of living as related to development. McGranahan follows the approach to
the definition and measurement of development as "economic
factors and level-of-living factors that may be viewed as inter-
dependent aspects of an evolving system which at the macrolevel cannot be properly broken down into factors that are
causes and those that are effects, or into inputs and outputs."
Under this conception, development comprises both economic
and social elements, which tend to change together as a complex. The volume examines economic and social indicators
(using 1960 data). A group of priority indicators has been
interrelated by a method of analysis called "correspondence
analysis." This type of analysis provides the basis for plot-
ting development profiles of individual countries against a
norm that changes with level of development. It also provides for typological analysis, showing how development
differs for different kinds of countries. The correspondence
system, plus scale transformations, further provides a means of
constructing a general or synthetic indicator of development,
which serves to predict missing scores better than does the per
capita gross national product, including scores on economic
as well as social variables.

By the use of these techniques of analysis, intended to make
the most of available data and involving no assumptions about
cause and effect, the author believes it is possible to gain a
somewhat clearer idea of what happens in development, and

thereby perhaps a better basis for understanding why develop-
ment happens. This is part of a project at the United Nations
Research Institute for Social Development on Contents and
Measurement of Socio-Economic Development.

594 Miller and Byrne, Inc. ANNOTATED BIBLIOGRAPHY: THE IMPACT OF
PUBLIC HEALTH SERVICE PROGRAMS ON STATE GOVERNMENT. Rockville, Md.: 1977. 183 p.

This volume is an annotated bibliography on the impact of four
federal health programs (Health Planning, Community Mental
Health Centers, Cooperative Health Statistics Systems, and
Nurse Training Grants) upon intergovernmental relations and
state health goals and activities.

595 Muller, Peter O. "The Evaluation of American Suburbs: A Geographical
Interpretation." URBANISM PAST AND PRESENT 4 (Summer 1977): 1-10.

Muller analyzes the development and sustained growth of city
fringes by using the U.S. Bureau of the Census studies beginning
in 1880. The article seeks to explain the forces underlying
this trend, especially certain intrametropolitan transportation
innovations.

596 Muller, Thomas. GROWING AND DECLINING URBAN AREAS: A FIS-
CAL COMPARISON. Washington, D.C.: Urban Institute, 1975. 121 p.

Of the twenty-seven American cities having populations over
half a million, thirteen increased their populations while fourteen declined from 1960 through 1973. This analysis provides
data on urban fiscal conditions and the available policy options.
Most of the cities with higher populations achieved this result
through annexation.

597 Muller, Thomas, and Dawson, Grace. THE FISCAL IMPACT OF RESIDEN-
TIAL AND COMMERCIAL DEVELOPMENT: A CASE STUDY. Washington,
D.C.: Urban Institute, 1972. 140 p.

This work predicts the fiscal impact of residential and commercial
development proposed in Albemarle County, Virginia, near
Charlottesville. The authors conclude that one large development will have a negative fiscal impact on the county.

598 New York City. Commission on the Delivery of Personal Health Services.
COMMUNITY HEALTH SERVICES FOR NEW YORK CITY: REPORT AND
STAFF STUDIES OF THE COMMISSION ON THE DELIVERY OF PERSONAL
HEALTH SERVICES. New York: Praeger, 1969. 696 p.

This is a report resulting from an investigation of health services
in New York City. It includes an analysis of services rendered
by public agencies and services delivered through voluntary and

private institutions. It also presents a model of the application of systems analysis to problems of health services in a metropolitan area. Topics covered are population characteristics and potential of municipal hospitals; medical manpower problems; the impact of city, state and federal funding and the functions and roles of city executive agencies in relation to health care services. Existing resources are reviewed and related to sources of new funds and technological advances in the medical and data processing field. Recommendations are offered and can be utilized by other cities in analyzing their own health care program.

599 Peskin, Henry M., and Seskin, Eugene P., eds. COST-BENEFIT ANALYSIS AND WATER POLLUTION POLICY. Washington, D.C.: Urban Institute, 1975. 370 p.

While the art of cost-benefit analysis has long been applied to water pollution studies, there still are difficulties of measuring both costs and benefits. This publication applies measures to practical pollution problems, and discusses who should pay (and how much) for water pollution abatement, what control mechanisms are feasible, and whether institutional changes are needed to protect natural resources.

600 Public Technology, Inc. HUD/PTI INFORMATION SYSTEMS IMPROVEMENT PROGRAM: CHIEF EXECUTIVE'S OVERVIEW. Washington, D.C.: 1977. 86 p.

This volume is part of a series of reports on the establishment of an information systems improvement program in local government. It deals with relevant information systems concepts, program organization, operations, and the factors involved in evaluating the costs and benefits of an improvement program.

601 Rokeach, Milton, and Parker, Seymour. "Values as Social Indicators of Poverty and Race Relations in America." ANNALS OF THE AMERICAN ACADEMY OF POLITICAL AND SOCIAL SCIENCE 388 (March 1930): 97-111.

The purpose of this paper is to describe a way of thinking about values and value systems and a way of measuring them so that they may be widely employed as social indicators of underlying social problems--specifically poverty and race relations and the issue of whether or not cultural differences exist between the poor and the rich and between Negro and white.

The Rokeach Value Survey consists of two sets of eighteen terminal (preferred end-states of existence) and eighteen instrumental values (preferred modes of behavior). The respondent's task is to rearrange each set of eighteen values in order of importance as "guiding principles in your daily life." Distinctive value patterns have been found for various groups such as hippies, policemen, prison inmates, college students, college professors, artists, and the religiously devout. The findings reported here lend support to the idea that considerable value differences do distinguish the rich from the poor, but not Negroes from whites. Differences found between the latter, for the most part, disappear when socioeconomic position is controlled.

602 Schaenman, Philip S. USING AN IMPACT MEASUREMENT SYSTEM TO EVALUATE LAND DEVELOPMENT. Washington, D.C.: Urban Institute, 1976. 106 p.

Schaenman reviews impact measurement systems as applied in Phoenix, Arizona; Indianapolis, Indiana; and Montgomery County, Maryland. He uses a checklist system to evaluate new developments. The measures attempt to determine if community goals will be advanced by the development. The volume provide guidelines for measuring impacts on the aged, the poor, and the handicapped.

603 Schiff, M. "Social Dysfunctions and Myths--Indicators of Social Malaise in Sweden and Other Industrialized Societies." AMERICAN JOURNAL OF ECONOMICS AND SOCIOLOGY 34 (July 1975): 281-94.

By comparative analysis of social indicators, this investigation attempts to clarify the dysfunctions of Swedish society in rela-tion to the popular mythology in Western and industrialized societies concerning the Swedish way of life. It finds that Sweden remains a capitalistic country in the forefront of pro-gressive reform despite the critics' beliefs that alleged socio-economic shortcomings in its welfare state have produced wide-spread social malaise and loss of capitalist incentive and indi-vidual initiative. The separation of dysfunction from myth pro-ceeds on two levels: (1) an examination of functional character-istics of and false assumptions regarding sexual liberation and the welfare state, and (2) a comparison of indicators of social malaise in Sweden and other industrialized societies.

604 U.S. Department of Health, Education, and Welfare. EVALUATION OF SERVICES INTEGRATION DEMONSTRATION PROJECTS. Rockville, Md.: 1976. 45 p.

An abstract bibliography on thirty-eight evaluation reports on human services integration projects funded by U.S. Department of Health, Education, and Welfare as part of Project Share. Projects are aimed at testing various human service linkage mechanisms such as integrated planning, new case manage-ment approaches, and integrated information systems. The documents range from evaluations of individual Services Inte-gration Targets of Opportunity (SITO) projects to aggregate evaluation.

605 Wholey, Joseph S., et al. FEDERAL EVALUATION POLICY: ANALYZ-
ING THE EFFECTS OF PUBLIC PROGRAMS. Washington, D.C.: Urban
Institute, 1970. 134 p.

> The study evaluates fifteen programs in the U.S. Department
> of Health, Education, and Welfare, the U.S. Department of
> Housing and Urban Development, the Office of Economic
> Opportunity, and the U.S. Department of Labor. It includes
> seventy-two specific program evaluation recommendations.

606 Winnie, Richard E., and Hatry, Harry P. MEASURING THE EFFECTIVE-
NESS OF LOCAL GOVERNMENT SERVICES: TRANSPORTATION. Washington, D.C.: Urban Institute, 1972. 84 p.

> This study is citizen oriented in that it tries to help consumers
> assess the quality of local transportation. The proposed system
> provides local officials with a mechanism for evaluating how
> well their transportation services are meeting the needs of
> citizens. Twelve measures of effectiveness are analyzed
> against goals such as safety, accessibility, convenience, travel
> time, and environmental quality. Communities are shown how
> to collect data for different transportation users. Recommenda-
> tions and cost estimates are provided.

607 Young, Dennis R. HOW SHALL WE COLLECT THE GARBAGE? A
STUDY IN ECONOMIC ORGANIZATION. Washington, D.C.: Urban
Institute, 1972. 83 p.

> The report provides urban officials with guidelines setting
> standards and levels of garbage collection, for monitoring the
> collection agencies, and for determining how to finance
> garbage collection.

Chapter 6

FUTURE OF URBAN INDICATORS

608 Alford, Robert R. "Data Resources for Comparative Studies of Urban Administration." SOCIAL SCIENCE INFORMATION 9 (June 1970): 193-203.

> Alford presents a summary of an informal meeting at the United Nations in 1969 of scholars in various pursuits related to the collection and utilization of data from all over the world. The article covers the need for such data for use in urban administration, how it might be collected and organized, and probable difficulties to be encountered.

609 Anderson, James G. "Causal Models and Social Indicators: Toward the Development of Social Systems Models." AMERICAN SOCIOLOGICAL REVIEW 38 (June 1973): 285-301.

> See 119.

610 Appelbaum, Richard P. "The Future is Made, Not Predicted: Technocratic Planners vs. Public Interest." SOCIETY 14 (May-June 1977): 49-53.

> The increasing input of experts who claim to have scientific knowledge about human behavior into the public decision-making process represents a threat to our freedom. The possibilities for expert, technical social science knowledge are severely limited by the very nature of such knowledge. Thus, belief in the possibility of finding technical solutions to all social problems is a myth with highly political consequences. To regain some measure of control over our lives, we must revise our theory of knowledge, rethink the differences between technical knowledge and political choices, and, in sum, re-politicize our lives.

611 Bauer, Raymond A. "Detection and Anticipation of Impact: The Nature of The Task." In his SOCIAL INDICATORS, pp. 1-67. Cambridge: MIT Press, 1966.

> See 5.

612   Bell, Daniel. "The Adequacy of Our Concepts." In A GREAT SOCIETY?, edited by Bertram M. Gross, pp. 127-61. New York: Basic Books, 1968.

In looking at social change and social values there is a need for a new calculus. The inadequacy of National Income and Product Accounts, National Wealth Accounting, gross national product, and so forth is pointed out. A system of social accounts is called for. This system would seek to measure social costs and net returns of innovations and to create indicators of economic opportunity and social mobility.

613   _____. "Notes on the Post Industrial Society (I)." PUBLIC INTEREST 6 (Winter 1967): 24-35.

The United States economy today is primarily a service rather than a manufacturing one. This is the result of the acceleration of technological development and diffusion, and the tremendous increase in the professional and technical work force. New theories of economic planning allow the government to induce growth, redirect resources and reshape the economy itself. New technology allows the government to conduct large-scale controlled experiments by computer and to plot alternative futures.

The author deduces that the intellectuals in government and the universities, the professional and technical sectors of society, will expand not only in number but in power. They will exert greater pressure on the government for objectives usually associated with the more highly educated: more social amenities, improved quality of life in the city, improved educational systems, enhanced cultural opportunities, and so forth. The universities will become the central institutions in America as the source of innovation and knowledge.

Nevertheless, the author concludes that the political arena will become even more significant because more policy decisions will involve national rather than private or local interests, more interest groups will assert their claim to national priorities, and because a technological society will require the government to do more government planning.

614   _____. "Notes on the Post Industrial Society (II)." PUBLIC INTEREST 7 (Spring 1967): 102-18.

The major concern of society today is no longer the production of goods but the improvement of services, education, and the amenities. Government by experts, advisors, and technocrats has replaced the market as the primary decision maker. However, some of society's problems cannot be readily resolved with technical criteria because they involve values and political choices and because there is presently no effective social calculus which can provide a true measure of the total social cost or benefit of a policy decision.

The author recommends a system of social accounts to broaden the scope of present economic accounting. The system would begin with a series of social indicators which would help to measure several factors: the social as well as the private cost of enterprises; the cost of social ills such as crime, juvenile delinquency, and disruption of the family; the quality of life in terms of health care, adequate housing, and so forth, and not just the standard of living; and human assets such as health and income earning capacity. The ultimate purpose of the system and the social indicators would be to clarify policy choices.

615 _____. "Toward a Social Report: I." PUBLIC INTEREST 15 (Spring 1969): 72-84.

See 9.

616 Boucher, Wayne I. "The Future Environment for Technology Assessment." In TECHNOLOGY ASSESSMENT IN A DYNAMIC ENVIRONMENT, edited by Marvin J. Cetron and Bodo Bartocha, pp. 401-14. New York: Gordon and Breach Science Publishers, 1973.

Boucher describes the internal and external pressures which he believes will contribute to a radical transformation of the science of technology assessment in the near future.

Boucher claims that in order for technology assessment (TA) to serve all its purposes well, TA will have to develop a reliable system of social indicators. Its uses will include the assessment of priorities for TA. The need for a social indicators system reflects the need to recognize new human imperatives and the need to explore "all forms of consciousness, all forms of expression, and all forms of institutions." Boucher explains that the social indicators analysis must be a creative and bold endeavor because it is the responsibility of the TA scientist to anticipate future social consequences of major technological advancements. However, Boucher warns that TA scientists will have to deal with the phenomenon of changing social values and pressures which will challenge the conclusions of the TA assessor.

Boucher believes that TA is not significantly different from systems analysis. In fact, he writes that some authors in the field feel that the principles of TA are not new, but the difference is that there is a greater commitment and emphasis being given to futures research. Boucher predicts that TA will receive institutional support (possibly the strongest from private corporations) which will eventually lead to an increased influence in contemporary decision making for TA.

617 Brady, Edward L., and Branscomb, Lewis M. "Information for a Changing Society." SCIENCE 175 (March 1972): 961-66.

The authors stress the need for improved mechanisms for developing information, performing social analysis, and making good decisions. They categorize the users of information: the researcher, the industrial engineer or other applier, the planner, the policymaker, the decision maker, the manager, and the public as consumer, beneficiary, and victim. The article summarizes the government's goals for a national policy on information, the objectives to meet the broader goals, and the report's conclusions.

618   Brouillette, John R. "The Department of Public Works: Adaptation to Disaster Demands." AMERICAN BEHAVIORAL SCIENTIST 13 (January-February 1970): 369-79.

This article begins with a description of public works departments in large cities pointing out several common characteristics: large bureaucracy, abundance of resources, highly trained personnel, and a well-developed communications system. The major tasks of the public works department are listed, and those which place special demands on the department during a crisis are discussed. These include: keeping the streets open, insuring the distribution of water to the community, and maintaining the sewer system in working order. There are four types of situations which might produce demands for changes in either the tasks or structure of public works organizations. They are normal periods, anticipated periodic emergencies, unanticipated disasters, and unanticipated disasters of a serious magnitude.

619   Cohen, Wilbur J. "Education and Learning." ANNALS OF THE AMERICAN ACADEMY OF POLITICAL AND SOCIAL SCIENCE 373 (September 1967): 79-101.

Cohen discusses the need for quantitative as well as qualitative indicators to measure progress toward educational goals. He sees the indicators on quality of education and educational opportunity as triggering change and modernization in the educational system.

620   _____. "Social Indicators: Statistics for Public Policy." AMERICAN STATISTICIAN 22 (October 1968): 14-16.

Wilbur Cohen talks about the kind of statistics that the secretary of HEW needs: (1) those illustrating present conditions in society, and (2) those that can suggest the cost and effectiveness of alternative means of resolving the problems that exist. He argues that there is a need for more indicators that will help policymakers; for example, indicators to measure the performance of teachers and the output of the educational system. He suggests a program that would assess the state of education. Social indicators could help prevent problems from

becoming serious by demonstrating clearly to policymakers that
the problem is developing. There is a need for new research
and speed in the delivery of information both to decision makers
and to the public. Administrators must be able to interpret
the numbers, and statisticans can make an important contribution in this regard.

621   Coleman, James S. RESOURCES FOR SOCIAL CHANGE: RACE IN THE
UNITED STATES. New York: Wiley-Interscience, 1971. 114 p.

Coleman develops a list of the political, economic, and social
resources that define the individual's position in American
society. He believes these resources represent the "focal points"
in social change for blacks since blacks have lower than average levels of nearly all these resources than whites.

The aim of racial social change in Coleman's estimation is to
reduce and eventually eliminate the differential between resources
held by the average white and the average black. Coleman's
purpose in writing this book is "to begin a description of that
system which will aid in the development of resources for
those groups in a society that currently experience the greatest
deficits, in particular Negroes in American Society."

Coleman distinguishes between two categories of social resources.
One type of resource is that which is of value in and of
itself. The second type of resource is that which is conver-
tible into resources of other types. The book gives a good
description of the comparative state of resources held by blacks
and whites. It presents a new approach to the theory of social
change by proposing a system of resource conversion as the
means of social reform.

622   deJouvenel, Bertrand. "A Letter On Predicting." AMERICAN BEHAV-
IORAL SCIENTIST 9 (June 1966): 51.

The author argues that it would be illuminating to aggregate
forecasts by a group of experts in some particular field and
then check them against forecasts made by a random group of
citizens with no special relevant expertise. He suggests that
by comparing the experts to three or four random groups of
citizens, ranked according to degree of general knowledge,
findings might indicate whether predictive ability increases or
decreases as general and special knowledge increases.

623   de Neufville, Judith Innes. SOCIAL INDICATORS AND PUBLIC POLICY:
INTERACTIVE PROCESSES OF DESIGN AND APPLICATION. New York:
Elsevier Scientific Publishing Co., 1975. 311 p.

See 149.

624   Dirasian, Henry A. "Water Quality: The State of the Art." URBAN
       AFFAIRS QUARTERLY 6 (December 1970): 199-212.

       Dirasian focuses on the problem of treating liquid and solid
       wastes. He describes the conventional processes of eliminating
       these wastes from our waterways as well as some recent tech-
       nological advances. Local jurisdictions are urged to recognize
       the seriousness of the problem and particularly the archaic
       means by which they are dealing with the problem. Water-
       way treatment is not a technological problem, it is one of
       reordering priorities to meet needs. Strong federal leadership
       is required or else it will be difficult to overcome the frag-
       mented efforts historically associated with environmental issues.

625   Downs, Anthony. "Alternative Futures for the American Ghetto."
       DAEDALUS 97 (Fall 1968): 1331-78.

       Downs discusses the possibility of various futures for American
       ghettos. He sees the need for the development of a single,
       long-range strategy to cope with social problems. He develops
       several alternative strategies for dealing with the problem of
       future ghetto growth. He discusses the present policy and
       four alternatives in the context of degree of concentration,
       degree of segregation, and degree of enrichment. His solution
       to the problem is integrated dispersal of Negroes out of the
       central city. He makes some program suggestions on how to
       do this, but they are not fully developed.

626   Drenowski, Jan. "The Practical Significance of Social Information."
       ANNALS OF THE AMERICAN ACADEMY OF POLITICAL AND SOCIAL
       SCIENCE 393 (January 1971): 82-91.

       This article is concerned with the needs for more extensive
       and reliable social information. It raises and attempts to answer
       two questions: "What kind of information on social matters
       is most urgently required, and why?" Drenowski criticizes
       the use of economic indicators in the social area and suggests
       several specific types of "social indicators," generally those
       which express "welfare of the population" and those which
       express or refer to the development process.

627   Dror, Yehezkel. DESIGN FOR POLICY SCIENCES. New York: Ameri-
       can Elsevier Publishing Co., 1971. 156 p.

       Dror presents the idea of "policy sciences" as the answer to
       the need for a different scientific approach to meet the needs
       of humanity. He contends that various sciences have been
       successful only in a limited way, and they have failed very
       badly in attempts at policy formation. The author presents a
       case for policy sciences in great detail-dimensions, analysis,
       so-called "megapolicy" and "metapolicy" political implications,
       and so forth.

628   Etzioni, Amitai. "Indicators of the Capacities for Societal Guidance."
       ANNALS OF THE AMERICAN ACADEMY OF POLITICAL AND SOCIAL
       SCIENCE 388 (March 1970): 25-34.

         See 156.

629   Etzioni, Amitai, and Lehman, Edward W. "Some Dangers in Valid Social
       Measurement." ANNALS OF THE AMERICAN ACADEMY OF POLITICAL
       AND SOCIAL SCIENCE 373 (September 1967): 1-15.

         This essay deals with dysfunctions that social measurement may
         have for societal planning. Problems examined include frac-
         tional measurement, indirect measurement, and formalistic-
         aggregative measurement. These problems may lead to invalid
         conclusions which could become the basis for erroneous policy
         decisions.

630   Fisk, Donald M., et al. HOW EFFECTIVE ARE YOUR COMMUNITY
       RECREATION SERVICES? Washington, D.C.: Government Printing
       Office, 1973. 89 p.

         This report proposes measures and procedures to collect effective-
         ness data on community recreation services.

631   Friedman, Lewis, and Marlin, John T. "Rating Cities Performance."
       NATIONAL CIVIC REVIEW 65 (January 1976): 12-19.

         Careful monitoring of local government performance is needed.
         Economy in government is one test of performance but other
         standards are needed to supplement it. Efficiency is best used
         to guide the everyday delivery of municipal services, but
         not to determine what programs should be funded at what levels.
         Evaluating program effectiveness is a new challenge to the
         current way of doing things. It is directed at uncovering
         which programs succeed in obtaining their goals and which ones
         do not. An accurate rating performance can help in setting
         city priorities and in allocating scarce resources to different
         departments and functions of government.

632   Glaser, Daniel. "National Goals and Indicators for the Reduction of
       Crime and Delinquency." ANNALS OF THE AMERICAN ACADEMY OF
       POLITICAL AND SOCIAL SCIENCE 371 (May 1967): 104-26.

         See 415.

633   Goldin, Harrison J. "Financial Problems of the Cities." BUREAUCRAT
       5 (January 1977): 377-90.

         Goldin describes the highly unorthodox fiscal procedures that
         New York City has used to manage its deficits: (1) Since
         there was no central accounting system, no one knew how much

expense the city had incurred at any particular time. (2)
Due to agency autonomy, the city had no precise information
on how many employees it had, how much money it actually
had. (3) The comptroller, who is elected, and the budget
director, who is appointed by the mayor, did not develop
common data bases. Lists ten concrete goals for helping New
York City, including that of a balanced budget by 1978 and
an unprecedented attempt to overhaul its accounting and budget procedures. Moreover, he argues that federal policies which
have encouraged suburban growth at the expense of the cities
must be drastically altered. Otherwise, what has happened to
New York will happen to every older major city in America.

634   Goldman, Nathan. "Social Breakdown." ANNALS OF THE AMERICAN
ACADEMY OF POLITICAL AND SOCIAL SCIENCE 373 (September 1967):
156-79. Reprinted in SOCIAL INTELLIGENCE FOR AMERICA'S FUTURE,
edited by Bertram M. Gross, pp. 375-404. Boston: Allyn and Bacon,
1969.

See 166.

635   Goldston, Eli. THE QUANTIFICATION OF CONCERN: SOME ASPECTS
OF SOCIAL ACCOUNTING. New York: Columbia University Press,
1972. 76 p.

This is a publication of three lectures, one each on social indicators, social responsibility, and social audit. In nontechnical fashion, Goldstein reviews the need for and efforts at
acquiring indicators and the many uses to which they can be
put. He also discusses the need that corporations have for the
knowledge that such indicators supply as well as, more generally,
the responsiblity corporations have to society.

636   Gordon, Ian. "Subjective Social Indicators and Urban Political Analysis:
Or, What Do We Need to Know about Who's Happy?" POLICY AND
POLITICS 5 (March 1977): 93-111.

Gordon argues that the field of subjective social indicators has
some utility for students of urban policymaking, but that it lies
outside the mainstream of traditional political science in its
psychological orientation and its concern for the nonpolitical
feelings or attitudes of nonelite actions. Some of the recent
works on subjective measures of well-being are reviewed, both
in terms of what they measure and what the measurements have
shown. Conclusions are then drawn regarding the relevance
of subjective social indicators for local political studies.

637   Gottehrer, Barry. "Urban Conditions: New York City." ANNALS OF
THE AMERICAN ACADEMY OF POLITICAL AND SOCIAL SCIENCE 371
(May 1967): 141-58. Reprinted in SOCIAL INTELLIGENCE FOR

AMERICA'S FUTURE: EXPLORATIONS IN SOCIETAL PROBLEMS, edited by Bertram M. Gross, pp. 472-94. Boston: Allyn and Bacon, 1969.

See 43.

638   Gottman, Jean. "The Present Renewal of Mankind's Habitat: An Overview of Present Trends of Urbanization Around the World." HABITAT 1 (September 1976): 157-63.

Urban theory is still based on the conception of towns as stable, rather homogeneous communities. Thus, it has difficulty measuring or even defining the realities of the modern city. Yet the large and growing cities of the world are the greatest laboratories for mass acculturation that ever existed. The time seems right for an attempt to formulate new methods of dealing with urban areas: density must be accepted and explained; the present waste of space, materials, and human time must be reduced and replaced with more economical consumption; and the amount of goods, machines, housing, transport, and space in general used by individuals must be cut back.

639   Gross, Bertram M. "The City of Man: A Social Systems Reckoning." In ENVIRONMENT FOR MAN: THE NEXT FIFTY YEARS, edited by William R. Ewald, Jr., 136-56. Bloomington: Indiana University Press, 1967.

Gross attempts to shock city planners to secure more attention to the human aspects of planning. He notes dangers as well as the potential of social systems accounting for urban areas. He urges that the United Nations broaden its state of the world surveys and that the president either broaden the Economic Report to Congress or the State of the Union Message or else establish a social report to cover progress on problems in social structure and development.

640   _____. "The Coming General Systems Models of Social Systems." HUMAN RELATIONS 20 (November 1967): 357-74.

Gross asks three basic questions: "Where have we been?" "Where are we going?" "Where do we want to go?" The thrust is that we see individual changes, but there is a great multiplicity of effects in different areas every time there is a change. He describes these as systems changes. Gross advises that a systems approach is needed. He explains different types of social accounting and emphasizes the need for general systems accounting and discusses such things as models, structure, and performance as well as dynamics and openness. The author relies on his own previous works extensively in this article.

641 _____. "The State of the Nation: Social Systems Accounting." In
SOCIAL INDICATORS, edited by Raymond A. Bauer, pp. 154–271.
Cambridge: MIT Press, 1966.

See 44.

642 Gross, Bertram M., and Springer, Michael. "New Goals for Social
Information." ANNALS OF THE AMERICAN ACADEMY OF POLITICAL
AND SOCIAL SCIENCE 373 (September 1967): 208–18.

The authors propose that a rational consideration of policy is
impeded by a domestic "intelligence gap." A dimension of
this gap is "concept lag," and its remedy is a table of "Indicator Suggestions" which should contribute to conceptual innovation and the upgrading of obsolescent data. New social
information is needed to overcome the "intelligence gap" that
inhibits the making of effective policy. Indicators and goals
must be developed and interrelated. Eight specific suggestions
are outlined for improving this situation and acquiring hard
data.

643 _____, eds. "Political Intelligence for America's Future." ANNALS
OF THE AMERICAN ACADEMY OF POLITICAL AND SOCIAL SCIENCE
388 (March 1970): entire issue.

This entire issue is devoted to a look ahead at the role that
social indicators and social reports may play in the development and management of American society. Special editors
Bertram M. Gross and Michael Springer were given the task
of assembling the study.

The work includes ten articles written by a dozen scholars
and is divided into three parts: "On Societal Guidance,"
"The Uses of Social Knowledge," and "On Social Accounts."
The contributors look at political, industrial, and urban institutions and examine both domestic and international factors
which affect the study of social indicators.

The articles address the fundamental questions facing proponents
of a social science of managerial rationality: what is to be
included under the label "social indicators," and how is this
social knowledge to be combined with conventional economic
analyses to and the process of policy formulation? The editors
and contributors give functional substance to what is too often
viewed as a purely "intellectual exercise"--the formulation
and use of social science indicators. A selected bibliography
is also included.

644 Haar, Charles M. SUBURBAN PROBLEMS. Cambridge, Mass.: Ballinger
Publishing Co., 1974. 212 p.

In October 1967, President Lyndon Johnson directed that a

national task force be created to study suburban problems. The task force report, completed in the waning months of the Johnson administration, profiled American suburbia and identified a number of existing problems as follows: (1) inflating land costs, (2) abuse of the countryside and pollution, (3) increased transportation costs, (4) escalating home costs and the exclusion of the disadvantaged, (5) psychological aimlessness, and (6) increasing expense of public services and education.

Three major recommendations are put forth to cope with these problems. First, creation of an urban development bank to open up new and larger sources of private and public capital for public investment. Second, development of a federal urban parklands corporation to monitor and more effectively control urban land use. And third, housing assistance for Vietnam veterans, the elderly, and other minorities to give them better access to suburban living.

645   Hatry, Harry P. "Issues in Productivity Measurement for Local Government." PUBLIC ADMINISTRATION REVIEW 32 (November-December 1972): 776-84.

Productivity measurements are important resources in determining how effective action taken by local governments has been. Yet productivity measurement programs in local government have not been implemented in large numbers. This article highlights the need for productivity measurement in cities and discusses the difficulties involved in trying to define and measure outputs in social service functions. The measurement of input is discussed by suggesting three alternatives: man hours or man years of effort, cost in constant dollars, and cost in current dollars without deflating for price level changes. The author presents an illustration of ten service functions and suggested workload measures, citizen impact measures, and pertinent local conditions that should be considered in measuring productivity. Two examples of solid waste collection and police crime control are presented.

646   Hatry, Harry P., and Fisk, Donald M. IMPROVING PRODUCTIVITY AND PRODUCTIVITY MEASUREMENTS IN LOCAL GOVERNMENT. Washington, D.C.: National Commission on Productivity and Work Quality, 1971. 73 p.

This study summarizes the major issues in productivity and productivity measures in local government with special emphasis on the comparisons between political jurisdictions. Reviewing current programs and practices, the authors do not find adequate comparative data or national data for any local governmental functions. They recommend approaches for developing such data to increase efficiency and effectiveness in local government and suggest problem areas to be considered when comparing productivity data in different local governments.

647   Hauser, Philip M. "Are the Social Sciences Ready?" AMERICAN SOCIOLOGICAL REVIEW 11 (August 1946): 379-84.

Hauser asks whether social scientists are ready for the opportunity and challenge of providing enough knowledge to prevent the suicidal anachronism represented by our social institutions and practices. He views the debate over the advisability of including a division of social sciences in the National Science Foundation as a symptom of the prevalent state of social disorganization. Hauser's study highlights considerations which should figure heavily in blueprints drawn for foundations sponsored research. Such projects will test whether the social sciences are ready with carefully planned, well-designed, far-reaching, and significant research objectives.

648   _____. "The Chaotic Society: Product of the Social Morphological Revolution." AMERICAN SOCIOLOGICAL REVIEW 34 (February 1969): 1-19.

Hauser discusses the impact on man and society of changes in size, density, and heterogeneity of population through consideration of four developments and their interrelationship: population explosion, population implosion (density), population diversification, and accelerated tempo of technological and social changes. He explores the role of social sciences in social accounting.

649   _____. "Statement of Dr. Hauser." Symposium on Communities of Tomorrow, December 11-12, 1976. In NATIONAL GROWTH AND ITS DISTRIBUTION. U.S. Department of Agriculture in cooperation with the Department of Commerce; Health, Education, and Welfare; Housing and Urban Development; Labor; and Transportation, April 1968, pp. 70-77.

Hauser was one of nineteen participants speaking before a gathering of scholars, business leaders, and government officials. Discussions and presentations centered on why and how growth is occurring and what it projects for the future.

The fundamental solution to the urban problem is implicit in a number of perspectives, he asserts, including the population explosion, the population implosion, population diversification, acceleration of technological change, our outmoded system of government, state government inattention to urban areas, fragmented metropolitan areas, misidentification of problems, and segregated housing patterns. He suggests in the future that we strive for the development of a national growth policy and national goals, the rationalization of the American system of government, and the placement of human rights as a first priority.

650   Hoch, Irving. "Quality of Life Related to City Size." HABITAT 2, nos. 1-2 (1977): 219-34.

Hoch discusses a number of factors which influence quality of life as they relate to city size. Some of the observations are that (1) wages are higher in large cities, (2) taxes increase with population size faster than does income, and (3) despite the presence of other factors, it is valid to say that crime is higher in larger cities. Cities can solve their problems, the author argues, without massive population redistribution.

651   Horowitz, Irving Louis. "Social Indicators and Social Policy." In his PROFESSING SOCIOLOGY: STUDIES IN THE LIFE CYCLE OF SOCIAL SCIENCE, pp. 328-39. Chicago: Aldine, 1968.

Horowitz asks several basic questions. (1) Can a useful national social accounting system be established? (2) How can we insure against violations of privacy considering the kind of data to be gathered? (3) What role might state and local governments play in formulating, implementing, and participating in creating a national social policy? (4) Should data collection be a state, regional, or national responsibility?

Horowitz argues that a council of social advisors must be established and some kind of social accounting operationalized. Flexible legislative guidelines need to be established to resolve real social problems. Social scientists must be given a role in shaping public policy. A social accounting act would be a step in the right direction.

652   Howard, William A. "City-Size and Its Relationship to Municipal Efficiency: Some Observations and Questions." EKISTICS 28 (November 1969): 312-15.

Howard's article concerns the relationship between size of city and cost of benefits per capita in a quantitative and qualitative sense. A good deal of research has been done on the former but little on the latter. The author notes a few places where some work has been done and continues to be done, but he advises that these are rather meager and involve very limited areas. Howard calls for additional information in the quality phase of measurements of municipal services.

653   Johnston, Denis F. "Forecasting Methods in the Social Sciences." TECHNOLOGICAL FORECASTING AND SOCIAL CHANGE 2 (July 1970): 173-87.

See 185.

654   Judge, Anthony J.N. "Information Systems and Inter-Organizational Space." ANNALS OF THE AMERICAN ACADEMY OF POLITICAL AND SOCIAL SCIENCE 393 (January 1971): 47-64.

The author describes the need for a worldwide information
collection system. He maintains that great amounts of data
are not being used efficiently and much of it not at all.
Judge outlines the difficulties and the waste this causes and
recommends solutions. His solutions involved more attention
to social aspects than economic aspects of growth and development as well as the use of computer systems. Judge outlines
details of his own system which would be useful in correcting
the problem of inadequate flow of information to policymakers,
primarily through what the author describes as "interactive
computer graphics."

655 Kangun, Norman, and Moyer, R. Charles. "The Failings of Regulation."
MSU BUSINESS TOPICS 24 (Spring 1976): 5-14.

Direct regulation of natural monopolies and more general anti-
trust regulation of American industry has been less than satisfactory. The classical dichotomy of pure competition and
monopoly continues to be the basis for regulatory theory even
though oligopoly and interdependence are the dominant characteristics of the contemporary industrial structure. Moreover,
the "economic man" model of consumer behavior is an unrealistic basis for many public policy actions. In addition, the
fact that public policy is made and implemented by lawyers,
whose training and habits are inadequate for effective policymaking, is an obvious problem. Lawyers are not trained in
economics, finance, or quantitative methods. Lawyers also
have an orientation toward winning cases, whereas rational
regulation and enforcement policy demands that resources be
directed toward problems where societal payoffs are likely to
be largest.

656 Kopkind, Andrew. "The Future-Planners." AMERICAN PSYCHOLOGIST
22 (November 1967): 1036-41.

Kopkind discusses new ways to analyze, anticipate, and control
the social environment, involving both central planning and
futurism. He gives a description of future-planning projects.
There is an assumption that government must increasingly inter-
vene to reform the social structure. There is a need for social
indicators as a base for future planning. The assumption of
future planning is that the lack of information is at the bottom
of society's problems.

657 Lee, Philip R. "Health and Well Being." ANNALS OF THE AMERICAN
ACADEMY OF POLITICAL AND SOCIAL SCIENCE 373 (September 1967):
193-207.

Lee describes health in the broad sense of absence of pain and
disease and feeling of well-being. He discusses relationships
between health and well-being and other factors such as

economic status, housing, education, social class and customs, and culture. The author proposes that techniques should be developed to measure these relationships in an effort to establish rational goals for health and well-being. He asserts that health status has generally been a negative function (measuring mortality, morbidity, and disability) and must change to provide an index of positive health and well-being--not just technical and scientific but social as well. Land calls for a system to measure quality of care, but does not provide any plan for achieving this.

658 _____. "A New Perspective on Health, Planning, and Health Policy." JOURNAL OF ALLIED HEALTH 6 (Winter 1977): 8-15.

Federal health policy in American should have two primary goals: (1) to improve the health of the people by attacking the changing causes of death and disability and by restoring the concept of individual responsibility for health, and (2) to make it possible for all Americans to have access to adequate health care, to be able to pay for necessary care, and, at the same time, to reform the system of health care financing so that its costs will not continue to escalate. If health policy is based on sound understanding of the biological, behavioral, sociocultural, and environmental determinants of health, it can lead to a more rational and economic use of America's health resources.

659 Liu, Ben-Chieh. "Economic and Non-Economic Quality of Life: Empirical Indicators and Policy Implications for Large Standard Metropolitan Areas." AMERICAN JOURNAL OF ECONOMICS AND SOCIOLOGY 36 (July 1977): 225-40.

Liu analyzes U.S. Standard Metropolitan Statistical Areas (SMSAs) with populations greater than five hundred thousand in an effort to quantitatively measure quality of life. Individual indicators such as income and wealth as well as community indicators such as industrial productivity and income distribution were used. The SMSAs were then classified in accordance with the index values of the indicators. The trade-offs between economic growth and changes in noneconomic conditions among the urban areas were studied, and policy implications were deduced and recommended.

660 Lucy, William H. "Metropolitan Dynamics: A Cross-National Framework for Analyzing Public Policy Effects in Metropolitan Areas." URBAN AFFAIRS QUARTERLY 11 (December 1975): 155-85.

Lucy's article calls for a "framework" to be used in analyzing the effects of public policies. The emphasis is on metropolitan areas, but the author asserts that the framework can be adapted to urbanized nations. He begins with a set of basic assumptions regarding individuals, public services, and policies. Lucy then builds ten propositions on top of that, from very basic personal relationships to interactions among other areas such as sociology, economics, and political science. He recommends additional studies along the same lines.

661 Madden, J. Patrick. "Social Change and Public Policy in Rural America: Data and Research Needs for the 1970's." AMERICAN JOURNAL OF AGRICULTURAL ECONOMICS 52 (May 1970): 308-14.

There is a need to monitor and understand trends in rural society. Rural society is experiencing an onslaught of urban influence, and rural development must be stimulated. Research and data are needed to improve rural economic opportunities, to improve institutions and the delivery of services, to meet housing needs, to deal with poverty, and to isolate barriers to change as well as determining ways of overcoming these barriers. Sociocultural components must be included in research and practice, and a multidisciplinary approach must be taken. Social indicators enable society to make changes according to normative criteria, and therefore they can be put to use in solving the problems of rural areas.

662 Mauro, John T. "Planning as an Instrument for Social Change." PLANNING 34 (January 1968): 59-67.

Social changes tend to be the result of political influences and short-term crises rather than long-range planning. Land use planning is an essential aspect of any social reform movement. City planners must learn to manage both land and money. Some suggested reforms include opening up suburban land to low and moderate income families, providing cheap mass transportation and resonable cost housing, starting public works programs, offering land and tax incentives for private industry, and using educational facilities for social services.

663 Michael, Donald N. "Social Engineering and the Future Environment." AMERICAN PSYCHOLOGIST 22 (November 1967): 888-92.

The author states that there is a need for social inventions to make the world more humane. The social technologies are just as important as the physical technologies. Social engineering is the deliberate application of systematically accumulated knowledge and theory about the nature of man and his institutions for the purpose of influencing man's behavior. The author summarizes past and present efforts in social engineering. In order to use scarce manpower efficiently and to allocate financial resources effectively, there is a need for more social research and application of findings. The computer will enhance research possibilities and the combination of government programs and funds, and social incentives. The computer will provide knowledge about the cumulative impact of changes.

664 Mindlin, Albert. "Improvements in Federal Statistical Programs for Small Areas." PUBLIC ADMINISTRATION REVIEW 33 (March-April 1973): 136-45.

Many local governments use statistical information generated by the federal government in order to research, plan, administer, and evaluate programs in their jurisdictions. In order to assist subnational units of government, the federal statistical system must become more attuned to the needs of these jurisdictions. The author surveys numerous organizations around the country to generate recommendations for changes in the federal government's statistical process. The major recommendations are the need for a quinquennial census, improved timeliness and coverage, better housing data, improved crime and criminal justice system data, improved data on income and labor force, improved geographic identification and better communication and organization of federal small area statistics programs. Each of the recommendations is discussed by the author.

665 Mondale, Walter. "New Tools for Social Progress." PROGRESSIVE 31 (September 1967): 28-31.

Mondale points out the value of social indicators in evaluating success of government programs. He specifies five purposes of social accounting: (1) to sharpen quantitative knowledge of social needs, (2) to measure more precisely our progress, (3) to evaluate efforts at all governmental levels, (4) to help in determining priorities, and (5) to help in the development and assessment of alternatives without waiting for failure.

666 _____. "Social Advisers, Social Accounting, and the Presidency." LAW AND CONTEMPORARY PROBLEMS 35 (Summer 1970): 496-504.

Former Senator Mondale sought to justify and explain his Full Opportunity and National Goals and Priorities Act which was passed by the Senate but not acted upon the House. The bill calls for a council of social advisers (CSA) composed of three of the nation's most gifted and respected social analysts. The CSA would be responsible for monitoring, on an ongoing basis, specific and actual conditions in the country which affect the social opportunity of the population. Developing a system of social indicators would be a principle task of the council.

The bill also called for the president to report annually on the nation's social status including such areas as education, health, housing, alienation, political participation, personal security, and social mobility.

667 _____. "Some Thoughts on Stumbling into the Future." AMERICAN PSYCHOLOGIST 22 (November 1967): 972-73.

Former Senator Mondale, sponsor of the Full Opportunity and Social Accounting Act, describes its intent to apply social data in forecasts of future behavior to help public officials understand change. The bill proposes a council of social advisers, an annual social report, and a joint congressional committee to carry out the task of social accounting.

668 Moynihan, Daniel P. "Urban Conditions: General." ANNALS OF THE AMERICAN ACADEMY OF POLITICAL AND SOCIAL SCIENCE 371 (May 1967): 159-77.

See 85.

669 Olson, Mancur, Jr. "An Analytic Framework for Social Reporting and Policy Analysis." ANNALS OF THE AMERICAN ACADEMY OF POLITICAL AND SOCIAL SCIENCE 388 (March 1970): 112-26.

See 209.

670 _____. "Economics, Sociology, and the Best of All Possible Worlds." PUBLIC INTEREST 12 (Summer 1968): 96-118.

Olson debates the need for interdisciplinary communication and collaboration with respect to Senator Mondale's bill providing for a council of social advisers. He defines the roles different social sciences should have in the policymaking process, and the futility of the division of labor among the social sciences, particularly the disciplines of economics and sociology, in that economic and sociological theory (particularly Parsonian theory) has important implications for all the other social sciences. The differences in method, preconception, and conclusion that distinguish modern economics and Parsonian sociology, and the need and special challenge for a social report which keeps both of the ideals in mind are discussed.

671 _____. "The Plan and Purpose of a Social Report." PUBLIC INTEREST 15 (Spring 1969): 85-97.

The author argues that there is a need for the federal government to issue regular social reports on the state of the nation. While national income reports measure the costs and activities of government, they do not measure the national welfare, that is, "the things that make life worth living," such as the success of education, the culture of the cities, and the strength of the family. Social indicators are needed to assess these conditions of society, to identify problem areas, and to evaluate the impact of social programs. Once indentified, statistics for social indicators ought to be produced as by-products of bureaucratic routine as are statistics for economic indicators.

672 _____ . "Toward a Social Report: II, The Plan and Purpose of a Social Report." PUBLIC INTEREST 15 (Spring 1969): 85-97.

Olson raises the question of whether the federal government should issue regular social reports on the state of the nation. He analyzes whether Planning, Programming, and Budgeting (PPB) is performing this report function. The author shows the inadequacy of current indicators, especially economic indicators. Pointing to the growth of public problems and causes of social conflict, he demonstrates the need for better information for policymaking.

673 Parker, John K. "Information Requirements for Urban Research Programs." In GOVERNING URBAN SOCIETY: NEW SCIENTIFIC APPROACHES, edited by Stephen B. Sweeney and James C. Charlesworth, pp. 241-50. Philadelphia: American Academy of Political and Social Science, 1967.

Urban research is conducted by a variety of academics including political scientists, economists, sociologists, psychologists, and anthropologists. Three types of information are needed to conduct urban research: published information, printed but unpublished information, and basic data. However, there are no integrated urban research libraries and the existence of potentially useful documents are known to very few. Examples of these types of materials are presented. Urban research is also hampered by a lack of data on our metropolitan regions. Much of the data that becomes available is often outdated before it can be fruitfully used. Metropolitan data banks could be useful components for urban researchers and practitioners. The major problem confronting the urban observatories will be to achieve effective access to available data.

674 Perloff, Harvey S. THE QUALITY OF THE URBAN ENVIRONMENT. Baltimore: Johns Hopkins Press, 1969. 332 p.

Three themes look at the quality of the urban environment in terms of a set of "new resources in the urban age": (1) natural resources of the urban environment–urban space including overground and underground, relatively "pure" air and water, and amenity resources, (2) man-made features as a microenvironment serving as actual or potential substitutes for the macroenvironment, and (3) measures of environmental condition and change. Perloff emphasizes the importance of providing a broad picture of the urban environment in terms of social indicators and social accounts as well as searching for better informational and measurement tools useful for decision making.

675 Rosenthal, Robert A., and Weiss, Robert S. "Problems of Organizational Feedback Processes." In SOCIAL INDICATORS, edited by Raymond A. Bauer, pp. 302-40. Cambridge: MIT Press, 1969.

See 322.

676 Sadacca, Robert; Loux, Suzanne B.; Isler, Morton L.; and Drury, Margaret J. MANAGEMENT PERFORMANCE IN PUBLIC HOUSING. Washington, D.C.: Urban Institute, 1974. 131 p.

> The authors propose indicators to evaluate the quality of housing project management, tenant complaints, the quality of maintenance, high operating costs, and the behavior of housing employees. However, some factors are beyond the influence of housing managers, such as the level of police and street cleaning services. Also, management style seems to be a factor. There is a correlation between tenant satisfaction, high managerial performance, and low operational costs.

677 Sadowsky, George. MASH: A COMPUTER SYSTEM FOR MICROANALYTIC SIMULATION FOR POLICY EXPLORATION. Washington, D.C.: Urban Institute, 1977. 158 p.

> The computer system known as MASH (MicroAnalytic Simulation of Households), was designed to implement DYNASIM (Dynamic Simulation of Income Model), described in POLICY EXPLORATION THROUGH MICRO-ANALYTIC SIMULATION, by Orcutt, Caldwell, and Wertheimer. The author comments on shortcomings of MASH that foreshadow still more sophisticated computer systems if microanalytic simulation proves useful as a social science tool. MASH permits social scientists to work directly with the computer.

678 Sheldon, Eleanor Bernert; Land, Kenneth C.; and Bauer, Raymond A. "Social Reporting for the 1970s." In THE PRESIDENT'S COMMISSION ON FEDERAL STATISTICS II, pp. 403-35. Washington, D.C.: Government Printing Office, 1971.

> See 99.

679 Sheldon, Eleanor Bernert, and Moore, Wilbert E., eds. "Monitoring Social Change in American Society." In their INDICATORS OF SOCIAL CHANGE: CONCEPTS AND MEASUREMENTS, pp. 3-26. New York: Russell Sage Foundation, 1968.

> The authors call for reviews of structural changes in American society through analysis of (1) the demographic base--its changing composition and distribution; (2) the ways in which a society produced goods, organizes its knowledge and technology, reproduces itself, and maintains order; (3) how the products of society are allocated; and (4) how the system as a whole changes from a social welfare perspective.

680 Sipel, George A. "Too Much Growth: Guidelines for Action." PUBLIC MANAGEMENT 56 (May 1974): 10-12.

The increasing deterioration in the quality of urban life demands that city policymaking bodies and administrative staffs make a major commitment to revitalize cities. Taxation and zoning laws need to be updated, as do current and proposed city policies. Effective planning, based on clearly defined goals and objectives, must take place. If controlling growth is desired, the purpose for doing so must be defined. Is it to allocate limited resources to serve an expanding population, or to prevent inefficient development patterns? Evolution of new growth management tools is encouraging, and success depends on how well these tools are used and programs are implemented.

681 Stagner, Ross. "Perceptions, Aspirations, Frustrations, and Satisfactions: An Approach to Urban Indicators." EKISTICS 30 (September 1970): 197-99.

Stagner argues that cities exist to provide satisfactions for their citizens and proposes social indicators that capture citizen-satisfaction levels. He notes the impact of different aspirations and reference groups.

682 Terleckyj, Nestor E. "Measuring Progress Towards Social Goals: Some Possibilities at National and Local Levels." MANAGEMENT SCIENCE 16 (August 1970): B765-79.

See 333.

683 Todd, Ralph H. "A City Index: Measurement of a City's Attractiveness." REVIEW OF APPLIED URBAN RESEARCH 5 (July 1977): 1-15.

See 242.

684 U.S. Congress. Senate. "Behavioral Scientists Urge Establishment of Council of Social Advisors." CONGRESSIONAL RECORD 117 (4 August 1971): 29283-89.

Former Senator Walter Mondale, Chairman of the Special Sub-committee on Evaluation and Planning of Social Programs of the Senate Committee on Labor and Public Welfare, placed in the CONGRESSIONAL RECORD testimony recorded at recent hearings before the subcommittee. Included are the following endorsements of the establishment of a council of social advisers: Testimony on "Full Opportunity and National Goals and Priorities Act," by Raymond A. Bauer; testimony by N.J. Demerath III; statement of Sol M. Linowitz, Chairman National Urban Coalition.

685 _____. "Introduction of the Full Opportunity and National Goals and Priorities Act." S.5 CONGRESSIONAL RECORD 117 (25 January 1971): 317-23.

This publication outlines Titles I and II of the bill. Title I asserts full social opportunity as a national goal, and provides for the staff offices to serve as leadership for it. Title II—National Goals and Priorities—discusses the purposes and functions of the office. It includes behavioral and social science recommendations of the national commission on the causes and prevention of violence.

686 U.S. Congress. Senate. Committee on Government Operations. Subcommittee on Government Research. FULL OPPORTUNITY AND SOCIAL ACCOUNTING ACT—SEMINAR. 90th Cong. 1st sess. Washington, D.C.: Government Printing Office, 1968.

Statements are included from Gerhard Colm, Bertram Gross, Preston Wilcox, Raymond Bauer, Francis Keppel, Harvey Perloff, Nelson Polsby, Mancur Olson, and others. Senator Fred R. Harris (Oklahoma) chaired the hearings. The committee proposed an annual social report by the president, to be prepared by a council of social advisers and submitted to the joint committee on the social report.

687 U.S. Congress. Senate. Committee on Labor and Public Welfare. FULL OPPORTUNITY ACT. REPORT TO ACCOMPANY S.5. 91st Cong. 2d sess. Washington, D.C.: Government Printing Office, 1970. 14 p.

A report recommending the Full Opportunity and Social Accounting Act calls for an annual report to Congress including the following: (1) a social analysis of budgeted programs, (2) examination of national resources and the potential costs and benefits of proposed programs, and (3) recommendations on priorities.

688 U.S. Congress. Senate. Committee on Labor and Public Welfare. Special Subcommittee on Evaluation and Planning of Social Programs. FULL OPPORTUNITY ACT. HEARINGS. 91st Cong. 1st and 2d sess. Washington, D.C.: Government Printing Office, 1970. 439 p.

These hearings on S.5, the Full Opportunity Act, include material submitted for the record. The appendix contains an annotated bibliography, including materials on social science policy, social accounting, social scientists and policymaking, interdisciplinary social science research, and social and political forecasting.

689 _____. FULL OPPORTUNITY AND NATIONAL GOALS AND PRIORITIES ACT. HEARINGS. 92d Cong. 1st sess. Washington, D.C.: Government Printing Office, 1971. 190 p.

This document includes statements from governmental agencies on the bill. The bill proposes a social report by the president, a council of social advisers, and a congressional office of goals and priorities analysis. The appendix includes an annotated bibliography on social science policy, social accounting, policy-making, interdisciplinary research, and forecasting.

690 U.S. Bureau of the Census. CURRENT POPULATION REPORTS. Series p-20 no. 132. "Educational Change in a Generation." Washington, D.C.: Government Printing Office, 1964. 18 p.

Upward educational mobility between generations is shown by comparing the educational attainment of men twenty to sixty-four years old in 1962 with that of their fathers. The statistics given show that the type of social environment in which a person is raised is related to his chances of surpassing the educational level of his father. Time trends appear to be much more important than the position of siblings in the family in explaining educational mobility between generations. Education differences between fathers and sons has not been as great for nonwhites as for whites.

A description of the terms used, and explanation of the source and reliability of the estimates, and the tables of statistics is given.

691 U.S. National Science Foundation. National Science Board. SCIENCE INDICATORS--1974. Washington, D.C.: Government Printing Office, 1975. 242 p.

See 108.

Appendix A
PERIODICALS WITH CONTENT RELEVANT TO
URBAN INDICATORS

ADMINISTRATION AND SOCIETY. Formerly JOURNAL OF COMPARATIVE
ADMINISTRATION. Beverly Hills, Calif.: Sage Publications, 1974--.
Quarterly.

ALBERTA STATISTICAL REVIEW. Edmunton, Alberta: Bureau of Statistics,
1967--. Monthly.

AMERICAN INSTITUTE OF PLANNERS JOURNAL. Washington, D.C.: American Institute of Planners, 1925--. Quarterly.

AMERICAN INSTITUTE OF PLANNERS NEWSLETTER. Washington, D.C.:
American Institute of Planners, 1966--. Monthly.

AMERICAN JOURNAL OF POLITICAL SCIENCE. Detroit: Wayne State
University Press, 1973--. Quarterly.

AMERICAN POLITICAL SCIENCE REVIEW. Menasha, Wis.: George Banta Co.,
1906--. Quarterly.

AMERICAN SOCIOLOGICAL REVIEW. Menasha, Wis.: American Sociological Society, 1936--. Bimonthly.

ANNALS OF THE AMERICAN ACADEMY OF POLITICAL AND SOCIAL SCIENCE.
Philadelphia: American Academy of Political and Social Science, 1890--.
Annual.

BLACK COMMUNITY PROGRESS REVIEW. Los Angeles: BCPR Communications,
1976--. Monthly.

CITY. Washington, D.C.: Urban America, 1967--. Annual.

COMMUNITY DEVELOPMENT SOCIETY JOURNAL. Columbia, Mo.: American
Press, 1970--. Semiannual.

Periodicals

COMPARATIVE URBAN RESEARCH. New Brunswick, N.J.: Transaction Periodical Consortium, Rutgers-The State University, 1972--. Biannual.

COMPARATIVE URBAN RESEARCH. New York: City University of New York, Comparative Urban Studies Center, 1972--. Semiannual.

COUNTY NEWS. Washington, D.C.: National Association of Counties, 1970--. Weekly.

DATA USER NEWS. Washington, D.C.: U.S. Bureau of the Census, 1975--. Monthly.

EDUCATION AND URBAN SOCIETY. Beverly Hills, Calif.: Sage Publications, 1968--. Quarterly.

EVALUATION QUARTERLY. Beverly Hills, Calif.: Sage Publications, 1977--.

HOUSING AFFAIRS LETTER. Washington, D.C.: Community Development Services, 1961--. Weekly.

JOURNAL OF REGIONAL SCIENCE. Philadelphia: Regional Science Research Institute, 1958--. Biannual.

JOURNAL OF URBAN ECONOMICS. New York: Academic Press, 1974--. Quarterly.

METROPOLITAN AREA PLANNING COUNCIL REGIONAL REPORT. Boston: Metropolitan Area Planning Council, 1971--. Monthly.

MONTHLY BULLETIN OF STATISTICS. New York: United Nations Statistical Office, 1947--.

NATION'S CITIES. Washington, D.C.: National League of Cities, 1963--. Quarterly.

NEWSLETTER. Washington, D.C.: Federal Statistics Users Conference, 1958--. Monthly.

POLICY ANALYSIS. Berkeley and Los Angeles: University of California Press, 1974--. Quarterly.

POLICY AND POLITICS. London: Sage Publications, 1972--. Quarterly.

POLICY SCIENCES. New York: American Elsevier, 1970--. Quarterly.

POLITICAL SCIENCE QUARTERLY. New York: Academy of Political Science, Columbia University, 1886--.

POLICY STUDIES JOURNAL. Urbana: University of Illinois, 1972--. Quarterly.

POLITY. Amherst: University of Massachusetts, 1968--. Quarterly.

PUBLIC ADMINISTRATION REVIEW. Washington, D.C.: American Society for Public Administration, 1940--. Bimonthly.

PUBLIC INTEREST. New York: National Affairs, 1965--. Quarterly.

PUBLIC MANAGEMENT. Chicago: International City Managers' Association, 1919--. Monthly.

SOCIAL INDICATORS RESEARCH: AN INTERNATIONAL AND INTERDISCI-PLINARY JOURNAL FOR QUALITY-OF-LIFE MEASUREMENT. Dordrecht, Holland: D. Reidel Publishing Co., 1974--. Quarterly.

SOCIAL SCIENCE QUARTERLY. Austin: Southwestern Social Science Quarterly and University of Texas, 1919--.

SOCIETY. Philadelphia: Transaction, 1972--. Monthly.

URBAN AFFAIRS QUARTERLY. Beverly Hills, Calif.: Sage Publications, 1965--.

URBAN DATA SERVICE REPORT. Washington, D.C.: International City Management Association, 1962--. Monthly.

URBAN LAND. Washington, D.C.: Urban Land Institute, 1941--. Monthly.

URBAN RESEARCH NEWS. Beverly Hills, Calif.: Sage Publications, 1966--. Semimonthly.

URBAN STUDIES BULLETIN. Ithaca, N.Y.: Cornell University, Program in Urban and Regional Studies, 1973--. Quarterly.

WESTERN POLITICAL QUARTERLY. Salt Lake City: Institute of Government, University of Utah, 1948--.

Appendix B
ABSTRACTS AND INDEXES

In recent years there has been a significant increase in the number of abstracts and indexes including items on urban indicators. There is no one abstract journal or index which deals exclusively with urban indicators.

AMERICAN DOCTORAL DISSERTATIONS. Ann Arbor, Mich.: Association of Research Libraries, 1955-56--. Annual.

COMPREHENSIVE DISSERTATION INDEX (1861-1972). Ann Arbor, Mich.: University Xerox. Annual updates.

CURRENT CONTENTS. Philadelphia: Institute for Scientific Information, 1961--. Weekly.

DISSERTATION ABSTRACTS INTERNATIONAL. Ann Arbor, Mich.: University Xerox, 1938--. Monthly.

INDEX TO CURRENT URBAN DOCUMENTS. Westport, Conn.: Greenwood Press, 1971--. Quarterly.

> This lists the official publications of the largest cities and counties in the United States and Canada.

INTERNATIONAL POLITICAL SCIENCE ABSTRACTS. Oxford: Blackwell, 1951--. Quarterly.

NEWSBANK. Greenwich, Conn.: 1970--. Quarterly.

> This is an indexed collection of articles from U.S. urban newspapers.

PUBLIC AFFAIRS INFORMATION SERVICE. New York: Public Affairs Information Service, 1915--. Weekly.

Abstracts and Indexes

SAGE PUBLIC ADMINISTRATION ABSTRACTS. Beverly Hills, Calif.: Sage Publications, 1974--. Quarterly.

SAGE URBAN STUDIES ABSTRACTS. Beverly Hills, Calif.: Sage Publications, 1973--. Quarterly.

This includes references to books, articles, and government publications.

SOCIAL SCIENCES CITATION INDEX. Philadelphia: Institute for Scientific Information, 1973--. 3 issues per year.

This provides access to material reviewed or mentioned by other sources.

SOCIAL SCIENCES INDEX. New York: Wilson, 1974--. Quarterly.

SOCIOLOGICAL ABSTRACTS. New York: Sociological Abstracts, 1952--. Frequency varies, approximately 6 issues per year.

URBAN AFFAIRS ABSTRACTS. Washington, D.C.: National League of Cities and U.S. Conferences of Mayors, 1971--. Weekly.

This monitors 800 periodicals, journals, and newsletters.

URBAN AFFAIRS REPORTER. Chicago: Commerce Clearing House, 1967--. Biweekly.

This provides loose-leaf information on federal programs affecting state and local governments.

Appendix C
URBAN PUBLIC INTEREST AND
PROFESSIONAL ASSOCIATIONS

American Institute of Planners
1776 Massachusetts Avenue NW
Washington, D.C. 20036

American Public Health Association
1015 Eighteenth St. NW
7th Floor
Washington, D.C. 20036

American Public Welfare Association
1155 Sixteenth St. NW
Suite 201
Washington, D.C. 20036

American Public Works Association
1313 E. Sixtieth St.
Chicago, Ill. 60637

    Washington office:
    1176 Massachusetts Ave. NW
    Washington, D.C. 20036

American Society for Public
  Administration
1225 Connecticut Ave. NW
Rm. 300
Washington, D.C. 20036

American Society of Planning
  Officials
1313 E. Sixtieth St.
Chicago, Ill. 60637

Council of State Community Affairs
  Agencies
1612 K St. NW
Rm. 906
Washington, D.C. 20006

Council of State Governments
Iron Works Pike
P.O. Box 11910
Lexington, Ky. 40511

    Washington office:
    444 N. Capitol St.
    2d Floor
    Washington, D.C. 20001

International Association of Chiefs
  of Police
11 Firstfield Rd.
Gaithersburg, Md. 20760

International Association of Fire
  Chiefs
1329 Eighteenth St. NW
Washington, D.C. 20036

International City Management
  Association
1140 Connecticut Ave.
Washington, D.C. 20036

International Personnel Management
  Association
1313 E. Sixtieth St.
Chicago, Ill. 60637

Associations

Washington office:
1176 Massachusetts Ave. NW
Washington, D.C. 20036

Labor-Management Relations Service
of Concerence of Mayors
1620 Eye St. NW
Rm. 616
Washington, D.C. 20036

Municipal Finance Officers Association
1313 East Sixtieth St.
Chicago, Ill. 60637

Washington office:
1730 Rhode Island Ave. NW
Suite 512
Washington, D.C. 20036

National Academy of Public Administration
1225 Connecticut Ave.
Rm. 300
Washington, D.C. 20036

National Association of Counties
1735 New York Ave. NW
Washington, D.C. 20036

National Association of Housing and
Redevelopment Officials
2600 Virginia Ave. NW
Rm. 404
Washington, D.C. 20037

National Association of Regional
Councils
1700 K St. NW
Rm. 1306
Washington, D.C. 20036

National Conference of State Legislatures
1405 Curtis St.
Denver, Colo. 80202

Washington office:
444 N. Capitol St. NW
Washington, D.C. 20001

National Governors' Conference
1150 Seventeenth St. NW
Washington, D.C. 20036

National Institute of Municipal
Law Officers
839 Seventeenth St. NW
Washington, D.C. 20006

National League of Cities
1620 Eye St. NW
4th Floor
Washington, D.C. 20006

National Municipal League
47 E. Sixty-eighth St.
New York, N.Y. 10021

National Recreation and Park Association
1601 N. Kent St.
Arlington, Va. 22209

National School Boards Association
1055 Thomas Jefferson Street
Washington, D.C. 20007

National Training and Development
Service for State and Local
Government
5028 Wisconsin Ave. NW
Washington, D.C. 20016

Public Administration Service
1313 E. Sixtieth St.
Chicago, Ill. 60637

Washington office:
1776 Massachusetts Ave. NW
Washington, D.C. 20036

Public Technology, Inc.
1140 Connecticut Ave.
Washington, D.C. 20036

United States Conference of Mayors
1620 Eye St. NW
Washington, D.C. 20036

AUTHOR INDEX

This index includes all authors, editors, compilers, and other contributors to the works cited in the text. References are to entry numbers unless preceded by a "p." and alphabetization is letter by letter.

A

B

Author Index

Author Index

Goodman, Leo A. 167-68
Goodman, Leonard H. 42
Gordon, Ian 295, 636
Gottehrer, Barry 43, 637
Gottman, Jean 420, 638
Grabosky, Peter N. 507
Graft-Johnson, K.T. de 381
Green, Miles 114
Greene, Kenneth V. 169
Greer, Scott 421
Greiner, John M. 585
Gross, Bertram M. 6-7, 43-49,
    159, 166, 170, 296-97, 612,
    639-41, 643
Gruber, Alan R. 173
Guest, Avery M. 422
Gurr, Ted Robert 172, 423-24, 507
Gustely, Richard D. 420, 583
Guttman, Joel 426
Guttman, Louis 194, 427

H

Haar, Charles M. 644
Hadden, Jeffrey K. 428-29, 485-86
Hahn, Harlan 516
Hamilton, Edward K. 430
Hansen, Kristin A. 553
Hanushek, Eric A. 431
Haran, E.G.P. 256, 298
Harland, Douglas G. 173
Harrison, Bennett 432, 586
Harrison, David, Jr. 50
Hartman, Gerald 581
Harvey, Robert O. 433
Hatry, Harry P. 51-52, 174-80,
    258, 260, 299, 434, 585, 587,
    606, 645-46
Hauser, Philip M. 53, 435, 647-
    49
Hauser, Robert M. 436
Hawes, Mary H. 437
Hawley, Willis D. 51
Hayes, Charles R. 438
Hearle, Edward F.R. 54
Heise, David R. 55
Henriot, Peter J. p. xix, 300
Henshel, Richard L. 56
Henson, Mary F. 551
Herrick, Neal Q. 439

Hill, Richard C. 440
Hinday, Virginia Aldise 441
Hirsch, Gary B. 181, 442
Hobson, Richard 182
Hoch, Irving 150
Hodge, Robert W. 231
Hoel, Lester A. 443
Holahan, John 558
Holleb, Doris 57, 301
Holtmann, A.G. 281
Hoos, Ida R. 302
Hoover, Edgar M. 444
Horowitz, Irving 303-4, 651
Horton, Frank E. 218
Howard, William A. 445, 652
Hudson, Michael C. 539
Hughes, James W. 58-59, 305,
    351, 446
Hula, Richard C. 507
Human Services Information System
    Project of Lancaster County.
    See Lancaster County, Pa.

I

Illinois Department of Local Govern-
    ment Affairs 589
Insel, Paul M. 493
Isler, Morton L. 447, 676
Isserman, Andrew M. 183

J

Jackson, Kenneth T. 448
James, Franklin J. 59
Janson, Carl-Gunnar 60
Jantsch, Erich 184
Johnson, David Richard 449
Johnston, Denis P. p. xix, 185,
    450, 653
Jones, Bryan D. 186
Jones, Charles O. 323
Judge, Anthony J.N. 654

K

Kain, John F. 50
Kaiser, Edward J. 369
Kania, Richard R.E. 451
Karnig, Albert K. 526

Author Index

Miller, S.M. 489
Miller and Byrne 489
Mills, Edwin S. 490
Milsum, J.H. 309
Minar, David 421
Mindlin, Albert 11, 133, 672
Minister of Industry. Trade and Commerce 491
Minns, R. 196
Missel, Muriel 84
Mitchell, Joyce 54, 82
Mitchell, William C. 82, 492
Moffitt, William 523
Moles, Abraham 199
Mondale, Walter F. 665-67, 687
Monts, J. Kenneth 83
Moore, John A. 375
Moore, Wilbert E. 8, 70, 82, 100, 154, 200, 228, 287, 324, 387, 492, 538, 679
Moos, Rudolf H. 493
Morgan, James N. 314
Morgenstern, Oskar 494
Moriyama, Iwao M. 200, 495
Morrey, C.R. 496
Morris, Cynthia Taft 344
Morrison, Peter A. 497
Morrison, W.I. 196
Morton, Robert T. 291
Moser, C.A. 84
Moyer, Charles 655
Moynihan, Daniel P. 85, 201, 315, 668
Muller, Peter O. 595
Muller, Thomas 202, 223, 316, 317, 596-97
Murphy, Raymond 203
Murphy, Thomas P. 86
Mushkin, Selma J. 204

N

National Goals Research Staff. See U.S. National Goals Research Staff
National Planning Association 205
National Research Council. Urban Information Systems Inter-Agency Committee (USAC)
National Wildlife Federation 498

Neenan, William B. 169
Neiman, Max 206
Newman, Sandra 207
New York City. Commission on the Personal Health Services 598

O

Obudho, Robert A. 208
Office of Management and Budget. See U.S. Office of Management and Budget
O'Kane, James M. 279
Olson, Kerry C. 143
Olson, Mancur 210, 319, 669-72
Ontell, Robert 87
Orcutt, Guy H. 211
Orleans, Peter 421
Orr, Larry L. 499
Ostrom, Elinor 212-13, 500
Ostrom, Vincent 275
Otis, Todd 501
Ott, Wayne R. 241
Ottensman, John R. 502
Oxanne, Larry 382

P

Pachon, Harry P. 503
Palisi, Bartolomeo J. 322
Palley, Howard A. 505
Palley, Marian Lief 505
Parker, John K. 88, 673
Parker, Seymour 601
Parson, Talcott 506
Patitucci, Frank 217
Peirce, David 507
Perkins, Dennis N.T. 214
Perle, Eugene D. 89
Perloff, Harvey S. 484, 674
Peskin, Henry M. 508, 599
Peterson, George E. 215
Peterson, John E. 385
Phares, Donald 509
Phillips, James E. 234
Plumlee, John P. 349
Popenoe, David 90
Powell, Dorian L. 510
Powers, Stanley 86, 165
Prescott, James R. 39
Public Technology, Inc. 600

Author Index

TITLE INDEX

This index includes all titles of books which are cited in the text. Titles of articles, enclosed in quotation marks, are also included. References are to entry numbers unless preceded by a "p." and alphabetization is letter by letter.

Title Index

Title Index

Title Index

Title Index

Title Index

Title Index

Title Index

SUBJECT INDEX

This index includes main areas of interest within the text. It is alphabetized letter by letter.

Subject Index

Subject Index

Subject Index